JN 1129.L32 HOW

How Labour Governments Fall

From Ramsay MacDonald to Gordon Brown

Edited by

Timothy Heppell
Associate Professor of British Politics, School of Politics and International Studies (POLIS), University of Leeds, UK

and

Kevin Theakston
Professor of British Government and Head of the School of Politics, University of Leeds, UK

First published 2013 by
PALGRAVE MACMILLAN

Palgrave Macmillan in the UK is an imprint of Macmillan Publishers Limited,
registered in England, company number 785998, of Houndmills, Basingstoke,
Hampshire RG21 6XS.

Palgrave Macmillan in the US is a division of St Martin's Press LLC,
175 Fifth Avenue, New York, NY 10010.

Palgrave Macmillan is the global academic imprint of the above companies
and has companies and representatives throughout the world.

Palgrave® and Macmillan® are registered trademarks in the United States,
the United Kingdom, Europe and other countries.

ISBN 978–0–230–36180–5

This book is printed on paper suitable for recycling and made from fully
managed and sustained forest sources. Logging, pulping and manufacturing
processes are expected to conform to the environmental regulations of the
country of origin.

A catalogue record for this book is available from the British Library.

A catalog record for this book is available from the Library of Congress.

Contents

Tables

Acknowledgements

The editors would like to thank the Centre for British Government within POLIS for providing funding to enable the 'How Labour Governments Fall' workshop to take place at Leeds University in December 2011. Particular thanks must be given to the contributors for delivering their papers at the workshop and for making our editorial role so straightforward. We would like to thank Amber Stone-Galilee, Liz Blackmore and Andrew Baird for their help and guidance throughout.

Contributors

Robert Crowcroft is Lecturer in Contemporary History within the School of History, Classics and Archaeology at the University of Edinburgh. He is the author of *Attlee's War* (2011).

Peter Dorey is Professor of British Politics within the School of European Studies at the University of Cardiff. He has published ten books, including (as author) *The Labour Party and Constitutional Reform: A History of Constitutional Conservatism* (2008) and (as editor) *The Labour Governments 1964–1970* (2006).

Timothy Heppell is Associate Professor of British Politics within the School of Politics and International Studies (POLIS) at the University of Leeds. He is the author of *Choosing the Labour Leader: From Wilson to Brown* (2010) and editor of *Leaders of the Opposition: From Churchill to Cameron* (2012).

Keith Laybourn is Professor of Modern British History within the Division of History at the University of Huddersfield. He is the author of *A Century of Labour: A History of the Labour Party* (2000) and *Marxism in Britain* (2005). He co-authored *Britain's First Labour Government* (2006) with Professor John Shepherd.

John Shepherd is Visiting Professor of Modern British History within the Division of History at the University of Huddersfield. He is the author of *George Lansbury: At the Heart of Old Labour* (2002) and co-author (with Professor Keith Laybourn) of *Britain's First Labour Government* (2006). He recently co-edited (with Jonathan Davis and Chris Wrigley) *Britain's Second Labour Government 1929–31* (2012) and is currently working on a monograph on the Winter of Discontent which is funded by the British Academy.

Kevin Theakston is Professor of British Government within the School of Politics and International Studies (POLIS) at the University of Leeds. He has published ten books, including *Winston Churchill and the British*

Constitution (2004) and *After Number Ten: Former Prime Ministers in British Politics* (2010).

Chris Wrigley is Professor of Modern British History within the Department of History at the University of Nottingham. He is the author of *British Trade Unions since 1933* (2002) and co-editor (with Jonathan Davis and John Shepherd) of *Britain's Second Labour Government 1929–31* (2012).

1
Introduction

Timothy Heppell and Kevin Theakston

The politics of New Labour from 1997 to 2010 are seen, by its advocates particularly, as the great exception within Labour's history. New Labour provided something that the party had never achieved before – a multi-term period in government. Victories at the general elections of 1997 (with a majority of 179), 2001 (a majority of 167) and 2005 (a majority of 66) enabled the party to govern uninterruptedly for 13 years. This was double the longest period of governance that it had ever experienced previously. That had been the six-year tenure under the leadership of Clement Attlee between 1945 and 1951, closely followed by the governments of Harold Wilson between October 1964 and June 1970. Advocates of New Labour took considerable pride in their era of electoral dominance and the comparison with Old Labour's record (Blair, 2010; Campbell, 2010, 2011a, 2011b; Mandelson, 2010). Between 1951 and 1997 Labour had contested 12 general elections and lost eight. Its defeats were, more often than not, substantial. The Conservatives secured three-figure parliamentary majorities in 1959, 1983 and 1987; three majorities of between 30 and 60 seats (1955, 1970 and 1979); and two majorities of between 15 and 30 seats (1951 and 1992). The electoral triumphs that Labour did achieve were less substantial. After losing office in 1951 its four victories prior to 1997 were, with the exception of 1966 (a majority of 97), narrow ones, with small single-figure majorities secured in October 1964 and October 1974. When Labour returned to office in March 1974 it was actually a minority administration.

The supposed triumph of New Labour was that it appeared to have challenged the assumption that the Conservative Party was the natural party of government (Bentley, 2007: 111). Labour MP Austin Mitchell, discussing what he called 'Labour's history of failure', once described it as 'the [twentieth] century's least successful major party' (Mitchell,

2000: 178). Indeed, in the 90 years since 1922, when Labour emerged indisputably as one of the big two parties in the British system (its leader either in government or heading the official opposition), it has been in government office for only 38 years (including the five years of the Churchill wartime coalition). In the year that Blair became Labour party leader, a group of political historians assembled by Anthony Seldon and Stuart Ball published a book that evaluated the reasons for the Conservative Party dominance of twentieth-century British politics (Seldon and Ball, 1994). The year after Blair ceased to be prime minister, Simon Lee and Matt Beech suggested that the 'Conservative century', as Seldon and Ball described it, had been transformed to such an extent that New Labour now represented the 'politics of dominance' (Beech, 2008: 1). However, the unfolding economic crisis would challenge the Beech claim and undermine the governing credentials of the post-Blair Labour party under Gordon Brown. Commenting upon the end of New Labour in 2010, Andrew Gamble attempted to place New Labour within a wider historical context:

> In the hundred years in which the Labour party has existed it has struggled to assert itself against a dominant Conservative party... For a time New Labour appeared to have changed that, but with the election of David Cameron in 2010 and the repositioning of the Labour party under Ed Miliband, many think the more familiar pattern of British politics has reasserted itself, with the Conservatives regaining their dominant position. If this turns out to be so the New Labour era will stand out in ever sharper relief as the one instance when Labour gained the ascendancy over the Conservatives and held it for a considerable period, establishing itself as the governing party.
>
> (Gamble, 2012: 492)

What factors explain why New Labour lost its status as the governing party, and are these any different from the factors explaining how and why previous Labour governments lost power? The following insight from Stuart McAnulla on pre-New Labour administrations would suggest that perceptions of economic competence were central:

> A large part of Labour's failure was perceived to be a result of the economic crises that had engulfed it each time it had been in power previously. On a number of occasions Labour governments had significantly boosted public spending on entering office only to be forced to reverse policies and make cutbacks when economic

problems emerged. Historically, financial markets had tended to lack faith in Labour governments and its perceived economic failure disillusioned voters, usually helping precipitate a quick exit from government.

(McAnulla, 2006: 122)

Austin Mitchell (2000: 178–80) similarly identified economic performance as central to the failure of Labour governments but framed the problems as 'an inability to manage the economy in such a way as to improve the lot and the living standards of the mass of the people' and a crippling deference to economic and financial orthodoxies (and particularly the interests of the City). Labour governments usually came to grief, he suggested, defending finance capitalism and the exchange rate. In a broader sense, comparative political science studies also suggest that government survival in office can be causally linked to economic indicators. While acknowledging that governments affect economic conditions as well as being affected by them, Paul Warwick, in his analysis of 16 West European parliamentary democracies from 1945 to 1989, argues that socialist or left-wing governments are actually more vulnerable if their performance is poor in terms of their record on inflation rather than unemployment (Warwick, 1992, 1994).

However, we would argue that parties lose office for more complex reasons than simply the performance of the economy. After all, John Major won an election for the Conservatives in the teeth of recession in 1992 and then lost office in the midst of an economic boom in 1997 (Sanders, 1993, 1999; Denver, 1998). Much of the political science literature on cabinet stability and government survival/termination focuses on modelling the specific attributes of the political actors and party and parliamentary factors in coalition situations, or on the disruptive effects of a range of critical 'events' and challenges arising in the external environment of government (such as political scandals, party factionalism, leadership struggles and clashes, intragovernmental policy disputes, wars and international crises, deteriorating relations with interest groups or clientele groups) (Browne et al., 1984, 1986). We share that focus on political and party factors and on the impact of 'events', but are not attempting an exercise in statistical modelling or game theory. Accordingly, this book takes an historical approach and aims to assess and compare the ways in which the different periods of Labour governance in Britain were brought to an end with election defeat or eviction from office in 1924, 1931, 1951, 1970, 1979 and 2010. It is concerned with understanding how and why these evictions occurred and the specific and particular factors that lay behind each of Labour's exits from government, and with the general factors and issues that might run across time. A distinction may be drawn between external factors that contributed towards the decline and fall of Labour governments (which may have been beyond the control of Labour as a party of government, and would have undermined any party of government irrespective of its political persuasion) and internal factors specific to Labour over which it did have some control, and therefore, arguably, culpability might be attached to the party. While the importance of economic competence and the impact of economic crises will be evaluated, other key questions will also be considered. For example, do Labour governments suffer from poor leadership and succumb to Cabinet splits or party revolts? Do they inevitably lose the trust of the electorate? Do they invariably run out of ideological steam and fresh ideas?

A key inspiration for this project was a book edited by Anthony Seldon entitled *How Tory Governments Fall: The Tory Party in Power since 1783*, which was published as the Conservative Party under John Major was on the brink of being removed from office after four successive terms (Seldon, 1996). In examining the fall of ten periods of Conservative governance over the last two centuries, the book picked out nine frequently recurrent factors: failure of leadership and a negative image of the party leader with the electorate; confusion over policy direction; manifest internal disunity; party organisation in the country being in disarray; depleted party finances; a hostile intellectual and media climate; the electorate's loss of confidence in the government's capacity for economic management; a strong feeling of 'time for a change'; and, finally, a revived and credible opposition. The argument was that rarely is any one of these factors alone strong enough to account for the defeat of Conservative governments – it is the combination that proves decisive, and the heaviest defeats that the Conservatives have suffered usually see more of the factors in evidence.

Although the aim of this book is to start an equivalent assessment of the factors that contribute to the fall of Labour governments in the twentieth century, our analysis will not replicate that of the Seldon book. This reflects the development of other interpretative models on governing failure that Seldon did not engage with. For example, similar assessments have been developed by Norton (1996: 234–44), Evans and Taylor (1996: 131–3) and Heppell (2008), with the final two models offering insights that were specific to the degeneration of long-serving governments.

However, before assessing these differing models, it is worth noting that they are all in some way influenced by the statecraft model advanced by the late Jim Bulpitt, which considers the methods used to win office (the politics of support) and then govern competently (the politics of power) (Bulpitt, 1986: 19–39). The statecraft model has the following dimensions, which, although listed sequentially, are evolving simultaneously (Hickson, 2005: 181). The first dimension of statecraft refers to party management – is the incumbent party leader able to present a united front to the electorate at election time, and, once the leader is prime minister, will the parliamentary party show the loyalty and discipline necessary to facilitate effective government? The second dimension of statecraft refers to what Bulpitt called political argument hegemony. In effect, this means ensuring that the party has acquired and can sustain dominance over the political agenda. Bale describes this as the 'struggle to establish a particular version of commonsense', so that the incumbent party is perceived to be the more plausible party in terms of policy solutions (Bale, 1999: 14). The third dimension of statecraft is whether the party, when in government, can demonstrate competence through its policy choices (Bale, 1999: 14). The fourth dimension of statecraft relates to electoral strategy. This is clearly not last in the sequence for a party that is in opposition and is seeking office, but for an incumbent party of government seeking another mandate this is when its party management, its dominance of political debate and its governing competence are either reaffirmed with another mandate or rejected, leading to the loss of office (Bulpitt, 1986: 21–2).

There is a clear overlap between the loss of the statecraft criteria (party management, political argument hegemony, governing competence and electoral strategy) and the factors that are identified in the models put forward by Norton, Evans and Taylor, and Heppell. Norton argues that for any party of government there are problems that can be grouped into three headings. First, there are problems that the party of government will face that would be problems for any party of government irrespective of its political persuasion. Norton suggests that this embraces the 'gap' between the expectations of the electorate and the resources available to government. This creates the conundrum that the electorate expects national governments to address problems, even though the capacity of national governments to do so is compromised by the fact that economic and political power has been flowing to multinational organisations and supranational institutions (Norton, 1996: 235–6). Second, there are problems specific to the party itself, or what might be described as intra-party factors. These relate to questions of competence; issues which may create an impression of party disunity; question marks surrounding leadership credibility; and concerns about the organisational apparatus of the party. Third, there are problems that relate to how the party of government compares with the opposition, or what might be described as inter-party issues. Here Norton argues that we need to note the existence (or not) of a renewed, competent, unified, well-led and organisationally secure opposition party (Norton, 1996: 234–44).

The models advanced by Evans and Taylor, and also by Heppell, are designed to address the specific circumstances that face long-term administrations. Evans and Taylor suggested that there was a clear comparison between the degenerative tendencies that were undermining the Major administration after 1992 and the circumstances that undermined the Macmillan/Douglas-Home administration in the period between 1961 and 1964. In constructing their framework for analysis they acknowledged that they were inspired by the musings of Alan Clark on what he called 'the destruct factors' in a *Sunday Times* article in late 1993 (Clark, 1993). 'All recent history shows that party government declines in effectiveness with the passage of time', argued Clark, noting that 'economic conditions' and 'government mishandling' of the economy can play a part, but placing most emphasis on the 'vicious circle' of political failures and mistakes (Clark, 1993). Evans and Taylor constructed a list of six indicators that were seen as symptomatic of degeneration. First, there was obsessive sensitivity to press criticism. Second, there can be high levels of mutual suspicion among party elites. Third, there can be a gravitational pull towards the loftier domain of foreign policy and high politics, and away from the mundane low politics of intractable domestic problems. Fourth, there can be inclination towards making concessions in policy development, with the rise of trade union power being cited as a dominant example when applied to the early 1960s. Fifth, there can be a gulf between the mindset of the parliamentary backbench of the party and its own frontbench, as ministers come to identify with their departments and prefer bureaucratic politics over party politics. Finally, the party can develop an inability to think and act strategically, and can become guided by the short term and tactical positioning (Evans and Taylor, 1996: 131–3).

As the Brown government began to experience governing difficulties, so Heppell (2008) sought to develop the Evans and Taylor model to compare and contrast the falls of the Conservatives in 1964 and 1997 with New Labour. This comparative historical approach sought to determine the extent to which New Labour was demonstrating comparable symptoms of governing degeneration. Here it was argued that there were six symptoms of degeneration for a party in government. First, it is undermined as the appropriateness of its policy objectives and its reputation for governing competence become questioned, especially in the sphere of economic management. Second, it suffers from increasingly negative perceptions of leadership credibility that undermine its electoral appeal as a governing party. Third, it experiences increasing levels of ideological division (manifesting itself in terms of both parliamentary rebellion and public disagreements showcased through the media) as the party becomes gripped by mutual suspicion and recrimination. Fourth, it finds its ethical conduct questioned by accusations of abuse of power as allegations of sleaze and corruption engulf it. Fifth, it is unable to avoid culpability for past mistakes and withstand the 'time for a change' argument. Finally, it struggles to adjust if faced with an increasingly unified, electorally appealing, politically renewed and credible main opposition party.

Within this model the analysis addresses two questions. Is there evidence to suggest that any of these degenerative tendencies are in existence; and, if any of them do exist, will this lead to electoral rejection? That is to say that this degenerative model is not a list of symptoms that are of equal value. Rather, it is the interrelationship between the degenerating symptoms that is crucial. The first stage within this model is to assess whether the governing party has lost credibility in terms of the first four symptoms – governing competence, leadership credibility, ideological division and abuse of power. The second stage relates to assessing whether the party of opposition can exploit any questioning of the governing party in relation to the above factors. Is the opposition sufficiently remodelled to enable it to make political mileage out of the degenerative symptoms that are becoming evident? Can it create a narrative that establishes the 'time for a change' argument? Thus, the degenerative model reflects the importance of the opposition, but also notes the centrality of competence. In other words, if a long-serving government is degenerating with respect to leadership credibility, ideological division and abuse of power, it has the capacity to withstand these degenerating symptoms if it can still retain governing competence.

What becomes apparent from these analyses and models developed by Seldon, Norton, Evans and Taylor, and Heppell is that they seem largely to relate to the Conservative Party studies literature. This reflects the fact that the Conservatives have been in government more often, and for longer, than Labour. However, while no historical comparative evaluation exists explaining why respective Labour governments have fallen, it does not mean that explanations for the fall of individual Labour governments have not emerged. Indeed, every time Labour has lost office there have usually been plenty of explanations, claims and scapegoats – often coloured by ideological and factional infighting in the party as it settles into, and eventually looks for a way out of, opposition. For example, the immediate aftermath of defeat in 1979 saw the publication of *What Went Wrong: Explaining the Fall of the Labour Government*, edited by Ken Coates. With a photograph of an authoritarian-looking James Callaghan on the cover, it was followed up with 200 pages of a left-wing ideological critique of the failures of the 1974–79 Wilson/Callaghan governments (Coates, 1979). Over a decade earlier Richard Crossman had written an essay entitled 'The Lessons of 1945', in which he attributed the loss of office in 1951 to the problems caused by the absence of detailed plans and blueprints developed before Labour took power; to the Attlee government's 'uncritical reliance' on the Whitehall bureaucracy; and to its inability to trust, involve and energise the wider party (Crossman, 1966). Of course, both the writers in the Coates collection and Crossman were approaching the issues from an ideological perspective and were primarily concerned to draw out political lessons for the future, and to set out stalls for what Labour should do next (in opposition and/or government). Both were expressions, too, of a tendency for Labour history in government to be written as 'a story of perpetual failure' (Brivati, 1997: 193).

Within this book each Labour government is considered, and explanations for their respective falls are provided. In Chapter 2, Keith Laybourn evaluates the circumstances surrounding the collapse of the first Labour government of Ramsay MacDonald in 1924. Inevitably, the first Labour government was faced with the constant problem that it was a minority government which could fall at any moment. The withdrawal of Liberal parliamentary support would at any point signal its end. The chapter outlines how, by pushing ahead with moderate social and political reform, the first Labour government's achievement was mainly one of showing that Labour could govern. When considering its removal from office, the chapter argues that charges of economic incompetence, a lack of direction over policy, internal disunity, depleted finances or a discredited party leader were of only limited significance. While acknowledging that there was criticism within the party over the failure of the government to press rapidly ahead with social reform, this chapter suggests that an overwhelming influence was the wider intellectual and political climate. Here its status as a minority administration was a central consideration. Its removal from office had little to do with the state of the Conservatives under Stanley Baldwin. Rather, it resulted from the attitudes among the Liberals towards Labour. It is argued that the failure of the first Labour government had more to do with the, almost irrational, fears about Marxism rising to power in Britain, as Marxism certainly had a major role to play in the withdrawal of Liberal Party support for the Labour government and ultimately its removal from office.

In Chapter 3 Chris Wrigley considers the collapse of the MacDonald government of 1929–31, for which an established narrative has developed. As the story goes, MacDonald's decision to form a coalition government with his erstwhile opponents amounted to a betrayal of his own party, a betrayal of the wider labour movement and a betrayal of the British working class. Labour, it was suggested, had been sacrificed to the vanity of its once esteemed leader; the intrigues of a bankers' ramp had constructed a crisis that served to divert Labour away from its chosen path of gradual and steady reform. All of this served a necessary political purpose. It allowed Labour to offload the blame for its failure in government onto a traitorous leadership that had since split from the party ranks. It also allowed Labour to distinguish – and set itself apart from – those (class) forces within capitalism that necessitated the reassertion of a practical, socialist alternative. Historically, however, such a narrative hides as much as it reveals. For, while it shows us much about the nature and trajectory of the Labour Party, it does little to explain why Labour fared so badly in office between 1929 and 1931. In reality, the failure of the Labour government of 1929–31 was a product of both external and internal factors. Its weak position as a minority government was compounded by evident limitation in terms of the governing criteria: by 1931 a credible argument can be made for stating that Labour had undermined its reputation for economic competence; that MacDonald had shortcomings in terms of party leadership; and that Labour was deemed to be lacking in a convincing sense of policy direction. Ultimately, however, the chapter argues that the Labour government's collapse was more a product of its minority position and its own inadequacies than of any obvious or credible alternative.

In Chapter 4, Robert Crowcroft and Kevin Theakston consider the fall of the Labour government of 1951. Elected in 1945, the Attlee government had a profound and far-reaching impact on Britain and left behind a legacy that would shape the framework of politics for a generation. In noting how its landslide majority disappeared after only five years, in the 1950 general election, and then how in 1951 Labour lost office altogether and was out of power for the next 13 years, the chapter makes the following conclusions with regard to its fall. The defeat was a narrow one and was not inevitable. Labour had some things going for it, including a broadly united party rank-and-file and party machinery, the support of the trade unions and a strong working-class mass vote. But crucial to its fall from power at this time were: the political and economic setbacks after 1947, including devaluation of the pound in 1949; a loss of political and ideological energy and a failure to renew the party and its programme in government; splits at the top over the future direction of policy and damaging Cabinet resignations after a battle over NHS spending in 1951; failures of leadership from Attlee himself, including poor election timing; and losing the propaganda battle against a revitalised opposition Conservative Party.

In Chapter 5 Peter Dorey analyses the fall of the Wilson government in 1970. He notes that, while the Attlee era shaped the contours of British economic, social and foreign policy for a generation, the Wilson era was geared towards modernisation in the hope of arresting decline. In governing terms, its ability to demonstrate economic competence was compromised by the devaluation crisis, while the sense that Labour had a clear policy direction was undermined by the limited impact of its trumpeted modernisation agenda when it entered office. The self-confident and optimistic oratory of Wilson had ceased to resonate by the end of his term in office. Damaged by the 'pound in your pocket' and the failure of 'In Place of Strife', his leadership was a source of feverish speculation in the 1968–69 period, although no formal challenge was made. Wilson was also absorbed in ongoing party battles and the time-consuming demands of balancing the competing needs (and egos) of right and left. The time devoted to manufacturing unity created a perception of a leader concerned with party rather than national needs, and focused on short-term tactical considerations rather than long-term strategy. The chapter identifies ongoing party divisions, leadership credibility, policy direction and economic competence as being more significant than any limitations within the party organisation or finance. In terms of the wider climate, it attributes defeat to the existence of an administration facing the electorate with a limited governing record to justify re-election, opposed by a competent, rather than inspiring, opposition, which was able to exploit the old maxim that oppositions do not win elections, governments lose them.

In Chapter 6 John Shepherd re-examines the circumstances surrounding the fall of the Callaghan government through a vote of no confidence in March 1979. The chapter emphasises the profound political (parliamentary) and economic constraints that the, then Wilson-led, government had when re-entering power in 1974. The chapter acknowledges that the Winter of Discontent, following on from the International Monetary Fund crisis and the collapse of the social contract, appeared to symbolise the crisis of Keynesian social democratic economic thinking; an over-bloated state and excessive trade union power. While accepting that perceptions of economic incompetence and a crisis of policy direction may have been prevalent, the chapter does not suggest that Callaghan as leader was a central consideration in its fall, or that any other Labour elite was better positioned to retain office. The chapter implies that the nature of party divisions over economic strategy, over the Common Market and defence, was compounded by a small and dwindling parliamentary majority. Although the party was financially less well equipped for electioneering than its Conservative counterpart, the chapter does not attribute defeat to organisational chaos or depleted party finances. Rather, it emphasises how the crises of social democracy, crystallised in the winter of 1978–79 and narrated effectively through the right-wing press, created an environment that suggested that the incumbent party was no longer a credible party of government.

In evaluating the fall of the Brown government in Chapter 7, Timothy Heppell recognises that there was a clear contextual difference when compared with the five previous Labour administrations. Whereas in 1924, 1929, 1945, 1964 and 1974 Labour had inherited office economically (and more often than not politically) constrained, New Labour benefitted from a benign economic inheritance and a weak and discredited Conservative opposition. Rather than explicitly focusing on Labour's political dominance between 1997 and 2007, Chapter 7 focuses on the 2007–10 stage of governance and its political degeneration. It draws this distinction because this era coincided with the leadership tenure of Gordon Brown: the economic crises and expenses scandal, which cumulatively did so much to undermine the credibility of Labour in its third term. While acknowledging the centrality of economic decline and a lack of policy direction to its fall, the chapter does place an emphasis on the significance of internal party disunity and its weak organisational and financial base. In addition to arguing that Labour was poorly equipped for electioneering, the chapter also emphasises the difficulties that the party was facing due to a hostile media and intellectual climate, and the rallying call of 'time for a change'. Ultimately, the chapter concludes, the perceptions of leadership ability were to be central. Despite the recession, Labour almost retained parity with the Conservatives on economic competence and other leading salient issues. This indicates that there were doubts about the narrative and image of the Conservatives. However, while their leader David Cameron had opinion polling ratings superior to those of the party that he led, Brown had the reverse effect.

Chapters 2–7 will, therefore, provide detailed appraisals of how and why the Labour governments fell in 1924, 1931, 1951, 1970, 1979 and 2010. The models identified earlier in the introduction help to inform the analysis, although editorially there has been no attempt to make contributors adhere to any particular model. Rather, contributors have been asked to show an awareness of the recurring themes and make reference to them if relevant to the fall of the government that they are analysing.

References

Bale, T. (1999), *Sacred Cows and Common Sense: The Symbolic Statecraft and Political Culture of the British Labour Party* (Aldershot: Ashgate).

Beech, M. (2008), 'New Labour and the Politics of Dominance', in Lee, S. and Beech, M. (eds), *Ten Years of New Labour* (Basingstoke: Palgrave).

Bentley, T. (2007), 'British Politics after Tony Blair', *British Politics*, Vol. 2, No. 2, 111–17.

Blair, T. (2010), *A Journey* (London: Hutchinson).

Brivati, B. (1997), 'Earthquake or Watershed? Conclusions on New Labour in Power', in Brivati, B. and Bale, T. (eds), *New Labour in Power: Precedents and Prospects* (London: Routledge).

Browne, E., Frendreis, J., and Gleiber, D. (1984), 'An "Events" Approach to the Problem of Cabinet Stability', *Comparative Political Studies*, Vol. 17, No. 2, 167–97.

Browne, E., Frendreis, J., and Gleiber, D. (1986), 'The Process of Cabinet Dissolution: An Exponential Model of Duration and Stability in Western Democracies', *American Journal of Political Science*, Vol. 30, No. 3, 628–50.

Bulpitt, J. (1986), 'The Discipline of the New Democracy: Mrs Thatcher's Domestic Statecraft', *Political Studies*, Vol. 34, No. 1, 19–39.

Campbell, A. (2010), *The Alastair Campbell Diaries: Volume 1. Prelude to Power 1994–1997* (London: Hutchinson).

Campbell, A. (2011a), *The Alastair Campbell Diaries: Volume 2. Power and the People 1997–1999* (London: Hutchinson).

Campbell, A. (2011b), *The Alastair Campbell Diaries: Volume 3. Power and Responsibility 1999–2001* (London: Hutchinson).

Clark, A. (1993), 'The Downing Street Disease', *The Sunday Times*, 26 December.

Coates, K. (ed.) (1979), *What Went Wrong? Explaining the Fall of the Labour Government* (Nottingham: Spokesman Books).

Crossman, R. (1966), 'The Lessons of 1945', in Anderson, P. and Blackburn, R. (eds), *Towards Socialism* (New York: Cornell University Press).

Denver, D. (1998), 'The Government that Could Do No Right', in King, A., Denver, D., Norris, P., Norton, P., Sanders, D. and Seyd, P. (eds), *New Labour Triumphs: Britain at the Polls* (London: Chatham House).

Evans, B. and Taylor, A. (1996), *From Salisbury to Major: Continuity and Change in Conservative Politics* (Manchester: Manchester University Press).

Gamble, A. (2012), 'Inside New Labour', *British Journal of Politics and International Relations*, Vol. 14, No. 3, 492–502.

Heppell, T. (2008), 'The Degenerate Tendencies of Long Serving Governments…1963…1996…2008?', *Parliamentary Affairs*, Vol. 61, No. 4, 578–96.

Hickson, K. (2005), 'Inequality', in Hickson, K. (ed.), *The Political Thought of the Conservative Party since 1945* (Basingstoke: Palgrave).

Mandelson, P. (2010), *The Third Man: Life at the Heart of New Labour* (London: HarperPress).

McAnulla, S. (2006), *British Politics: A Critical Introduction* (London: Continuum).

Mitchell, A. (2000), 'Reinterpreting Labour's History of Failure', in Brivati, B. and Heffernan, R. (eds), *The Labour Party: A Centenary History* (London: Macmillan).

Norton, P. (1996), 'Conclusion: Where from here?' in Norton, P. (ed.), *The Conservative Party* (London: Harvester Wheatsheaf).

Sanders, D. (1993), 'Why the Conservative Party Won – Again', in King, A., Newton, K., Crewe, I., Norton, P., Denver, D., Sanders, D. and Seyd, P. (eds), *Britain at the Polls 1992* (London: Chatham House).

Sanders, D. (1999), 'Conservative Incompetence, Labour Responsibility and the Feel Good Factor: Why the Economy Failed to Save the Conservatives in 1997', *Electoral Studies*, Vol. 18, No. 2, 251–70.

Seldon, A. (1996), *How Tory Governments Fall: The Tory Party since 1783* (London: Fontana).

Seldon, A. and Ball, S. (1994), *Conservative Century: The Conservative Party since 1900* (Oxford: Oxford University Press).

Warwick, P. (1992), 'Economic Trends and Government Survival in West European Parliamentary Democracies', *American Political Science Review*, Vol. 86, No. 4, 875–87.

Warwick, P. (1994), *Government Survival in Parliamentary Democracies* (Cambridge: Cambridge University Press).

2

The Fall of the First MacDonald Government, 1924

Keith Laybourn

On leaving his Whitehall office on a cold January evening in 1924, Thomas Jones, assistant cabinet secretary, saw the newspaper placards announcing 'Lenin Dead (official), Ramsay MacDonald Premier' (Jones, 1960: 266). This juxtaposition of two monumentally important headlines was unfortunate, but remarkably apposite in the short history of the first Labour government, whose fortunes were very much determined by the relationship between Britain and the Soviet Union, although that was played out within the context of a nine-month-long minority socialist Labour government dependent upon the Liberal Party to maintain it in power.

After six weeks of uncertainty and rumours following the indeterminate December 1923 general election, Britain's first-ever Labour government took office on 22 January 1924, with Ramsay MacDonald as both its prime minister and foreign secretary. Just over nine months later, on 29 October 1924, despite increasing its vote by over a million, the Labour Party's first government suffered a decisive general election defeat which saw Stanley Baldwin's Conservative government return to power. Shortly after that defeat the Labour Cabinet held a meeting, at 10.30 am on 31 October, on the reasons for its defeat, the Zinoviev Letter and the role of the Foreign Office (Jones, 1960: 298–9). In the following days the Labour Cabinet members held their own post-mortem on the Zinoviev Letter, which had been published during the general election to destructively suggest that the Labour government was the tool of communism. But it was reported at the final Labour Cabinet meeting on 4 November that there was no conclusive proof of the authenticity of the document, and a public communiqué was issued to that effect. To this day, despite several investigations, there has been no clear evidence of the authenticity of the Zinoviev Letter (Bennett, 1999). The enduring interest of the Labour Party in the Zinoviev Letter clearly suggests that some have seen it as the cause of Labour's defeat. Yet this is undoubtedly an exaggeration, for the collapse of the Labour government has to be viewed in the much wider political context into which it fitted. Above all, the Labour government of 1924 was a minority government, dependent upon the support of the Liberal Party for its continued existence. There was, however, no coalition government, and throughout its brief existence the first Labour government was precariously positioned because of its insistence upon pushing forward with an Anglo-Soviet Trade Treaty. This was unpopular with both the Liberal and Conservative parties, who, over the infamous Campbell case, finally took the decision to ditch the Labour experiment. But was it pushed, as Lord Beaverbrook suggested in his article 'Who Killed Cock Robin?' or did it jump out of power, as Andrew Thorpe and others suggest? (Beaverbrook, 1924, and Beaverbrook Papers, BBK/G12/6; Thorpe, 1997, 2000: 328–9). This chapter will argue that it was probably pushed out of power by the opposition parties, for it is difficult to underestimate the fear of international communism, to which Labour seemed attached, in Britain in the early 1920s, and what is remarkable is that the first Labour government lasted even nine months.

The formation of the first Labour government and the threat of socialism

No assessment of the 1924 administration and its collapse can ignore its antecedents or avoid the question of how far its beginnings configured its political trajectory. Formed in 1900 as the Labour Representation Committee, an alliance between working-class trade unions as socialists, the emergent Labour Party had not expected parliamentary victory so early. However, the December 1923 general election had proved inconclusive, even though the Conservatives had won 258 seats to Labour's 191 and the Liberals 158 (Shepherd and Laybourn, 2006: 41–2). The Liberals were reluctant to support Baldwin's Conservative administration – Asquith stating that he would not 'stir a finger to save' the Conservatives and telling Liberal MPs that 'they really controlled the situation' and 'if a Labour government (were) ever to be tried ... it would hardly be ... under safer conditions' (*Manchester Guardian*, 19 December 1923). In other words, Asquith and the Liberals saw support for the Labour government as some sort of safe experiment. Inevitably, the first Labour government had to live with the fact that it was a minority government which could inevitably fall on the withdrawal of Liberal parliamentary support. The fundamental question, then, is why, in the autumn of 1924, after just over nine months, did the first socialist Labour government fall?

From the start, there had been concerns that a Labour government committed to socialism might be a danger to British politics and society. In December 1923 Lord Haldane – the former Liberal Imperialist soon to be Labour Lord Chancellor – wrote to his 99-year-old mother at his home in Scotland. 'The City is in panic at the thought of a Labour government and is cursing Baldwin for bringing an election. All the old ladies are writing to their brokers beseeching them to save their capital from confiscation.' He added that 'I have had a letter from Baldwin begging me to join the Labour Government and help them out' (Maurice, 1929: passim). Asquith, his former leader, also agreed, and later reflected upon his post bag being filled with letters 'to save the country from the "horrors of Socialism and Confiscation"' (Earl of Oxford and Asquith, 1928: 207–8). Even more famously, after inviting MacDonald to form an administration, King George V wrote in his diary: 'Today 23 years ago dear Grandma died. I wonder what she would have thought of a Labour government?' (Nicolson, 1952: 384).

Between the indecisive general election of 6 December 1923 and the formation of the first Labour government on 22 January 1924, Baldwin had held on to power with the hope that he could muster support to oppose the Labour Party with the fear that Ramsay MacDonald 'might introduce a Levy on Capital, increased income tax and death duties' (*Memorandum By Lord Stamforsham*, 10 December 1923, RA PS/GV/K 1918/34). Without Liberal support, however, it was impossible for him to implement his general election programme, which included the idea of tariff reform and protection which was rejected by both the Liberal and Labour parties. It soon became obvious that Labour would have to form the new administration, and equally clear that the fear of a confiscating and nationalising Labour administration would be an exaggeration. As MacDonald drew up plans for his Cabinet, it became obvious that he was playing down the potential socialist aspirations of his anticipated administration. Notable left-wingers such as George Lansbury, the pacifist and later Labour Leader, and E. D. Morel, a leading figure in the anti-war movement and opposed to the Treaty of Versailles Union of Democratic Control, were either not going to get a seat in the Cabinet or be marginalised to less important roles. The reality was that MacDonald's Labour Party was going to temper its socialist optimism to establish its credentials as a party of government.

This policy was firmly established on 12 December, less than a week after the 1923 general election, when Ramsay MacDonald dined at

Sidney and Beatrice Webb's London house with Philip Snowden, Jimmy Thomas, Arthur Henderson and J. R. Clynes. The Labour leader put before his future Cabinet colleagues a memorandum of what they might achieve in government. He committed his future administration to a modest domestic programme of tackling unemployment, improving the housing stock and widening educational opportunities. These policies were presented to both the General Council of the Trades Union Congress and the National Executive Committee of the Labour the next day, 13 January 1924, and endorsed by them in a statement.

> That this joint meeting of the General Council and National Executive of the Labour Party registers its complete confidence in Mr. Ramsay MacDonald, MP as Leader of the Parliamentary Labour Party, being sure that should he be called upon to assume high office he will in all his actions consider the well-being of the nation in seeking to apply the principles of the Labour Movement.
>
> (National Executive Committee Minutes of the Labour Party, 13 January 1924)

In other words, the Labour Party was committed to a course of action whereby it would accept office and consider the introduction of moderate social reforms in line with the needs of the nation. This intended moderation became even more evident at Labour's 'Victory Rally' at the Albert Hall on 8 January 1924. The aspirations of the Labour Party had been dampened by the prospect of becoming a minority government, and the mood of the party was caught by H. W. Massingham's spellbinding reflection upon Labour's hopes and realities. He wrote that in a mood of buoyancy and seriousness:

> Mr. MacDonald had come to say a difficult word to an idealistic audience. The word was moderation.... The effort of the Labour ministry to establish itself as a governing force would, he made clear, establish a new concordat of peace, based upon the immediate recognition of Russia and an attempt to bring Germany back to the European system. And it would make an offer with capital to engage with it in a great scheme of productive employment.... Impatient idealism may have revolted, and had it done so, the life of the Labour government, if it had ever begun, would have dwindled in a short and inglorious episode. But the response was perfect. The enthusiasm of the meeting was restrained and enhanced; and it was clear that the new Government, basing itself not on the class war, but on cooperative and even

the religious instincts of the whole nation, would have behind it the wonderful movement, which brought it into being.

(H. W. Massingham article in *Nation*, 6 February 1924, Labour Party National; Executive Committee. Minute Book, Box VI)

The moderation of Labour's domestic policy

The minority Labour government did, indeed, pursue limited social reform, rather than the social reconstruction of society. In education C. P. Trevelyan, Labour's President of the Board of Education, aimed to raise the school-leaving age to 15 and to extend secondary educational opportunities for all, along the multilateral lines advocated by R. H. Tawney in his Labour Party policy document *Secondary Education for All* (Tawney, 1922, 1988). Instead, Trevelyan achieved some modest reduction in class sizes in elementary schools, made efforts to reduce the number of unqualified teachers, improved school accommodation, raised the number of local education scholarships to secondary schools from 25 per cent to 40 per cent, and restored state scholarships from state-aided schools to universities (*Labour Magazine*, March 1924). The Labour Party Conference of October 1924 reiterated these aims and claimed to embody 'all practical steps towards the ideal of securing to all children the same choice of advanced education as the children of the rich' (Twenty-Fourth Annual Conference of the Labour Party, London, Labour Party, 1924: 125). However, there was little significant change, and Labour's words were mere window dressing.

In housing, the Glasgow Independent Labour Party activist John Wheatley introduced a Housing Bill that provided subsidies for the building of local authority rented housing, probably the Labour government's most significant domestic achievement. The 'Wheatley' Housing Act of 1924 effectively subsidised those houses let at a fixed rent to the tune of £9 per year in urban areas and £12 10s in agricultural parishes for 40 years to offset the interest rates charges raised for house construction. Yet there was no pretence that this was a socialist policy, and Wheatley told the House of Commons on 26 March that Labour's housing plans did not amount to socialism: 'I wish this country were ready to receive a Socialist programme and we would show you how much easier it is to solve the housing problem...than trying to patch up the capitalist system...' (*Hansard Parliamentary Debates* (1924), vol. 174, cols 1667–98, 15 May 1924).

The Labour government made minor achievements in other areas of domestic policy. Philip Snowden, who became chancellor of the exchequer, was a reassuring figure for financiers and capitalists in Britain. He was impeccably orthodox in his economic thinking, committed to free trade, balanced budgets and cuts in public expenditure. For Snowden, socialist policies could only be financed out of a budget surplus. In effect, the chancellor of the exchequer's approach severely curtailed the scope of the government's domestic programme, particularly in relation to mass unemployment.

On 11 December 1923, Beatrice Webb, the famous Fabian socialist, predicted that Labour would dash expectations that unemployment would be tackled. She wrote that:

> What came out was that Snowden, who thinks he has the right to be Chancellor of the Exchequer, is chicken hearted and will try to cut down expenditure. He even demurred to a programme of public works for the unemployed. Where has the money to come from? He asked with a Treasury clerk's intonation.
>
> (Mackenzie and Mackenzie, 1984: 11 December 1923)

Indeed, on becoming shadow chancellor, Snowden had declared: 'we shall always have the problems of unemployment with us under a system of competitive capitalism' (Cross, 1966: 185). Although he did, on occasion, envision the end of capitalism, he was committed to deflationary policies, balanced budgets, and paying off the National Debt, through the so-called Sinking Fund. He felt that a diminishing national debt would allow interest rates to fall and encourage industrialists to borrow money to invest in the growth of the economy. The fact that policies of sound capitalist finance might have been anathema to socialism did not appear to occur to him. The Conservative MP Robert Boothby recalled the Labour chancellor's obsession with the shibboleths of nineteenth-century economics. 'Economy, Free Trade, Gold – these were the keynotes of his political philosophy and deflation the path he trod with almost ghoulish enthusiasm' (Laybourn, 1988: 38).

Most of the Labour Party thinking appeared to accept that unemployment was inevitable under capitalism and that only socialism would solve the problem of poverty – of which unemployment was but a part. Like many other members of the Labour Party, Snowden rejected the more expansionary policies of David Lloyd George, John

Maynard Keynes and other Liberals, which he regarded as palliatives, not solutions. J. A. Hobson, a Liberal economist, suggested that the tendency for capital to over-save in slumps might be rectified by taxation, which would permit governments to restore the normal saving–spending ratios and help economic recovery. But this was generally rejected as reformist tinkering, and the Labour government generally accepted the need to alleviate the conditions of workers who were unemployed (Booth and Pack, 1985: 136). Indeed, it abandoned most other distinctive socialist policies that had marked Labour off from the Liberal and Conservative parties before 1924.

The Labour Party manifesto of 1923 failed to mention nationalisation, in a desire to produce a non-controversial programme which would not damage Labour's chances at the 1923 general election. Snowden's commitment to raise a capital levy – an idea which first emerged in 1915 to regain interest and profits from the pockets of businessmen, financiers and industrialists by introducing a capital levy on fortunes over £1,000 – had effectively been kicked into the long grass of politics, since MacDonald thought that it would cost Labour about 50 seats in the 1923 general election (Snowden, 1934: 595). The abandonment of the proposal – to be replaced by a committee of businessmen led by the cotton tycoon Lord Colwyn, to consider alternative ways to tackle the National Debt – was one of Labour's first financial pronouncements in office in February 1924. In the end, all that Labour could offer to the poor and unemployed was a modestly more caring attitude towards their plight.

In contrast to the Conservative government's 'Big Business Budget' of 1923, which cut rates in the super-tax on the rich, Snowden's 'Housewife's Budget' of 29 April 1924 used a surplus £40 million to reduce indirect taxation on food, 50 per cent of which was spent on almost halving the tax on sugar. He also spent £500,000 removing the duty on motor vehicles. The Labour government also set up a sub-committee on housing and unemployment, presided over by Sidney Webb, president of the Board of Trade, which was then split up into two sub-committees, for housing (John Wheatley) and unemployment (Tom Shaw). Regarding the latter, it quickly became evident that the public works schemes of the early 1920s were to be the main solution to unemployment and that the sub-committee placed reliance upon a revival of world trade based upon free trade and the restoration of the Gold Standard (Cabinet 23/27 (11) (24), 10 February 1924).

After meeting Sidney Webb, Thomas Jones remarked on Labour's dearth of ideas for the workless. 'We then talked of Unemployment, and it was rather disappointing to find Sidney Webb, the author of pamphlets innumerable on the cure of unemployment regardless of cost, now as Chairman of the Unemployment Committee, reduced to prescribing a revival of trade as the one remedy left to us' (Jones, 1960: 269, 1 February 1924).

Nevertheless, Labour did have some solutions beyond the conventional nostrum of public works. In April 1924 the government planned to create work through the electrification of the railways, though this was later abandoned. Instead, MacDonald's idea of the electrification of Britain was presented to the House of Commons on 29 May 1924, and on 30 July Snowden informed the House of Commons of the aim to construct a National Grid, financed by the Exchequer, to redistribute the nation's electrical output (*Hansard Parliamentary Debates*, 5th Series, vol. 174, cols 645–60 and vol. 176, cols 2091–2114, 30 July 1924; Cabinet 23/47 (40) (24), 9 July 1924; Cabinet 23/47 (35) (24), 30 May 1924; Cabinet 23/47 (40) (24), 5 August 1924).

Even if largely bereft of new ideas to solve the intractable problems of unemployment, Labour had always been more progressive about the relief of the workless. By 1924 two systems of unemployment provision existed, the contributory system and the uncovenanted system, or dole, which was provided for those out of benefit.

When Labour came to office in 1924 the government was naturally expected to improve conditions for the unemployed. The administration introduced an Unemployment Insurance Act that effectively created a statutory right to benefit, recognising only two kinds of benefit – standard and extended – to which all workers were entitled. The Act, introduced in April, amended the eligibility rules of the 1920 measure and extended the benefits from 26 to 41 weeks. Benefit levels for both men and women were increased. However, the new Act also introduced the 'genuinely seeking work' clause by which applicants had now to prove that they were actively seeking employment.

There were many other aspects of domestic development in the short lifetime of the first Labour government, but none of them threatened to shake the fabric of British society or the resolve of the Liberal Party to support the first Labour government. Indeed, it was defeated on 13 occasions, in connection with the Agricultural Wages Bill, the Housing Bill, the London Traffic Act and other legislation (Shepherd and Laybourn, 2006: 120). The first 11 occurred between 13 March 1924 and 28 July 1924. None of these was a challenge to the government. However, the last two, on 8 October 1924, were censure motions on the famous Campbell case, whereby the withdrawal of a prosecution of

J. R. Campbell, of the Communist Party of Great Britain, brought the
end of the first Labour government.

The dangers of foreign policy and of recognising
the Soviet Union

On 12 February 1924 MacDonald informed the House of Commons
that 'the position of this country in Europe has become so unsatisfac-
tory that I believed that it would be a great advantage if, whoever was
Prime Minister was also Foreign Secretary, in order to give weight of
office to any sort of policy that one might devise' (*Hansard Parliamentary Debates*, vol. 169, col. 767, 12 February 1924; Nicolson, 1952: 385).
And, indeed, MacDonald had compelling reasons for ring-fencing the
Foreign Office for himself; for, ten years before, he had opposed the
outbreak of the Great War as an Edwardian progressive who detested
war. He had resigned from the leadership of the parliamentary Labour
Party and joined others – such as E. D. Morel, Charles Trevelyan,
Norman Angell and Arthur Ponsonby – in forming the Union of Democratic Control (UDC). Unlike the Fellowship of Reconstruction and the
No-Conscription Fellowship, the UDC was not another 'stop-the-war'
organisation, but a group of Liberals, radicals and intellectuals who
opposed the war and worked for peaceful settlement of the conflict.
Their key demands were expressed in four cardinal points: no transfer
of territory without a plebiscite; parliamentary control of British foreign policy; the formation of an international council to maintain world
peace; and comprehensive disarmament combined with the nationalisation of the armaments industries. By the early 1920s the UDC, with
a greatly increased membership, had become a significant voice within
the Labour ranks on international policy (Winkler, 1956, 1994, 2005;
Sylvest, 2006).

Labour was also influenced by the Labour Advisory Committee on
International Questions (ACIQ), which provided the forum for debat-
ing international questions within the party. The secretary was Leonard
Woolf, author of the *International Government* (1916) alongside Philip
Noel-Baker and Noel Buxton. Arthur Henderson, Labour's home secretary, who would have been foreign secretary had not MacDonald taken
the position, did not attend the meetings, but took on the Committee's advice in moving Labour towards support of the League of Nations
and a system of collective security during the 1920s. However, ACIQ
was less active during MacDonald's stewardship of foreign policy, as was
the non-partisan League of Nations Union (LNU), of which MacDonald

was unique among British prime ministers in refusing the position of honorary president.

MacDonald was an instinctive internationalist and was essentially committed to the pacification of Europe. He came from a socialist and anti-imperialist background, and viewed as barbaric the conflicts between capitalist nations. He viewed a successful foreign policy as being a way to stimulate international free trade and thus the nation's general economic prosperity, but he was also an impassioned believer in disarmament.

There is no need here to go into the minute detail of MacDonald's foreign policy. It is sufficient to say that he was faced with an unstable European situation in which the French and Belgians had occupied the heavily industrialised Ruhr region in 1923 when Germany had defaulted on reparation payments of timber and poles. In addition, a combined industrial commission of French and Belgian engineers and technicians had taken over strategic Ruhr mines and factories (O'Roirdon, 2001). In response to these developments, MacDonald attempted to tackle the problem of reparations, which he saw as counter to stability in Europe, and the need for disarmament. He supported the Dawes Report, for rescheduling German reparation debts, and sought to end the French occupation of the Ruhr at the bitterly fought Inter-Allied Conference in London in July and August 1924. A new arrangement on reparations was agreed here, which was associated with the gradual withdrawal of the French troops from the Ruhr and the move towards the establishing of collective security through the League of Nations in September 1924, which later emerged as the 21-point 'Anglo-French' Geneva Protocol. The Protocol offered to introduce an arrangement of arbitration between nations in which those who refused to agree to the decision would be deemed aggressors and punished by sanction or force. Effectively, the French thought that this meant that Britain would support them in opposition to any future German aggression, though the wider details of this arrangement were to be settled at a future disarmament conference (the Locarno Conference, as it became) in June 1925. Collective security was to be the solution to international conflict, although the Locarno conference did not endorse MacDonald's scheme (Shepherd and Laybourn, 2006: Chapter 6). Nevertheless, the Geneva Protocol was MacDonald's finest hour, a month before he fell from power, although other aspects of the Labour government's foreign policy, in connection with the Empire and colonial lands, had come under criticism from the left-winger George Lansbury, the Independent Labour Party and the Communist Party of Great Britain.

In accepting the need for a system of collective security, MacDonald had, in fact, moved Labour's foreign policy from that of the UDC, with its greater emphasis upon free trade and a more democratic approach to domestic policies being sufficient to avoid wars, towards the more Gladstonian internationalism, which favoured nations uniting together to prevent war. This had been encouraged by Arthur Henderson, after his visit to Russia in 1917, and grudgingly accepted by MacDonald. By 1924 MacDonald, and the Labour Party, felt that collective international action might preserve the peace which the continuing reparation settlements of the Treaty of Versailles threatened (Brigden, 2009).

The downfall of the first Labour government

Clearly, the first Labour government was successful in areas such as house building and foreign policy. It was not particularly threatened by charges of economic incompetence, a lack of direction over policy, internal disunity, and depleted finances. It did face criticism from within its own ranks for failing to press rapidly ahead with social reform, but even George Lansbury, through the *Daily Herald*, the Independent Labour Party and the Communist Party of Great Britain were prepared to support the government, although they held some misgivings over its economic policy. MacDonald was also a remarkably able party leader and prime minister whose reputation had yet to be soured. His attempts, as foreign secretary, to bring about lasting peace in Europe had helped gain him international respect and recognition.

Instead, the failure of the first Labour government had more to do with the, almost irrational, fears about Marxism rising to power in Britain. Although Thomas Jones, assistant cabinet secretary, soon found that Labour ministers were more moderate, describing John Wheatley as 'Pale Pink' rather than 'Turkey Red', there was concern over the government's recognition of the Soviet Union through negotiating the Anglo-Soviet Treaties (Jones, 1960: 270, 1 February 1924).This divided the Liberal Party and led to David Lloyd George leading a section to support the Conservative Party in order to overthrow the Labour government. The arrest and then release of J. R. Campbell, assistant editor of the Communist *Workers' Weekly*, which had published, on 25 July 1924, an 'Open Letter' asking British troops not to fire on fellow workers, led to further Liberal disaffection. The letter was considered treasonable and treacherous, while the Labour government was increasingly seen as falling within the purview of Moscow. Liberal support for Labour was withdrawn, and a general election took place, in which the Zinoviev

Letter, or 'Red Letter Scare', perhaps further reduced Labour's appeal. The detail of these events reveals the fear that the Russian revolutions inspired among the British establishment.

The fall of the Labour government was serpentine in character and open to several interpretations. Beatrice Webb, the historian of Labour, and wife of a member of the first Labour Cabinet, felt that the elusive mystery of MacDonald's leadership may have played a part in Labour's downfall, especially in his mishandling of the Campbell case. Others, such as J. R. Clynes, Lord Privy Seal and Deputy Leader of the House of Commons, where he was thus effectively deputy prime minister, considered that Stanley Baldwin and H. H. Asquith felt that Labour had done so well that if action were not taken 'Labour would be in power for many years to come' (Clynes, 1937: 64–5). Others, such as the leading figures in the Independent Labour Party, felt that it failed because it did not deliver socialism. Some of these explanations are implausible, given the political climate operating at the time. Full-blooded socialism was not a realistic proposition in 1924, as MacDonald recognised on the formation of the Labour government. Also, few would have suggested that the Labour Party had done terribly well, although it had achieved some minor successes. It was the opposition to the Soviet Union, not domestic policy, that united the two other major political parties against the vulnerable minority Labour government.

One of the cardinal points of MacDonald's foreign policy was *rapprochement* with Soviet Russia. Before taking office, and from Lossiemouth, MacDonald confided his policy on Russia to the editor of the *Nation*, H. W. Massingham, who was his intermediary with Rakovsky, the Russian charge d'affaires in London, and stated that he wished to get matters rolling to recognise the Soviet Union (Letter from MacDonald to Massingham, 19 December 1923 and Massingham to MacDonald, 21 December 1923, Massingham Papers). The Labour government then established formal diplomatic relations with the Soviet Union, but wished to go further to settle compensation claims with British bondholders and the negotiation of commercial transactions. Earlier MacDonald had expressed his pleasure at the amnesty granted in Russia by the Soviets to the Social Revolutionaries. As he took office, he received an assurance from Rakovsky that the release of prisoners would follow the amnesty (Letter of Rakovsky to MacDonald, 22 January 1924, National Archives, formerly the Public Records Office, PRO, 30/69/1264).

In February 1924 MacDonald told the Commons that there would soon be an Anglo-Soviet Conference in London to settle outstanding

differences (*Hansard Parliamentary Debates* (1924), vol. 169, cols 768–9).
In April he opened this conference with a firm speech, listing the differences between the British and Soviet systems of government, objecting
to how the Communist Third International had misrepresented him,
and forcefully pressing the interests of the Council of Anglo-Soviet
Foreign Bondholders and the Association of British Creditors in Russia
(Hutt, 1937: 90–1). After the first meeting, Arthur Ponsonby was left
by MacDonald with the main responsibility of leading the negotiation team.

There were two major issues at the Anglo-Soviet Conference – the goal
of settling the outstanding differences between Britain and the Soviet
Union, and the economic need to conclude a commercial treaty that
would benefit international trade. The desire to retrieve the position of
British bondholders with claims on pre-revolutionary Russia that were
repudiated by the Soviet regime had a high priority. As time went on,
however, it became necessary for the Cabinet to agree to a £30 million
loan to the Soviets in return for two-thirds of it being spent on British
manufacturers and a satisfactory settlement to the bondholding issue
(Cabinet 44(24), 30 July 1934). This proved a contentious issue, since
Philip Snowden was opposed to it, believing that the Russians would
not pay compensation to the British bondholders. Eventually a compromise was agreed whereby there would be both a commercial treaty and
a separate treaty, subject to further negotiations, that would be agreed
between the bondholders and the Russian government. Once at least
half of the outstanding capital value claimants agreed to the terms of the
Russian government, the British government would guarantee the loan.

The settlement was put before the House of Commons for 21 days,
which effectively ensured that it would not be ratified until after the parliamentary summer recess. By that time, stiff opposition was developing.
Conservative opponents of the treaty were joined by leading Liberals,
including Sir John Simon, Walter Runciman and David Lloyd George.
On 3 September the Liberals published a pamphlet, *The Sham Treaty*,
which was followed on 8 September by a series of articles in the *Daily
Chronicle* entitled 'In Darkest Russia'. In response, Ponsonby put up a
stout defence of the Treaty, particularly the loans to the Soviets. In an
interview with the political correspondent on the *Manchester Guardian*,
he emphasised the benefits to British trade and European peace that normal relations with Russia would bring (*Manchester Guardian*, 3 September
1924). He wrote optimistically to MacDonald about the splits in Liberal
ranks over the Treaty:

Even Mond says nothing about a vote...LLG's pretence of 'consulting' the party is pure bunkum...Asquith is silent. [T]o reject a Treaty would be unprecedented – a most serious step to take. At the general election which would follow they would be split finally and irretrievably...I think my interview with the *M. G.* did some good.

> (Ponsonby to MacDonald, 14 September 1924,
> MacDonald Papers, National Archives, formerly the
> Public Records Office, PRO 30/69/1264)

In addition, the General Council of the Trades Union Congress and the National Executive of the Labour Party decided, on 2 September, to mount a strong campaign for the Anglo-Soviet Treaty in the face of the opposition of the capitalist press.

Eventually, on 22 September, Asquith, the Liberal leader, wrote to *The Times*, denouncing the treaties as 'crude experiments in nursery diplomacy', although he did allow that the treaties might be amended rather than rejected outright. Asquith was then mindful of the strong likelihood that the defeat of the Labour government would result in a third general election in less than three years, for which the Liberal Party was ill-prepared.

MacDonald, however, believed strongly in the Russian treaties and was not prepared to compromise, feeling that the Liberals were being dishonest in their tactics. On 26 September he stated that 'I am inclined to give the Liberals an election if they force it' (MacDonald Diary, 26 September 1924, in the National Archives). On 27 September he made a speech at Derby in which he stated forcefully that the Russian treaties might become the basis of a general election:

> We shall take no words from the House of Commons or party leaders like 'I am in favour of trade with Russia and peace with Russia, but I am not going to accept the treaties'...An agreement with Russia on these lines, embodied in our two draft Treaties...is now an essential part of the Labour Party's policy and if the House of Commons will not allow it, the House of Commons had better censure us [loud cheers].

> (*The Times*, 29 September 1924)

On 1 October, at a party meeting, the Liberals decided to oppose the loan guarantee, and it looked certain that the Labour government would collapse (Lyman, 1957: 164). Four days later, Austen Chamberlain, the Conservative shadow foreign secretary, wrote to his sister Ida:

> Meanwhile . . . I take it that we are in for a general election. I think the Govt. would be beaten on Wednesday [on the Campbell case] – I only wish that they would accept that defeat – then, if they last so long, beaten again on the Russian Treaty. They must resign or dissolve on the second, if not the first, defeat & then the deluge! I find myself absolutely unable to predict what will happen.
>
> (Self, 1995: AC5/1/334, letter to Ida, 5 October 1924)

As it happened, it was the infamous Campbell case, not the Russian treaties, that became the summer madness that led to the autumn general election. Predictions of a Labour defeat at Westminster were rife in the press at the beginning of October 1924. On 2 October Sidney Webb, president of the Board of Trade, informed his wife that 'I have no inside news to tell you; but it is generally assumed that "our number is up": I am inclined to doubt whether we shall be defeated next Tuesday or Wednesday on the Communist prosecution motion.' He added that 'On the whole I expect the defeat to take place on Thursday 30 October', actually only six days before Labour's fall. Though, for good measure, Sidney Webb added: 'If I am wrong, it might well happen three or four weeks earlier' (Mackenzie and Mackenzie, 1984: 216–17, Sidney Webb to Beatrice Webb, 2 October 1924).

G. D. H. Cole, the famous historian, reflecting upon Labour's 1924 defeat in the late 1940s, wrote:

> Then came the sad bungle of the Campbell prosecution accompanied by signs that MacDonald was suffering from a bad attack of anti-bolshevism which was aggravated instead of being corrected by the campaign carried on in the press and in Parliament against the Russian Treaties. If the Campbell episode was bad, that of the alleged 'Red Letter', which occurred during the election campaign, was infinitely worse he declared.
>
> (Cole, 1928; Shepherd and Laybourn, 2006: 162)

The Campbell case was the *cause celebre* that brought down the first Labour government (Newark, 1969: 19–42). At the end of July 1924 the Director of Public Prosecutions (DPP) drew the attention of the Attorney General, Sir Patrick Hastings, to an article published in the 25 July issue of the *Workers' Weekly*, an obscure Communist newspaper. On its front page, the left-wing Glasgow paper had carried an 'Open Letter' with a plea to British soldiers not to shoot fellow workers, citing previous examples of them firing upon the workers and noting how the first Labour government had threatened to use naval men in the dock strikes. J. R. Campbell hammered home his key message: 'Let it be known that neither in class war nor in military, will you turn your guns on your fellow workers.' Campbell was, therefore, prosecuted under the antiquated Sedition to Mutiny Act of 1797.

In parliament on 29 July Sir Frederick Hall, the Conservative MP, declared that he would put down a private notice on the 'Open Letter', and Rhys Davies, under-secretary for the Home Office, replied that he was considering action (*Hansard Parliamentary Debates*, vol. 176, col. 1897, 29 July 1929). Shortly afterwards the Attorney General instructed the DPP to take criminal proceedings against Campbell in Bow Street Magistrates Court, which prompted John Scurr to ask the Attorney General in the House of Commons of the circumstances of the police raid on the officers of the *Workers' Weekly*, the details of which produced animated debate in the House. It has since become clear that Special Branch were deeply involved in the decision to prosecute Campbell; Childs, the Head of Special Branch, had provided the Labour Cabinet with weekly reports on revolutionary groups and British Communist connections with the Soviet regime (Barnes, 1979).

Recently released files in the National Archives reveal how the Campbell case was mishandled. Six detectives raided the London officers of the *Workers' Weekly* and discovered that Rajani Palme Dutt, the editor, was ill and that Campbell was temporarily in charge. This meant that they had to wait two hours to get a warrant to arrest him, which was a maladroit move, since Campbell had a distinguished war record. In fact, he had been invalided out of the Royal Naval Volunteer Reserve after the amputation of all his toes on both feet, and his Military Medal had been bestowed for bravery in the field (National Archives: KV2/1186).

At the Cabinet meeting at 6.00 pm on 6 August, the case was discussed, and MacDonald claimed that he had not known about the arrest of Campbell before it occurred. It was here that the decision was taken, on account of the apology of the publishers of the *Workers' Weekly* and the willingness of Campbell to apologise, that prosecution would be dropped, as it eventually was on 13 August. However, the *Workers' Weekly* immediately published the banner headline 'Working Class Agitation forces Government surrender' (*Workers' Weekly*, 15 August 1924).

The summer break allowed the case to subside for a time, but when parliament reconvened at the end of September the issue was hotly debated. Hastings, the Attorney General, took full responsibility for the arrest and the release of Campbell and, responding to a question from Sir Kingsley Wood, MacDonald, unbelievably, denied any part in deciding not to prosecute and any awareness that he might be called to court to give evidence. He told the House of Commons that:

> I was not consulted regarding either the institution or the subsequent withdrawal of proceedings. The first notice which came to my knowledge was in the Press. I never advised its withdrawal, but left the whole matter to the discretion of the Law Officers, where that discretion properly rests. I never received any intimation, nor even a hint, that I should be asked to give evidence. That also came to my attention when the falsehood appeared in the paper.
>
> (*Hansard Parliamentary Debates*, 5th Series, vol. 177, cols 8–16, 30 September 1924)

MacDonald's forthright denial of any responsibility came as a thunderbolt to Cabinet officials. 'When I heard it, as I did in the House, a shiver went down my spine', Tom Jones recalled on 15 October. In his diary he noted Hankey's statement that MacDonald's explanation was 'a bloody lie' (Jones, 1960: 296, 15 October 1924). The fact is that, when the King first heard of the Campbell case, MacDonald had written to him to apportion blame elsewhere: 'I knew nothing about it until I saw it in the newspapers. I then sent for the Attorney General and Public Prosecutor and gave them a bit of my mind.' He added that he told them 'as they had begun, they had to go through with it' (Marquand, 1977: 364–70; Nicolson, 1952: 398–9). In his view, only Campbell's offer of a written apology, which was never received, was an adequate reason to abandon the prosecution. However, Labour ministers feared a court case, because the Communists would have summoned MacDonald to give evidence and answer some awkward questions. In the end, MacDonald blamed inexperienced ministers and inefficient civil servants for the botched affair (MacDonald to Stamfordham, 22 August, RA PS/GV/K 1958/4).

Jones's diary reveals that Sir Maurice Hankey had made an attempt to get MacDonald to check the accuracy of his statement on 2 October, noting that he had put a draft minute in front of MacDonald after a meeting following the Cabinet meeting on 6 August, and after a meeting at the House of Commons concluded at 11.00 am on 7 August. Jones showed Jimmy Thomas, a cabinet minister, the rough notes of the meeting on

6 August, which led Thomas to suggest that 'unfortunately "Mac" had gone beyond the truth and we had all got to try to pull things together.' He himself did not want an election (Jones, 1960: 295–7).

As already indicated, the Campbell sideshow was fought in the context of the Anglo-Soviet Treaty. In the end, it was the position of the leaders of the three political parties over this issue that was the crucial factor in the downfall of the Labour government. Among the opposition leaders, no one was more opposed to the Russian Treaty than David Lloyd George. Although he had been positive about the idea of appeasement of Russia in 1921, he was now opposed to the idea of a loan to Russia. He had attacked the commercial treaty as 'fake' in the House of Commons on 6 August, and he approached Winston Churchill, now back with the Conservatives, about the possibility of a Tory–Liberal combination to oust Labour (*Westminster Gazette*, 8 July 1924; *Daily Chronicle*, 8 August 1924; Campbell, 1977, 1999: 85–9). At that point he wrote to his daughter, Megan, stating that:

It looks now as if we are in for another General Election. I have done my best to precipitate it. Labour had its chance and with a little more wisdom and what the old puritans sagely called 'Grace of God' they could have remained in another three years and formed a working alliance with Liberalism that would have ensured a progressive administration of this country for 20 years. But they have lost their heads as men and women will from sudden elevation. Hence their fall.

(David Lloyd George to Megan, 2 October 1924;
Morgan, 1973: 204)

On 1 October Beatrice Webb predicted the collapse of the Labour government over either the 'silly little issue' of the Campbell case or the Russian treaties (Cole, 1956: 44). Nine days later she noted:

The end of the tale of the Parliament of 1923–24 and of its Cabinet is soon told. The two Oppositions decided to kill the Government on the Campbell issue. Some say they drifted into their decision: others that the Russian Treaty proved [un]expectedly popular and that the Liberals, in particular, would have lost, not fourteen, but fifty, in the division lobbies, if they had stuck to demanding the Treaty. Anyhow the Conservatives ran away from their direct censure, and beat the Government by the meaner Liberal way of the Court of Enquiry which the Cabinet could not accept without lowering its prestige a few weeks before it was to be sent to the country on the Russian issue [*sic*].

(Cole, 1956: 44)

In truth, however, MacDonald had expected the fall of the Labour government, and informed the Labour Conference on its opening day, 7 October 1924, which happened to be the eve of the crucial Campbell debate, that the Liberals

> have decided to have an election in three weeks, if they can force it. In preparation for it, they are laying their traps, and when I saw the newspapers this morning, and especially the Liberal Press, the shaking of heads about an election, I really wondered did they think that all their readers were fools. There has been a trumped up stunt about the dropping of a certain prosecution. What a chance for a worry! What a chance for a humiliation! What a chance for the wiles of a pettifogging lawyer!
>
> (Twenty-Fourth Annual Conference of the Labour Party, Report, 7–10 October 1924, London, Labour Party: 110–11)

The end of the Labour government finally came when the administration lost a vote of confidence in the House of Commons on 8 October 1924. MacDonald had made it clear that in these circumstances he would ask for a dissolution of parliament from the King and seek a new mandate at the general election. On 2 October he reported to the King that the end of the Labour government was in sight. His opponents' attack over the withdrawal of the Campbell prosecution, followed by the Liberal Party resolution to reject the Russian Treaty, was part of a more general move to destroy the administration.

Yet opinion was divided on the precise reason for Labour's defeat. Beatrice Webb felt that 'the silly little issue' was perhaps at best a pretext for bringing down the Labour government. J. R. Clynes went further, and felt that the withdrawal of the Campbell prosecution provided the pretext for the opposition parties to combine against the government because they believed that Labour was 'doing too well' (Clynes, 1937: 64–5). Philip Snowden believed that it was MacDonald's fault because of his inaccurate statement in the House of Commons on the Campbell case, his subsequent vague apology to the House on 8 August, and the scandal of Sir Arthur Grant, the head of the biscuit firm McVitie & Price, giving MacDonald 30,000 shares in his company and the donation of a Daimler motor car. Grant's subsequent baronetcy in the Honours list led to taunts of 'biscuits' in the House of Commons during MacDonald's' speeches. Bitterly, Snowden felt after watching MacDonald's performance in the Commons on 8 October – which led John Wheatley to whisper to Snowden that 'I never knew a man who could succeed so well, even if he is telling the truth in giving the impression he was not doing so' – the fate of the Labour government was sealed (Snowden, 1934: 850). More recently, however, Andrew Thorpe has seen the Campbell case as a timely opportunity to leave office (Thorpe, 1997, 2000: 328–9). John Beckett, sometime Labour activist and Fascist, also reflects in his unpublished memoirs that MacDonald seemed tired and perhaps lacked the willingness to continue (J. Beckett unpublished manuscript in the Labour Study Archive, People's Museum, Manchester). The issue comes down to whether or not it was a conspiring opposition or a spent Labour leader that allowed the Campbell case to bring about the collapse of the first Labour government.

There is evidence to suggest that MacDonald was tired, and it was he, after all, who made the Campbell case an issue of confidence in the government. However, in the final analysis, it was the opposition that decided the fate of the first Labour government. Lord Beaverbrook, the press baron, wrote in his article 'Who Killed Cock Robin' that the Labour government fell because of political manoeuvres and a series of accidents and blunders by MacDonald, Baldwin and Lloyd George. Convinced that his administration would be defeated over the Russian Treaties, MacDonald chose to stand his ground on the withdrawal of the Campbell prosecution, which, according to Beaverbrook, led to the early end of a government whose commitment to the Russian Treaties would have ended as a result of the Zinoviev Letter (Beaverbrook, 1924). Instead, Beaverbrook felt that Baldwin wanted the Labour government to continue; on 30 September he offered to postpone the Campbell debate until 18 November. MacDonald rejected this, and on 8 October the Conservatives put down a vote of censure and the Liberals opted for an amendment requesting a select committee of inquiry. If the voting had gone along party lines, both would have been defeated with the government still intact, since the Conservatives were not prepared to support the Liberal amendment. However, Lloyd George, totally opposed to the Russian Treaty, attempted to get the Conservatives to abandon their motion of censure and, after some political machinations, got Baldwin to agree that the Conservatives would vote for the Liberal amendment.

Indeed, Beaverbrook may well have been right. While the crucial debate was in progress, the Cabinet met at 8.45 pm to confirm that it would continue to oppose the motion and the amendment (Cabinet 23/48 (53) (24), 8 October 1924). As the censure motion and the amendments were both matters of confidence, Baldwin's announcement sounded the death knell of the government. In winding up for Labour, J. H. Thomas censured the Conservatives' action as 'a mean and contemptible party manoeuvre', but to no avail. The Speaker put the question 'That the words proposed be left out stand part of the question', and the Liberal amendment was carried – Ayes 198 to Noes 359. The amended motion asking for a select committee of inquiry was then put and, although, remarkably, 14 Liberals and two Conservatives went into the same lobby with the Labour MPs, the result of 364 votes to 198 meant defeat for the first Labour government. The Cabinet met briefly at 11.30 pm to note that MacDonald would see the King at Buckingham Palace the next morning at 10.00 am to work for the immediate dissolution of parliament (Cabinet 23/48 (54) (24), 8 October 1924).

The October 1924 general election

George V was reluctant to grant a dissolution on the minor issue of the Campbell case, although he knew that it was inevitable, since neither Baldwin nor Asquith would take office and a coalition government was unlikely (Nicolson, 1952: 398–400). Labour immediately produced an election manifesto which toasted the first Labour government's success in housing and foreign policy and offered a moderate programme which included the reorganisation of the mining industry, a national electricity generating system, taxation of land values, and the establishment of a royal commission on the licensing laws.

Labour was attacked by the Conservatives on the issue of the Russian Treaties and its failure to find a solution to unemployment. The Conservatives offered improvement in education and agricultural rate relief, while the Liberals focused upon free trade, temperance and education pensions. MacDonald made a radio speech attacking the opposition parties for bringing down the government, while his opponents focused their attack upon the Anglo-Soviet treaties and Baldwin showed his relaxed mastery of radio broadcasting. However, the 1924 general election will always be remembered for the notorious Zinoviev Letter. It was revealed four days before polling day by the *Daily Mail*, whose sensational headlines were 'Civil War Plot by Socialists' Masters': 'Moscow Orders to Our Reds: Great Plot Disclosed' (*Daily Mail*, 25 October 1924). The infamous 'Zinoviev Letter' called upon the British Communists to stir up insurrection and revolution. To the Labour movement this has become a plot by the Tory press, the Conservative central office, and members (or former members) of MI6 (Secret Intelligence Service) to bring down the government and to restore the Tory Party to office. All these groups hated Russian Communism and were highly suspicious of the Labour government's recognition of the Soviet regime and the attempts to promise commercial links between Britain and Russia. The Special Intelligence Service submitted copies of the Zinoviev Letter to the Foreign Office and other ministries. The Foreign Office felt that it was genuine, but MacDonald, who received a copy of it while campaigning in Manchester, warned about its authenticity. And ever since, though it has proved impossible to examine the original letter, it has been the subject of intense debate and scrutiny. The Conservative government's investigation in 1928 pronounced it genuine, while the second Labour government's investigation suggested that it was a forgery, as have investigations in 1967 by the *Sunday Times* and the more recent report compiled by Gill Bennett in 1999. It seems that it might have been produced by a forgery ring in the Baltic and circulated by some members of British Intelligence, although the operational activities of MI6 seem to be missing (Shepherd and Laybourn, 2006: 182–3).

Whether or not the Zinoviev Letter made any difference to Labour's 1924 general election defeat is debatable (Table 2.1). Labour gained more than 1 million votes extra, while the Liberal vote fell by about 1,400,000 votes. Indeed, it was the Liberal Party that was the great loser in this election, which returned 419 Conservative MPs, 151 Labour MPs and 40 Liberal MPs. Labour thus lost 40 seats and the Liberals 118. This precipitated a brief scurry of activity within the Labour Party against MacDonald, although he soon re-established his position within the party and was to lead a second minority Labour government between 1929 and 1931.

Table 2.1 The general election of 1924

Party	Votes won	MPs elected	Share of vote (%)
Conservative	7,418,983 (5,286,159)	412 (258)	46.8 (38.0)
Labour	5,281,626 (4,267,831)	151 (191)	33.3 (30.7)
Liberal	2,818,717 (4,129,922)	40 (158)	17.8 (29.7)
Others	336,889 (225,105)	12 (8)	2.1 (1.6)

Note: Figures for 1923 in brackets.
Source: Craig, 1987.

Conclusion

Who, then, killed Cock Robin? Was it MacDonald himself, weary of power as Andrew Thorpe suggests? Was it because of political manoeuvres and a series of accidents and blunders by MacDonald, Baldwin and Lloyd George? Was it a deliberate ploy of the opposition parties?

What is clear is that the first Labour government could have been defeated at any point, since it was a minority administration dependent upon the support of the Liberal Party. From the start its uncompromising opposition to the Anglo-Soviet Treaty, or Treaties, in the face of a hostile Liberal Party, sensitised by the opposition of David Lloyd George, ensured that there was always an opportunity for the withdrawal of Liberal support. In the end, however, it was the bungled handling of the Campbell case that gave the Conservative Party the opportunity to press for a motion of censure on the first Labour government and to switch to the Liberal amendment, of forming a select committee to investigate the handling of the Campbell case, and force MacDonald to resign on an issue on which he had said he would resign. In the end, it would seem that Labour expected to be defeated and that the Conservative Party, amid political bungling, made the decision that its days were numbered. However, though defeated in the 'Red Letter' campaign, Labour in 1924 had established itself as a party of government, whereas the decimated Liberal Party was never to assume office again in twentieth-century Britain.

References

Barnes, T. (1979), 'Special Branch and the First Labour Government', *Historical Journal*, Vol. 22, No. 4, 941–51.

Beaverbrook, B. (1924), 'Who Killed Cock Robin?', *Sunday Express*, 23 November 1924.

Bennett, G. (1999), *A Most Extraordinary and Mysterious Business: The Zinoviev Letter of 1924* (London: Historian, LRD).

Booth, A. and Pack, M. (1985), *Employment, Capital and Economic Policy* (Oxford: Blackwell).

Brigden, P. (2009), *The Labour Party and the Politics of War and Peace, 1900–1924* (London: Royal Historical Society and Boydell).

Campbell, J. (1977, 1999), *Lloyd George: The Goat in the Wilderness, 1922–1931* (Aldershot: Gregg Revivals).

Clynes, J. R. (1937), *Memoirs 1924–1937* (London: Hutchinson).

Cole, G. D. H. (1928), *A History of the Labour Party* (London: Routledge & Kegan Paul).

Cole, M. I. (1956), *Beatrice Webb Diaries 1924–1931* (London: Longman).

Craig, F. W. S. (1987), *British Electoral Facts 1832–1987* (Aldershot: Dartmouth).

Cross, C. (1966), *Philip Snowden* (London: Barrie & Rockliffe).

Hutt, A. (1937), *The Post-War History of the British Working Class* (London: Left Book Club, Gollancz).

Jones, T. (1960), *Whitehall Diary Vol. 1 1916–1925* (London: Oxford University Press).

Laybourn, K. (1988), *Philip Snowden: A Biography* (Aldershot: Temple Smith/ Gower/Wildwood).

Lyman, R. (1957), *The First Labour Government* (London: Chapman and Hall).

Mackenzie, N. and Mackenzie, J. (1984), *The Diary of Beatrice Webb. Volume Three, 1905–1924* (London: Virago).

Marquand, D. (1977), *Ramsay MacDonald* (London: Jonathan Cape).

Maurice, F. (1929), *Haldane 1916–1928* (London: Faber and Faber).

Morgan, K. (ed.) (1973), *Lloyd George Family Letters, 1885–1936* (Cardiff and London: University of Wales Press and Oxford University Press).

Newark, F. (1969), 'The Campbell Case and the First Labour Government', *Northern Ireland Legal Quarterly*, Vol. 1, No. 1, 19–42.

Nicolson, H. (1952), *King George V: His Life and Reign* (London: Cassell).

O'Roirdon, E. Y. (2001), *Britain and the Ruhr Crisis* (Basingstoke: Palgrave Macmillan).

Self, R. C. (1995), *The Austen Chamberlain Diary Letters: The Correspondence of Sir Austen Chamberlain with his sisters Hilda and Ida, 1916–1937*, Vol. 5 (5th Series) (Cambridge: Cambridge University Press).

Shepherd, J. and Laybourn, K. (2006), *Britain's First Labour Government* (Basingstoke: Palgrave).

Snowden, P. (1934), *An Autobiography: Volume Two, 1919–1934* (London: Nicolson & Watson).

Sylvest, C. (2006), 'A Commanding Group? Labour's Advisory Committee on International Questions, 1918–1931', in Corthorn, P. and Davis, I. (eds), *The British Labour Party and the Wider World* (London: I. B. Tauris).

Tawney, R. H. (1922, 1988), *Secondary Education for All: A Policy for Labour* (London: Labour Party; Hambledon Press).

The Earl of Oxford and Asquith (1928), *Memories and Reflections 1852–1927*, Vol. 2 (London: Cassell).

Thorpe, A. (1997, 2000), *A History of the British Labour Party* (Basingstoke: Palgrave Macmillan).

Winkler, H. R. (1956), 'The Emergence of a Labour Foreign Policy for Britain', *The Journal of Modern History*, Vol. 28, No. 3, 247–58.

Winkler, H. R. (1994), *Paths Not Taken: British Labour and International Policy in the 1920s* (Chapel Hill, NC: University of North Carolina Press).

Winkler, H. R. (2005), *British Labour Seeks a Foreign Policy, 1910–1940* (London: Transaction Publishers).

3
The Fall of the Second MacDonald Government, 1931

Chris Wrigley

The fall of the second Labour government was but a matter of time from when James Ramsay MacDonald formed a minority government in June 1929. The length of the government was always likely to be determined by when the Liberals would combine with the Conservatives to eject Labour. This was likely to be determined when the two parties were ready to face the electorate again, in terms of both enhanced political appeal over 1929 and adequate finances, and when Labour appeared sufficiently discredited to justify its removal part way through a five-year electoral term.

The intrinsic weakness of the government was later obscured by various myths ascribed to its fall within the Labour movement, and later by historians and political scientists (Webb, 1932; Bassett, 1958; Berkeley, 1976, 1978; Marquand, 1977). Most of the 'myths' have centred around MacDonald and his closest associates, and, in particular, whether MacDonald's 'treachery' in dumping the Labour government for the National government was a long-planned move or was a result of his speedy reaction to a rapidly developing crisis. Sidney Webb wrote of the crisis that it 'was foreseen in advance...only by the statesman who was at once its author, its producer, and its principal actor' (Webb, 1932) However, since this assertion and some other claims in 1931–32, there have been few later statements of this kind; the most notable, by McKenzie, was effectively dismissed by Bassett in 1958 (McKenzie, 1955; Bassett, 1958, Appendix VI). The balance of opinion is firmly against a long-planned move to end the Labour government in favour of a National government. The notion of a Machiavellian MacDonald plotting at length to replace the second Labour government has been fully and adequately rebutted by, among others, Bassett, 1958, Marquand, 1977, Thorpe, 1991, and above all by Williamson, 1992. However, there are many historians who are critical of MacDonald's weakness, if not treachery, in calling a general election in late 1931 and thereby severely damaging the Labour Party and many of his associates of three decades and more.

The myths of 'the betrayal' of 1931 were explored at the time of the centenary of the formation of the Labour Representation Committee (forerunner of the Labour Party) by Jon Lawrence (Lawrence, 2000: 342, 351–4). Drawing on Labour autobiographies, Lawrence made clear how 1931 could be interpreted later to give legitimacy to conflicting views about the 1931 crisis. However, the partial recollections of many autobiographies, while of use for studying myths, are otherwise more notable for revising the past to serve the present. Morrison in his autobiography is unequivocal as to 'The 1931 Betrayal', and emphasises that he was the first in the Cabinet to criticise MacDonald for not resigning office. At the time, as his biographers Donoughue and Jones have shown, Morrison was equivocal about joining MacDonald's National government and, quite possibly, favourable at first (Morrison, 1960: 126–9; Donoughue and Jones, 1973: 162–7).

If one focuses more on the trade union leadership, and especially Ernest Bevin, it is clear that many were disillusioned earlier, seven years before 1931, by MacDonald's anxiety to keep the trade unions at a distance during the 1924 Labour government (Bullock, 1960: 236–47; Laybourn and Shepherd, 2006: 68–72) and by his failure to deal effectively with the so-called Zinoviev Letter during the 1924 general election campaign. Similarly, long before 1931, he had lost the support of the Labour Left. Nevertheless, that many in the Labour movement were shocked by MacDonald's departure to head a National government is undeniable.

MacDonald remains the prime minister from the most impoverished background. Yet part of his problem in the Labour Party was to do with his attitudes after bettering himself. This he did partly through self-help, partly through moving from Scotland to Bristol, then London, and partly through marriage to the upper-middle-class Margaret Gladstone. He came to see himself as a cosmopolitan European labour leader, a substantial intellectual, and he often did not conceal his disdain for the trade unionists in the parliamentary Labour Party. For Sidney Webb and George Bernard Shaw (both Fabians), MacDonald was part of 'the professional proletariat'. There was always something of the pupil teacher about him, a didactic urge to educate and elevate worthy trade unionist parliamentary colleagues. This was often combined with a preference for the company of Liberal intellectuals or former middle-class Liberals who had joined the Labour Party (Marquand, 1977; Wrigley, 1999). The disdain MacDonald and Philip Snowden, chancellor of the exchequer, showed for the Trades Union Congress leaders and most of the MPs who came from trade union activist backgrounds made for a lack of empathy between them during the critical days in summer 1931.

In spite of doubts about MacDonald's leadership during the first Labour government, MacDonald in 1929–31 was still greatly admired by much of the Labour movement. He was a speaker of charisma, something rare in the parliamentary Labour Party. The German author Egon Wertheimer, a perceptive commentator on the British Labour Party, wrote in the second edition of his *Portrait of the Labour Party* (May 1930) of the first edition (Germany, May 1929; UK, June 1929): 'Possibly it did not convey a sufficiently clear idea of the exceptional position occupied by MacDonald within the party, and did not sufficiently reveal the power which emanates from him.' This esteem carried many of his Cabinet colleagues with him for a few more days in late August 1931 than otherwise might have been the case. However, Wertheimer also commented, 'Sustained by the consciousness of success and recognition, he excels himself; in an atmosphere of criticism and misunderstanding, his energy and initiative seem to flag' (Wertheimer, 1930: xxx and 279). Macdonald was to experience precious little adulation but much criticism in the second half of the second Labour government. Responding to the call for a national government of individuals to rescue the nation appealed to his romantic self-image of a noble self-sacrificing patriot: pleasingly, very much a contrasting image of him to that held by many of the British people in 1914–18.

While many of the accounts of 'the betrayal' of 1931 have unsurprisingly focused on Ramsay MacDonald, the survival of the second Labour government depended on much else. Given the Conservative Party's rhetoric of 'Bolshevism' and 'The Red Peril', the Conservatives were unlikely to do otherwise than oppose the government on many issues, at least after a few months. In contrast, the second Labour government's fate lay for most of 1929–31 in the hands of the Liberals.

The minority Labour government and the Liberals

Why did the Liberals tolerate Labour in office much longer than they had in 1924? After the 1923 general election Baldwin had not resigned, but had gone to the House of Commons. In effect, this forced the Liberals to put the Conservatives out and Labour in. In 1929 Baldwin resigned soon after the general election result was known, so the Liberals did not need to take positive action to install Labour in office, and thus felt less responsible for the government's actions. While in 1924 the Conservative Party was the biggest party in the House of Commons, in 1929–31 Labour was in this position. This allowed the Liberals to abstain in parliamentary votes and Labour still to survive in office.

Beyond this, there were four key areas which influenced Liberal parliamentary support for the Labour government. These were the finances of the Liberals, the party's performance in by-elections, the acceptability of Labour's policies in parliament and the credibility of Labour in dealing with the developing international economic crisis. The finances of the Liberals were a sensitive area. After running 513 candidates in 1929 and spending some £400,000, the Liberal Party had no wish for a further general election soon. As well as £320,000, or possibly £425,000, for the 1929 general election, Lloyd George provided an annual £60,000 over several years to the party organisation until June 1930 and £2,000 per annum to the parliamentary party until 1931 (Douglas, 1971: 200, 209–10). Having long relied on money from sales of honours from Asquith's, then Lloyd George's, premierships, the Liberal Party's central organisation was unused to raising sizeable sums of money. As a result of the much smaller inflow of finance, full-time members of staff were made redundant over a period of time, with the Eastern Counties Federation having to part with all of its officials, and even in the South-West organisation collapsing in some seats (Cook, 1976: 112; Thorpe, 1991: 58; Tregidga, 2000: 58).

The Liberals faced major problems in funding by-election candidates, so the party did not contest 18 of the 31 by-elections of the period of the second Labour government (but nine of these had not been contested in the 1929 general election). Where the Liberals did compete, the party experienced bad results from August 1929 to September 1930, though it increased its share of the poll at Shipley and Whitechapel in November and December 1930 (coming near to winning), but had further poor results in the first half of 1931 (Cook and Ramsden, 1973: 366–7). For the Liberals the formation of the National government in August 1931 was something of a 'Get Out of Jail Free' card, in that it provided them with some government posts without initially having to fight a general election.

As well as the issue of weak finances and poor by-election results, the Liberals (or many of them) were not willing to oust Labour quickly, as they had greater hopes of securing policies that they wanted from Labour than from the Conservatives. More than that, the Conservatives wished to introduce tariffs. This was a policy that had hitherto been

anathema to Liberals. In the early days of the second Labour government, most of the Liberals viewed the Conservative Party as 'discredited
after five years in office' (Samuel, 1944: 199). When the Liberals did not
like Labour government proposals they faced, as Samuel later recalled, 'a
choice between two evils – agreeing to proposals that we did not think
were good, or else voting with the Conservatives to defeat the Ministry'
(Samuel, 1944: 199).

Lloyd George was notably more favourable to Labour than the Conservatives in 1929–31. At times there was even speculation that Lloyd
George would join the Labour Party. In 1925 the veteran Independent
Labour Party (ILP) stalwart Joseph Burgess even published a book, *Will
Lloyd George Supplant Ramsay MacDonald?* There were rumours in 1925
that the right wing of the Labour Party was considering a coalition with
the Liberals after the next general election if the Conservatives were in
a minority in parliament. The ILP took a strong line against such talk,
even expelling from the ILP Ben Spoor, who had been chief whip during
the 1924 Labour government (Burgess, 1926: 35–6). Burgess argued in
his book that, if the Labour right should reject the ILP's policies, then
'the next election will be fought on a Labour programme so timid that
the Lloyd George Land Policy restored to its original form, will pave
the way for a Coalition of Lib-Lab forces after the election' (Burgess,
1926: 48). Lloyd George's original mid-1920s land proposals had called
for a form of land nationalisation which looked back to the role of the
state under the Corn Production Act, 1917. Lloyd George's radicalism
had consistently included land reform, but the mid-1920s proposals
were too much for some Liberals (Douglas, 1976; Packer, 2001). The
land proposals were soon watered down, but not until they had provided the occasion for Alfred Mond and Hilton Young to defect to the
Conservatives (Campbell, 1977: 119–25).

There was renewed talk of Lloyd George joining Labour, either in
office or as a leading member of the party, in the later stages of the
1929–31 government. As Ben Pimlott has commented, 'long before the
collapse of August 1931 a demoralisation and a sense of purposelessness
had permeated all levels of the Party' (Pimlott, 1977: 9). In contrast,
Lloyd George had energy and ideas, especially in the areas of unemployment and agriculture. George Lansbury, on his own initiative, wrote to
Lloyd George on 13 February 1931, urging: 'I have thought of writing
to you many times during the past few years. Why won't you join the
Labour Party?' Lloyd George replied three days later, ' "Coming over"
is not the best way to help. It would antagonise millions of Liberals
with hereditary party loyalties...I am sure I can render more effective

assistance where I am' (Postgate, 1951: 265–6; Shepherd, 2002: 267). This was an interesting development, not least as that earlier socialist saint, Keir Hardie, had appealed to Lloyd George in 1903 to lead a Progressive Alliance of Radicals, Irish and Labour (Wrigley, 1976: 21–3). Had MacDonald died in mid-1923 he would have been a third socialist saint, not the sinner of post-1931 legend. Lansbury was not alone in thinking Lloyd George might 'come over'. Henderson talked of this in July to Hugh Dalton. Dalton noted in his diary: 'his vitality is amazing and his recent speeches have made a tremendous appeal to our people in the House' (Pimlott, 1986: 147).

In 1923–31, while Lloyd George sometimes appeared to favour seeking agreement with the Conservatives as he had done in 1916–22, more often he favoured a progressive coalition, reverting back to the left of centre politics before the First World War (Wrigley, 1991: 49–69). Lloyd George pressed for electoral reform, being willing to trade Liberal support for the Labour government for proportional representation. MacDonald was more willing to consider the alternative vote, which would also have had advantages for the Liberals. Pressed by Arthur Henderson, who wanted Liberal support for a measure replacing the Conservatives' Trades Disputes and Trade Union Act 1927, MacDonald agreed in December 1930 to introduce a measure of electoral reform that included the alternative vote. This was done in early 1931 with the Representation of the People (Number 2) Bill. There was little or no Labour enthusiasm for even the alternative vote, but it was supported, as it was recognised that the House of Lords would delay the measure for two years. While Lloyd George sought electoral reform, he remained keen to mould a new progressive alliance. Frances Stevenson had noted earlier, on 15 May 1926:

> D's idea is to go definitely towards the Left, and gradually to co-ordinate and consolidate all the progressive forces in the country, against the Conservatives and reactionary forces. Thus he will eventually get all sane Labour as well as Liberalism behind him.
>
> (Taylor, 1971: 246)

However, while Lloyd George was keen to influence unemployment, agricultural and other policies of the second Labour government as well as securing electoral reform, his ability to provide support was weakened by the crumbling coherence of the 59-strong parliamentary Liberal Party. For Sir John Simon and others, the natural enemy was the Labour Party, not the Conservative Party. Simon had produced a legal argument against the legitimacy of the General Strike in 1926, and he remained hostile to the trade unions. At the start of the second Labour government Lloyd George made it very clear that Labour should not take his support for granted. He flexed his muscles, making it very clear that he could and would give such under-performing Labour ministers as J. H. Thomas, Margaret Bondfield and Wedgwood Benn a hard time. He was particularly effective in criticising the Coal Mines Bill, taking a stance as a defender of the consumer against the self-interests of Labour and capital (Wrigley, 1991: 64–5).

However, on 25 October 1930 Sir John Simon wrote to Lloyd George making clear his hostility towards further support for the Labour government, and in particular his opposition to reversing the post-General Strike Conservative trade union legislation, the Trade Disputes Act, 1927, when it became an imminent issue that December. As David Dutton has observed, the major issue separating Simon from the Conservatives was free trade, and from early 1931 he appeared to prefer a protectionist government to Labour (Dutton, 1992: 104). By March 1931 he began to move towards supporting tariffs. Simon departed from the main Liberals in June 1931, ostensibly over land taxation, an issue long close to Lloyd George's heart (Snowden, 1934: 906–15; Dutton, 1991: 83–6). The Labour government's measure was very much in line with past Liberal aspirations (Douglas, 1976; Packer, 2001). Liberal disintegration in the last ten months of the second Labour government weakened one of its supports, but the government's collapse occurred before Lloyd George or Samuel could no longer carry sufficient of their party to keep it in office. With hindsight, it might have been better for the Labour Party had Simon convinced a majority of his colleagues to pull the plug on the second Labour government in late 1930 or early 1931.

So the length of the life of the second Labour government depended on the support of Lloyd George and the majority of Liberal MPs who continued to follow him. In February 1931 Lloyd George called for the government to introduce public expenditure cuts, preferring such cuts to be carried out by Labour without involving another general election. While Lloyd George responded to the growing mood for public expenditure reductions, as he had in 1921–22, he still hoped for more imaginative responses to growing unemployment. The sudden and severe illness of Lloyd George on 27 July 1931 removed not only the most sympathetic to Labour of the leading Liberals, but also the remaining major proponent of the 1929 Liberal economic policies. Bernard Wasserstein, whose judgements are usually shrewd, is most probably wrong to state that 'Lloyd George no more believed in Keynesianism *in principle* than the Celt in him believed in leprechauns' (Wasserstein, 1992: 312). Perhaps his notions were not formally Keynesian, but he had long had reflationary impulses, not least in believing that, had the First World War gone on longer, finance would have been found to continue it, and, as it had not, if the political will was there reconstruction could and should go ahead. Indeed, Lloyd George's proposed and actual state economic initiatives, from the time of the development aspects of his 1909 'People's Budget' to other proposals in 1921–22, were drawn on by Keynes and Lloyd George in their late 1920s proposals to deal with unemployment.

However, with Lloyd George in hospital and with the escalating crisis of summer 1931, the main group of Liberals under Herbert Samuel were very happy to join a national government which at the time was pledged to be only for a short time and not to involve an immediate expensive general election. Samuel was very quick to assure Ramsay MacDonald on 13 August that the Liberal Party was supportive of substantial cuts, just as it had been since at least February. Philip Williamson has seen Samuel's position as confirming support for Labour to carry out the cuts and for the Liberals to 'remain independent' of the Conservatives, who 'would try to force a general election, kill off electoral reform, and impose protection' (Williamson, 1992: 300). Also, Samuel's support for cuts was in line with his long-held Gladstonian economic beliefs (Wasserstein, 1992: 312–14). As Andrew Thorpe has observed of the Liberals after Lloyd George's illness, 'the Liberals' positive policy of 1929 was nowhere to be seen. In its place ... was an unreconstructed and unattractive Gladstonianism' (Thorpe, 1991: 62). Hence, MacDonald found his allies were now closer to Snowden in espousing economic orthodoxy than Lloyd George had been most of the time.

There was a large fragment of the Liberal Party that was more willing than Samuel to work with the Conservative Party. This was true, from the outset of the second Labour government in 1929, of such former Cabinet ministers as Walter Runciman and Sir John Simon. These Liberals were attracted to the talk of a national government which was in the air in autumn 1930. That October, Lloyd George had been at a dinner organised by Lord Reading and J. E. B. Seely, at which a paper had been given in favour of a national government (Thorpe, 1991: 55). Simon and Reading had talked of a national government on 27 November 1930. In the last months of 1930 this was common currency in some right of centre political circles, ranging from the newspaper editor J. L. Garvin, John Buchan, and General J. E. B. Seely to Sir Oswald Mosley, who was steadily moving away from the left (Williamson, 1991: 331–2;

1992: 148–56). However, the Conservative leadership was not enamoured of such talk. Their public speeches threw cold water on the notion. They wanted a general election, as they fully expected to win with a good majority, as in 1924. They were confident that it was better for them that Labour should suffer the opprobrium of slashing public expenditure before a general election (Ball, 1986: 160–2). There remained a substantial obstacle to the right-wing Liberals and the Conservatives coming together, and that was the issue of free trade or tariffs. As Philip Williamson has argued, Baldwin was happy to wait on events and in due course form a purely Conservative government committed to tariffs (Williamson, 1992: 160–1).

Economic and political crisis

The second Labour government continued to try to deal with the growing international economic crisis within free trade economics. While other parties could agree with Snowden's Gladstonian policies of cutting public expenditure and maintaining the gold standard, support for his other economic fundamental, free trade, soon dwindled even in part of the Liberal Party in the face of the increasingly severe downturn in international trade.

Within the Labour movement there were some doubts about the efficacy of orthodox economics. Ernest Bevin, Walter Citrine and some other trade unionists believed (as Jack Beard of the Transport and General Workers' Union put it at the 1930 TUC) 'in interference with the so-called "immutable economic laws"', just as trade unionists had done in 1850–75 when faced with the unpleasant consequences of belief in the 'iron law of wages' (*Times*, 3 September 1930). Critics of the Treasury view on the Macmillan Committee on Finance and Industry (November 1929 – June 1931), notably J. M. Keynes, Ernest Bevin and Reginald McKenna, the former Liberal chancellor of the exchequer, saw reducing unemployment as a priority and called for policies to expand trade rather than to drive down wages and salaries. Keynes and Bevin believed that Britain's 1925 return to the gold standard had been at too high a parity with gold and that this had played a very substantial role, along with similar action by other countries, in the international fall in price levels (Clarke, 1988: 73–225; Wrigley, 2011: 45–53). For Bevin and some other socialists, the alternative response to deflation should involve state economic planning, as had been the case during the First World War, notably at the Ministry of Munitions, more generally in wartime controls and post-war economic reconstruction, and was happening in the later 1920s in the Soviet Union and fascist Italy (Ritschell, 1997: 1–126). From January 1931, in the Society for Socialist Inquiry and Propaganda, Bevin and the socialist intellectuals R. H. Tawney, G. D. H. Cole and Margaret Cole discussed alternative policies, often involving economic co-operation, as 'the present system is rapidly breaking down' (Cole, 1977: 190–203).

MacDonald himself had serious doubts about free trade in such adverse conditions. Looking back, albeit with bitterness towards MacDonald, Snowden believed that in 'the latter part of the summer of 1930…MacDonald's mind was turned towards Protection'. Then, according to Snowden, he was hoping to win a majority in the next general election on a policy of not cutting the social services, adopting a 'forward programme' on unemployment and proposing a 10 per cent all-round revenue tariff (Snowden, 1934: 923). Earlier, in February 1930, he had urged the consideration of protecting British grain producers from subsidised external competition by a mix of subsidies and tariffs, but had backed away in the face of Snowden's and the Treasury's hostility (Marquand, 1977: 557–60; Griffiths, 2011). Clement Attlee, chancellor of the Duchy of Lancaster, observed that Snowden's arguments could equally damn the sugar beet subsidy, the government's coal proposals 'and most Socialist proposals' (Marquand, 1977: 560). MacDonald, however, agreed with Snowden on the desirability of public expenditure cuts and, by early 1931, he was backing proposals to economise on benefits to unemployed people. Privately, though, he felt that cuts should be accompanied by tariffs. With the May Report he hoped the severe welfare cuts could be balanced with tax rises. In this he was influenced by Keynes, who, in reply on 5 August to his request for his views on the May Report, had warned that the recommendations in it were 'an effort to make the existing deflation effective by bringing incomes down to the level of prices' and, if unaccompanied by other changes, would result in 'a most gross perversion of social justice' (Marquand, 1977: 386–8, 610; Williamson, 1992: 296–8).

In their explorations of alternatives to public expenditure cuts and deflation, Bevin and Citrine were asserting that the Labour Party did not have to penalise working people twice for the banking and other problems. They believed this penalisation was being brought about, first, by the sizeable job losses resulting from rationalisation of the old staple industries and, second, by the proposed major cuts in unemployment benefits. Between November 1929 and November 1930, the number of people unemployed rose by nearly 80 per cent to 2.4 million. As Bevin and the TUC put it in a manifesto immediately after the fall of the second Labour government, 'the proposals to economise at the expense of the poor are not only unjust but economically unsound. They will increase unemployment and aggravate the basic problem underlying the present crisis by reducing the consuming power of the masses' (Wrigley, 2011: 50).

The existence of such a critique of orthodox economic policies within the TUC emboldened ministers with major trade union backgrounds in the second Labour government to resist the severe cuts proposed for unemployed people. Rationalisation had been largely paid for by the workforces laid off, and Bevin had fruitlessly hoped that employers might help those made redundant by rationalisation and that the government might treat these people differently from others unemployed. There was a warning from abroad against the Labour movement treating some working people as less important than others. In Germany the socialist (SPD) trade unions had looked primarily after skilled male workers when redundancies occurred, while unskilled, young and female workers and unemployed people had not been treated equally with these workers, and consequently some had become supporters of the communists (KPD). Those Labour ministers who voted against MacDonald and Snowden's emergency cuts were unwilling to make the poorest pay proportionately most in attempting to recover the confidence of international finance (Wrigley, 2011: 53–4).

That the Labour ministers split and Ramsay MacDonald did not leave office after tendering the Labour government's resignation was due, of course, to the seriousness of the economic crisis. Labour's policies for dealing with unemployment might have cut back the existing high level of unemployment when it took office, but these policies were swamped by the rapidly deteriorating situation. In the 1929 election manifesto Labour had stated that it 'gives an unqualified pledge to deal immediately and practically with this question' and it offered a three-pronged approach: 'national and trade prosperity', 'maintenance' and helping the young in the labour market, and providing 'proper provision' for 'thousands of aged persons now compelled by poverty to struggle for employment' (Labour Party, 1929). Well before the summer of 1931 the Labour government's actions to carry out its pledges appeared feeble.

By 1929–31 Britain was no longer the predominant financial power that the country had been before 1914. While the City of London remained a major world financial centre, it was no longer the centre. Britain had been overtaken by the US as the greatest financial power. When Britain tried to assist German and Austrian banks in 1931, it did not have the financial strength to be effective. The City of London had been the source for short-term loans for countries experiencing economic difficulties. Such loans would have been backed by foreign deposits in London, but there had been a net outflow amounting to some £350 million between June 1930 and the end of 1931. Following on from the British financial help given to Central European banks, there was, for the first time, a loss of confidence in the liquidity of London. This loss of confidence was followed by a fall in sterling and a run on British gold reserves (Williams, 1963; Williamson, 2002: 259–66). Britain soon joined ten countries with banking crises that exacerbated the world economic downturn. Charles Kindleberger, in his influential study of the international economy in the decade from 1929, argued that 'part of the reason for the length, and most of the explanation for the depth of the world depression, was the inability of the British to continue their role of underwriter to the system and the reluctance of the United States to take it on until 1936' (Kindleberger, 1973: 28). In some socialist circles there was a belief that the problem of confidence was, at least in part, the fault of the British bankers. Beatrice Webb expressed this in her diary on 22 August 1931: 'the bankers have let us in for it by their £150 million long-term credits to Germany. While accepting short-term deposits of £200 million from other countries, the German credit cannot be withdrawn while other countries are withdrawing their deposits' (MacKenzie and MacKenzie, 1985: 252). While there was an element of truth in her comment, it missed the point that British banking had long supplied loans to economies under pressure.

The Wall Street Crash in 1929 had triggered the recession in the US, exposing speculation in property and other weaknesses in the economy. The US's problems had added to substantial weaknesses in Europe and among countries hit hard by the fall in primary product prices. The over-production of primary goods and currency instabilities were part of the problems created or made worse by the First World War.

The second Labour government did not cause the wider crisis of 1931. No British government of any political complexion would have escaped the international economic adversity. However, the second Labour government could have done better. The weakness of the Labour government's performance during the 1931 economic crisis was, in part, due to its continuing lacklustre approach to unemployment. The soaring levels of unemployment put a huge increased burden on the cost of unemployment benefits. The government simply did not have an adequate policy to reduce unemployment, and so social welfare costs rose rapidly. The cost to the Exchequer of unemployment benefits had shot up from £12 million to £125 million between 1928 and 1931 (McKibbin,

1975: 215). The problem of the government's economic performance was also in part to do with Philip Snowden's determined orthodoxy in prioritising the defence of free trade and the inflated parity of the pound to gold above all else. Most politicians of other parties accepted Snowden's orthodox views on public finance, Lloyd George being the great exception. Indeed, Snowden was probably the most Gladstonian of the 1920s chancellors of the exchequer, and was generally at one with the Treasury officials and the Bank of England. Hence, the government was not criticised by politicians of other parties over his desire to cut public expenditure and maintain the gold standard, but differed on the scale of reductions to the cost to the Exchequer of mass unemployment, as well as over tariffs. Snowden was willing to act on the funding of unemployment benefits. He firmly believed that working people would suffer badly if free trade and the gold standard were abandoned, and that public expenditure cuts were a lesser evil.

When the Liberals and the Conservatives put down motions in the House of Commons in February 1931 on restricting public expenditure, MacDonald, Snowden and their Cabinet colleagues agreed to the Liberal motion calling for the setting up of an independent committee to advise Snowden on how to carry out 'all possible and legitimate reductions in the national expenditure consistent with the efficiency of our services' (Committee on National Economy, 1931: 5). The critical phase of the government's economic problems came when the report of the Committee on National Expenditure under Sir George May was published on 31 July 1931.

The Conservative and Liberal members of the May Committee, all orthodox financiers, called for a very substantial public expenditure cut in the face of an estimated £119 million (rounded up to £120 million) budget deficit for 1932–33. As well as rounding up, the financiers counted in £50 million for the Sinking Fund, which was not usually counted in this way; indeed, payments to the Sinking Fund were often suspended in times of adversity. The political parties were admonished in the report for buying votes with welfare provision, and the majority report called for only some £23 million to be raised by taxation but £96.5 million to be saved in immediate cuts, of which £66.5 million was to be saved on unemployment insurance. In contrast to the majority, the two Labour members of the May Committee called for higher taxes on those holders of the National Debt and other fixed-interest-bearing bonds. As Philip Williamson has observed of the majority view, 'the proposals constituted an attempt to reverse much of the post-war social and employment policies' (Williamson, 2002: 267–73). Indeed, the majority of the May Committee had a long-term economic agenda, indicated in the observation that 'only by the strictest regard to economies and efficiency over a long period can the trade of the country be restored to its pre-war prosperity and any substantial number of the unemployed be reabsorbed into industry.' The majority of the committee concluded the report by stating that such a solution 'has to be found if democracy is not to suffer shipwreck on the hard rock of finance' (Committee on National Expenditure, 1931: 15, 215–23).

The publication of the May Report, alongside the European liquidity crisis, made the big issue for the Labour government not whether there should be public expenditure cuts, but the scale of these cuts. Snowden was not averse to this report putting pressure on Labour MPs to fall into line and do what Snowden wished. However, the May Report delivered a sufficient 'frightener' not only to alarm MPs but also to alarm overseas money markets. So the scale of the cuts had to be sufficient both to ensure that a majority of the House of Commons backed them and to impress overseas financiers that enough was being done. However, having long kept the trade union leadership at arms' length, MacDonald and Snowden had little cause to expect TUC sympathy for their arguments for massive cuts. As Neil Riddell has commented, the far from harmonious relations with the TUC leaders were in 'large part a problem of the government's own creation, the breakdown in relations with the trade unions would now play a pivotal role in its collapse' (Riddell, 1999: 200). The members of the TUC General Council, when meeting with the Cabinet Economic Committee and the National Executive of the Labour Party (at Henderson's suggestion) on 20 August, urged the suspension of the payment of £50 million to the Sinking Fund (which fitted the financiers' arguments that non-essential payments should not be made) and, in line with the May Committee's talk of fairness to all groups in society, opposed the big cuts directly affecting the unemployed, pensioners and public sector workers (notably teachers) and looked for a much larger part of the remaining gap to come from new taxation. While the government could not expect to come through the economic crisis without bigger public expenditure cuts than the TUC would accept, its collapse came on Snowden's proposals on unemployment benefits. However, as Ross McKibbin has observed, had the government not resigned, 'it would have been forced out anyway once the Liberals deserted – as they did desert – to the Conservatives' (McKibbin, 1975: 218).

That the Labour Cabinet would split to the extent that the government could not continue was not apparent early on in the crisis.

Henderson, the foreign secretary, had no distinctive economic policy and early on was willing to accept a revenue tariff and some unemployment benefit cuts as well as tax increases. At the first meetings of the Cabinet Economy Committee (set up to consider the May Report) on 12 and 13 August, MacDonald reassured Henderson and Willie Graham, President of the Board of Trade, that he would ensure 'equal sacrifices' and not just measures which would hammer unemployed and low-paid working people. He was clearly acting on Keynes's warning of a week earlier. Henderson, the most powerful Labour figure after MacDonald and an archetypal Labour loyalist, was very reluctant to harm a Labour government. As he said at the time, just as when first in the Cabinet in 1915–16, he was torn between his 'loyalty to his Cabinet colleagues and loyalty to the Movement outside' (Dalton, 1953: 269; Thorpe, 1988: 121–2; Wrigley, 1990: 175–6). The Labour MP Molly Hamilton later observed: 'His entire life had been given to the practice of co-operation' (Hamilton, 1944: 252). He had practised conciliation between employers and unions in his early career and then had become adept at securing co-operation between the Labour Party, the unions and the co-operative movement.

As Philip Williamson has observed in *National Crisis and National Government*, his account of the 1931 crisis (and much more), which has largely superseded earlier accounts, in mid-August all the party leaders 'expected the linked sterling and budget crisis to be solved through all-party agreement to a Labour Cabinet programme of "equal sacrifice"' (Williamson, 1992: 303). At the penultimate meeting of the Cabinet Economy Committee on 17 August, Henderson was very uneasy that the focus was on the cuts and asked that the 'whole scheme' be presented for discussion (by which he wanted the tax increases considered first) (Marquand, 1977: 615–16). At the Cabinet meeting on 19 August to consider economies, Henderson, aware of the Labour movement's hostility to substantial cuts in unemployment benefits, opposed a 10 per cent cut but was willing to accept some reductions on the principle of 'equal sacrifice' and even a revenue tariff to offset lower cuts for those unemployed. Any tariff was anathema to Snowden, who, with five others, opposed such a breach of free trade, and Snowden threatened resignation. MacDonald and Snowden saw Neville Chamberlain, Samuel Hoare (Conservatives), Herbert Samuel and Sir Donald Maclean (Liberals) on 20 August, giving them the details of the possible £78.5 million reductions in expenditure. Faced with a revised budget deficit of £170 million, the other party leaders demanded the full May Committee recommended cuts, and Samuel made clear he would not accept a revenue tariff. Henderson successfully appealed for loyal support from the Labour Party's National Executive Committee that day, but in so doing suggested that a revenue tariff would offset the need for benefit cuts. However, the TUC General Council wanted no cuts in public sector pay or welfare, and made their hostility clear when a deputation saw senior Labour ministers that evening (20 August). MacDonald, who had never had much time for the TUC, went ahead with tougher cuts in an effort to maintain international confidence in sterling. Now, as Marquand emphasised, MacDonald faced a political as well as a financial crisis (Marquand, 1977: 618–21; Williamson, 1992: 304–16).

Possibilities of such figures as Arthur Henderson accepting the cuts that Snowden deemed necessary dwindled as it became clearer by 21 August just how large cuts would have to be to satisfy opposition politicians and secure overseas and domestic financial confidence. After the TUC deputation, Henderson tried to secure a new compromise between cuts and other measures, while MacDonald and Snowden manoeuvred towards achieving support for higher cuts. At the Cabinet on 21 August, 11 Cabinet members accepted a 10 per cent cut in unemployment benefits but nine, including Henderson, did not. The Labour ministers soon found that leading Bank of England figures judged their modified package, which contained lower cuts in unemployment insurance, to be inadequate, as did the Conservative and Liberal leaders (Williamson, 1992: 317–19). Henderson, for one, came to believe that the opposition leaders were moving the level of cuts up and up in order to maximise splits in the Labour movement. His determination to oppose the level of cuts required by 22 August came, Andrew Thorpe has argued, 'not because of TUC dictation but as an angry response to the behaviour of the Opposition leaders' (Thorpe, 1988: 122). Most likely, the TUC meeting pushed Henderson towards the policies expected by the Labour Party National Executive Committee and TUC, with this move against major unemployment benefit cuts firmed up by the attitudes of the opposition leaders. In his eyes, they made it clear that they were not putting the nation before party advantage over Labour. With the collapse of the Labour government through divisions, the party leaders tried to resolve the issue of confidence in sterling through the formation of a National government, under Ramsay MacDonald, on 23 August.

Henderson, as usual, was in tune with the bulk of the Labour Party membership and the trade union movement. Labour Party branches were quick to support Henderson and the others against MacDonald and his small band of supporters. The Edinburgh Trades and Labour

Council, for instance, sent its support to those who had left office 'rather than agree to a policy of economy which had for its object the reduction of the already meagre allowance paid to unemployed workers' (Worley, 2005: 137).

Labour's record on unemployment on the economy was an easy target for critics on the left as well as on the right. The far left, in the form of the Socialist Party of Great Britain, had confidently predicted the failure of the second Labour government at its outset: 'no matter how able, how sincere, and how sympathetic the Labour men and women may be who undertake to administer capitalism, capitalism will bring their undertaking to disaster' (Socialist Party of Great Britain, 1929: 153). Not surprisingly, the Socialist Party exulted over the collapse of the government in August 1931, claiming: 'it has lived dishonestly and dies meanly and unlamented' (Socialist Party of Great Britain, 1931: 9). Far more damaging at Westminster were the radical critiques of Lloyd George and Mosley when calling for more dynamic policies (Skidelsky, 1967; Garside, 1990; Williamson, 2002; Ritschell, 2011).

Explaining the fall of the second Labour government

As in 1924, Labour's fall from office was a matter of bitterness for Labour loyalists. In 1924 Labour was deemed to have been unfairly beaten in the general election because of the Conservative Party's use of the alleged Zinoviev Letter. This made it harder to criticise MacDonald and his colleagues afterwards. In the electoral rejection of 1931 that followed shortly thereafter (Table 3.1), there was a choice of scapegoats for Labour's failure.

Table 3.1   The general election of 1931

Party	Votes won	MPs elected	Share of vote (%)
Conservative	11,377,022 (8,252,257)	470 (260)	55.0 (38.1)
Liberal	2,108,276 (5,014,638)	67 (59)	10.2 (23.6)
National Labour	316,741	13	1.5
National	100,913	4	0.5
National government overall	13,902,952	554	67.2
Labour	6,339,306 (8,048,968)	52 (287)	30.6 (37.1)
Others	405,588 (279,645)	9 (9)	2.1 (1.2)

Note: Figures for 1929 in brackets.
Source: Craig, 1987.

The 'betrayal' of MacDonald and Snowden provided a shield behind which other former ministers could shelter from criticism, and there were also the supposed machinations of bankers. Dalton, for example, publicly stated that 'the first Labour Government was destroyed by the Red Letter and the second by a Bankers' Order' and that Labour 'would not stand idly by and see our social services butchered to make a bankers' holiday' (Pimlott, 1985: 200–1). Historians have not been at all impressed by 'bankers' ramp' arguments, and at the time, as Bassett has commented, such notions were 'soon relegated well into the background'. The idea has been effectively demolished in recent times by Philip Williamson (Bassett, 1958: 173–6, 179–80, 408; Williamson, 1984).

Generally, the judgements of contemporaries and later historians have been markedly unfavourable to the second Labour government. Their assessments have often come close to suggesting that the government's fall was almost the equivalent of merciful euthanasia. Yet former certainties that the Labour government failed to take up viable alternatives have, at least partly, been undermined since Robert Skidelsky's seminal work *Politicians and the Slump* (1967), in which he observed that in the US, Germany, France and Sweden 'what might loosely be termed Keynsian policies' were adopted in spite of the 'absence of developed Keynsian theory' (Skidelsky, 1967: 387). Ross McKibbin has argued against viewing the US New Deal as a model of expansionism policies, while suggesting that Sweden is at least a doubtful case, given that it was to some extent enmeshed in German rearmament (McKibbin, 1975: 201–4). Skidelsky's admiration for the ' "bold" men of the 1929 Parliament' – Lloyd George and Mosley – was overdone, especially in the case of Mosley (Ritschell, 2011). Skidelsky was more convincing in his argument that MacDonald's failure had been in the two years previous to the August 1931 crisis rather than in the crisis itself. Future revisionism on 1931 is unlikely to be favourable to the financial stewardship of Snowden at the Exchequer, mostly backed by MacDonald as prime minister. Snowden was the iron chancellor, firm in avoiding consideration of other economic possibilities which would undercut free trade and adherence to the inflated 1925 parity of the pound to gold (Laybourn, 1988: 133–9).

Stuart Ball, when writing on how Conservative governments fell in 1916–29, argued that there were often several common factors in their defeats. He pointed to (i) a failure of leadership, (ii) the economic situation and the level of public's confidence in the government's ability to deal with it, (iii) confusion or lack of sufficient clarity in policy direction, (iv) a sense of stagnation and widespread belief in time for a change of government, (v) internal disunity, (vi) poor party organisation, (vii) lack of funds, (viii) hostile media and intellectual climate and (ix) strength and credibility of the opposition parties (Ball, 1996: 276–7). Several of these features were present in 1929–31. There was much criticism of MacDonald's leadership, as there had been in 1924, as being too timid to consider fresh ideas and sometimes indecisive. By the latter half of this short government there were widespread perceptions of drift and fatalism. There were divisions within the parliamentary Labour Party, most apparent in the complaints and minor rebellions of the ILP members. While party organisation was usually weak away from strong trade union branches and funds were relatively low after the 1929 general election, Labour's problems were not as great as the Liberals' worries in these areas. Labour, as always, faced a predominantly highly hostile press, a matter well explored by Laura Beers (Beers, 2010). The Conservatives had recovered from the 1929 election defeat by summer 1931 and were very confident of winning a big majority, as in 1924, at the next general election. They were eager to introduce tariffs at last, after 28 years of arguing the case, and were buoyed up by an awareness that the tide was turning against free trade. However, the second Labour government was not defeated in a general election but collapsed beforehand.

In making comparisons with the fall of other governments, more might be made of other occasions when governments collapsed before facing the electorate. In just over a quarter of a century between 1905 and 1931, this happened three times: in 1905, 1922 and 1931. In 1905 Arthur Balfour resigned following bitter divisions within the Conservative Party over economic policy. The government appeared tired after the Conservatives had been in office for a decade (and 17 of the previous 20 years) and had lost several leading figures, notably Joseph Chamberlain and the Duke of Devonshire. Balfour had hopes that an early resignation would exacerbate the recent deep divisions over imperialism among the Liberals. In 1931 there were serious divisions over economic policy. These were over the scale of public expenditure cuts, though there was friction over free trade or protection. In 1931 the Labour government did not suffer from longevity, but it did appear washed out and dispirited, and many of its leading figures were elderly (Lansbury) and had either retired (Passfield, Buxton, Turner), were likely to before long (Parmoor) or sought a more peaceful time in the House of Lords (Henderson). Ramsay MacDonald almost certainly intended resignation in August 1931 but, like Asquith in December 1916, had a high view of his near indispensability and so agreed to serve for a short while longer. At nearly 65, he did not expect another four years in the premiership. Unlike 1905, the 1931 collapse was primarily brought about by the international economic crisis and the weakened British financial sector.

In 1922 the government collapsed because a majority of the MPs of the larger coalition partner no longer wished for it to continue. For these Conservative MPs there was no longer a fear of the Labour movement, the 1921–22 recession had undercut trade union strength, there was anger over the Irish settlement, hostility to trade with the Soviet Union, a desire for tougher imperial policies, not least in India, distaste for the sale of honours to persons deemed unsuitable, and much else. It was a revolt for Conservative independence and a rejection of coalition politics.

In 1931, until late August, the Conservative Party still rejected coalition politics, and was only swayed to agree to join a national government by the scale of the economic crisis and the difficulty of rejecting the patriotic appeal of the King and others. The collapse of the Labour government was not primarily due to the strength of the Conservative opposition but to its being engulfed by the economic crisis. For many, the scale of social welfare and wage cuts was unacceptable, being contrary to what the Labour movement stood for. There is something in Robert Skidelsky's view that Labour had tried to 'govern without conviction a system it did not believe in but saw no real prospect of changing. It struggled to defend the working class as long as it knew how, and when it could defend them no longer it resigned.'

However, the Labour leaders from the outset knew that as a minority government they were living on borrowed time. In 1924 the electoral consequences were bad, but the 1924 general election damaged the Liberals more. In 1931 the electoral consequences were far worse, not least because the bulk of the Liberal Party opposed Labour in conjunction with the Conservatives.

References

Ball, S. (1986), 'The Conservative Party and the Formation of the National Government, August 1931', *Historical Journal*, Vol. 29, No. 1, 159–82.
Ball, S. (1996), '1916–1929', in Seldon, A. (ed.), *How Tory Governments Fall: The Tory Party in Power since 1783* (London: Fontana).
Bassett, R. M. (1958), *Nineteen Thirty-One: Political Crisis* (London: Macmillan).
Beers, L. (2010), *Your Britain: Media and the Making of the Modern Labour Party* (Cambridge: Harvard University Press).

Berkeley, H. (1976), 'The Day of the National Government', *The Times*, 14 August.
Berkeley, H. (1978), *Myth That Will Not Die: The Formation of the National Government 1931* (London: Croom Helm).
Bullock, A. (1960), *Ernest Bevin. Volume 1: Trade Union Leader 1881–1940* (London: Heinemann).
Burgess, J. (1926), *Will Lloyd George Supplant Ramsay MacDonald?* (Ilford: Burgess).
Campbell, J. (1977), *Lloyd George: The Goat in the Wilderness 1922–1931* (London: Jonathan Cape).
Clarke, P. (1988), *The Keynesian Revolution in the Making 1924–1936* (Oxford: Oxford University Press).
Cole, M. (1977), 'The Society for Socialist Inquiry and Propaganda', in Briggs, A. and Saville, J. (eds), *Essays in Labour History*, Vol. 3 (London: Croom Helm).
Committee on National Expenditure (1931), *Report* (London: HMSO, 1930–31, Cmd 3920).
Cook, C. (1976), *A Short History of the Liberal Party 1900–1976* (London: Macmillan).
Cook, C. and Ramsden, J. (1973), *By-elections in British Politics* (London: Macmillan).
Craig, F. W. S. (1987), *British Electoral Facts 1832–1987* (Aldershot: Dartmouth).
Dalton, H. (1953), *Call Back Yesterday: Memoirs 1887–1931* (London: Frederick Muller).
Donoughue, B. and Jones, G. W. (1973), *Herbert Morrison: Portrait of a Politician* (London: Weidenfeld and Nicolson).
Douglas, R. (1976), *Landpeople and Politics: A History of the Land Question in the United Kingdom, 1878–1952* (London: Alison and Busby).
Dutton, D. (1991), 'Lloyd George, John Simon and the Politics of the Liberal Party', in Loades, J. (ed.), *The Life and Times of David Lloyd George* (Bangor: Headstart).
Dutton, D. (1992), *Simon: A Political Biography of Sir John Simon* (London: Aurum).
Garside, W. R. (1990), *British Unemployment 1919–1939: A Study in Public Policy* (Cambridge: Cambridge University Press).
Griffiths, C. (2011), 'Making Farming Pay: Agricultural Crisis and the Politics of the National Interest, 1930–31', in Shepherd, J., Davis, J. and Wrigley, C. (eds), *Britain's Second Labour Government, 1929–31: A Reappraisal* (Manchester: Manchester University Press).
Hamilton, M. A. (1944), *Remembering My Good Friends* (London: Jonathan Cape).
Kindleberger, C. P. (1973), *The World In Depression 1929–1939* (London: Allen Lane).
Labour Party (1929), *Labour's Appeal to the Nation* (London: Labour Party).
Lawrence, J. (2000), 'Labour – the Myths it has Lived By', in Tanner, D., Thane, P. and Tiratsoo, N. (eds), *Labour's First Century* (Cambridge: Cambridge University Press).
Laybourn, K. (1988), *Philip Snowden: A Biography* (Aldershot: Temple Smith).
Laybourn, K. and Shepherd, J. (2006), *Britain's First Labour Government* (Basingstoke: Palgrave).
MacKenzie, N. and MacKenzie, J. (eds) (1985), *The Diary of Beatrice Webb*, Vol. 4: 1924–1943 (London: Virago).
Marquand, D. (1977), *Ramsay MacDonald* (London: Cape).

McKenzie, R. (1955), *British Political Parties* (London: Heinemann).

McKibbin, R. I. (1975), 'The Economic Policy of the Second Labour Government, 1929–31', *Past and Present*, Vol. 68, No. 1, 95–123.

Morrison, H. (1960), *An Autobiography* (London: Odhams Press).

Packer, I. (2001), *Lloyd George, Liberalism And The Land: The Land Issue and Party Politics in England 1906–1914* (Rochester, NY: Royal Historical Society/Boydell Press).

Pimlott, B. (1977), *Labour and the Left in the 1930s* (Cambridge: Cambridge University Press).

Pimlott, B. (1985), *Hugh Dalton* (London: Jonathan Cape).

Pimlott, B. (1986), *The Political Diary of Hugh Dalton, 1918–40, 1945–60* (London: Jonathan Cape).

Postgate, R. (1951), *The Life of George Lansbury* (London: Longmans, Green).

Riddell, N. (1999), *Labour in Crisis: The Second Labour Government 1929–31* (Manchester: Manchester University Press).

Ritschell, D. (1997), *The Politics of Planning: The Debate on Economic Planning in the 1930s* (Oxford: Oxford University Press).

Ritschell, D. (2011), 'Why was there no Keynesian Revolution under the Second Labour Government? A Reassessment of Sir Oswald Mosley's Alternative Economic Agenda in 1930–31', in Shepherd, J., Davis, J. and Wrigley, C. (eds), *Britain's Second Labour Government, 1929–31: A Reappraisal* (Manchester: Manchester University Press).

Samuel, V. (1944), *Memoirs* (London: Cresset Press).

Shepherd, J. (2002), *George Lansbury* (Oxford: Oxford University Press).

Skidelsky, R. (1967), *Politicians and the Slump: The Labour Government of 1929–31* (London: Macmillan).

Snowden, P. (1934), *An Autobiography*, Vol. 2: 1919–1934 (London: Ivor Nicholson and Watson).

Socialist Party of Great Britain (1929), *The Socialist Standard*, 25 June, 298.

Socialist Party of Great Britain (1931), *The Socialist Standard*, 28 September, 325.

Taylor, A. J. P. (ed.) (1971), *Lloyd George: A Diary by Frances Stevenson* (London: Hutchinson).

Thorpe, A. (1988), 'Arthur Henderson and the British Political Crisis of 1931', *Historical Journal*, Vol. 31, No. 1, 117–39.

Thorpe, A. (1991), *The British General Election of 1931* (Oxford: Oxford University Press).

Tregidga, G. (2000), *The Liberal Party in South-West Britain since 1918* (Exeter: University of Exeter Press).

Wasserstein, B. (1992), *Herbert Samuel: A Political Life* (Oxford: Clarendon Press).

Webb, S. (1932), 'What Happened in 1931: A Record', *Political Quarterly*, Vol. 3, No. 1, 1–17.

Wertheimer, E. (1930), *Portrait of the Labour Party*, 2nd edition (London: Putnams).

Williams, D. (1963), 'London and the 1931 Financial Crisis', *Economic History Review*, Vol. 15, No. 3, 513–28.

Williamson, P. (1984), 'A "Bankers' Ramp": Financiers and the British Political Crisis of August 1931', *English Historical Review*, Vol. 99, 771–806.

Williamson, P. (1991), '1931: The Political Realities', *Twentieth Century British History*, Vol. 2, No. 3, 328–38.

Williamson, P. (1992), *National Crisis and National Government: British Politics, The Economy and Empire 1926–32* (Cambridge: Cambridge University Press).

Williamson, P. (2002), 'The Conservative Party 1900–1939: from crisis to ascendancy', in Wrigley, C. (ed.), *A Companion to Early Twentieth-Century Britain* (Oxford: Historical Association and Blackwell).

Worley, M. (2005), *Labour Inside the Gate: A History of the British Labour Party Between the Wars* (London: I. B. Tauris).

Wrigley, C. (1976), *David Lloyd George and the British Labour Movement: Peace and War* (Hassocks: Harvester Press).

Wrigley, C. (1990), *Arthur Henderson* (Cardiff: University of Wales Press).

Wrigley, C. (1991), 'Lloyd George and the Labour Party after 1922', in Loades, J. (ed.), *The Life and Times of David Lloyd George* (Bangor: Headstart History).

Wrigley, C. (1999), 'James Ramsay MacDonald 1922–31', in Jeffreys, K. (ed.), *Leading Labour: From Keir Hardie to Tony Blair* (London: I. B. Tauris).

Wrigley, C. (2011), 'Labour dealing with Labour: aspects of economic policy', in Shepherd, J., Davis, J. and Wrigley, C. (eds), *Britain's Second Labour Government, 1929–31: A Reappraisal* (Manchester: Manchester University Press).

4
The Fall of the Attlee Government, 1951

Robert Crowcroft and Kevin Theakston

The Attlee Labour government of 1945–51 ended more with a whimper than with a bang. In contrast to the break-up of the MacDonald Labour government in 1931, there was no 'bankers' ramp' or dramatic and overwhelming financial crisis. There was nothing like the self-destructive trade union protests and strikes of the 1979 'Winter of Discontent' that fatally damaged Callaghan's government. There was no electoral meltdown. Instead, a small shift of votes – an average swing of just 0.9 per cent from Labour to the Conservatives – was enough to tip Labour out of office in the general election held in October 1951. On a high turnout, Labour's tally of votes had actually increased in absolute terms (to 13.9 million, compared with 13.2 million in the 1950 general election and 11.9 million in 1945) and it won 230,000 more votes (0.8 per cent) than the Conservatives, though the Conservatives came out ahead in seats, making 23 gains and ending up with a House of Commons majority of 17. It was a close-run defeat that seemed like a victory of sorts: the outgoing Labour leaders were relieved that it had not been worse (Hugh Dalton called the results 'wonderful'), believed the Conservatives would quickly encounter economic and political problems, and thought (wrongly) they would be back in office sooner rather than later (Pimlott, 1986: 567).

The end of the Attlee government was a process rather than an event, taking place over several instalments (including the two general elections of 1950 and 1951) and with multiple background and contributory factors, both internal to the government and the Labour Party and external, in the shape of political and economic events and forces beyond its control or influence. The interaction between diverse economic forces, social pressures and political decisions is central to understanding the end of the Attlee government. For the first two years – up to

61

1947 – the Labour government elected in 1945 was 'triumphant and seemed unshakeable', as one of its Conservative frontbench opponents put it (Macmillan, 1969: 48). It had a parliamentary majority of 146, it pushed strongly ahead with its programme, and the opposition was shell-shocked and ineffective. But from 1947 onwards the government started to run into difficulties, and its reputation for competence took a battering as it struggled with economic crises and other problems (notably the fuel crisis and convertibility in 1947, and devaluation in 1949). There were Conservative opinion poll leads for most of the period from the second half of 1947 through to January 1950, and Tory advances at Labour's expense in local government elections in 1947 and 1949, but, remarkably, Labour lost no parliamentary by-elections to the Conservatives (though often seeing large swings against them). However, the general context of 'austerity' and media and party-political criticisms of bureaucracy, nationalisation, government mismanagement, red tape, queues, shortages and rationing sapped Labour's popularity. Added to this, by the late 1940s, and very obviously in 1950–51, Labour seemed to have run out of steam; it displayed few new policy ideas, its leaders were physically exhausted, and factional splits were emerging. Even so, its electoral support remained strong to the end, and particularly in its working-class heartlands.

The blame game

Numerous hypotheses have been put forward for the decline and fall of the Attlee government. In isolation, none of them are terribly convincing. There are the ideologically motivated explanations – which usually translate into a charge that Attlee's administration was insufficiently 'socialist', and this sentenced it to a decline and fall worthy of Gibbon. Ralph Miliband, the most influential example of this tendency, blamed Morrison's 'consolidation' approach to policy post-1948 as lacking in energy and drive; the party leaders proved to be compromisers with capitalism. Miliband also attributed the government's defeat to 'business and financial interests' (especially steelmakers, insurance companies, and Tate & Lyle), which behaved exactly as capitalists are supposed to according to Marxist theory and poured 'enormous resources' into a propaganda campaign to promote 'free enterprise' and discredit nationalisation. Thus, Labour's aspirations were attacked and the public misled. Moreover – and equally predictably in the context of a Marxist framework – according to Miliband the Labour Party and even the British state itself (through its information services) proved to be no match for the arrayed representatives of the capitalist order – the Conservative Party, big business and 'their public relations experts' (Miliband, 1961: 298–302, 304–5). Perry Anderson echoed this argument, seeing a successful capitalist campaign to shift the 'equilibrium' back towards the 'hegemonic class'. 'Socialism had never been on the agenda of the Attlee government', which had failed to modify 'the basic coordinates of British capitalism' (Anderson, 1992: 43, 165, 169). David Coates (1975) later put forward a similar analysis of the failures of 'labourism'.

Contemporaries had their own take on things. They were keen to use the decline to bolster their positions in increasingly fraught political feuds. For instance, following the 1950 election the result was instantly explained by the emerging factions according to their own perspectives. For the left-wing Aneurin Bevan, the collapse of Labour's majority was an indictment of 'consolidationism'. Yet the party leadership drew precisely the opposite conclusion from the results: the fact that Labour's vote held up was interpreted as an *endorsement* of consolidation. That meant that the party should move further away from overt 'socialism'. The leaders also reckoned that offensive speeches by Bevan (that the middle classes really complained about austerity because they desired servants to order around, and that Conservatives were 'lower than vermin') had cost the party at least 2 million votes (Foot, 1975: 247; Williams, 1983: 167). Whatever their merits, these were, of course, self-serving explanations.

No more worlds to conquer?

By 1948–49 the Attlee government had largely passed the legislation it had been elected to enact. Landmark reforms – on the welfare system, health, public ownership and more – were being implemented. Moreover, many of these innovations were things that the Labour party had been seeking since its inception; they carried a powerful and visceral appeal for the party. But passing legislation based on these aspirations generated an acute problem. A New Jerusalem did not suddenly spring up in the green and pleasant land. Human nature did not change or improve, and people were not being remade as a result of government action. Britain was a bit different, to be sure, but not radically so. In essence, this was not what a socialist, or social democratic, country was supposed to look like. On one level, this highlights the inevitable gulf between intention and outcome in governing; and, in the case of the Attlee government, the gulf was a profound one. Converting values and aspirations into, first, actionable policies and, second, social outcomes is rather more difficult than is popularly appreciated (Whiting, 2000), and, while Labour had certainly come up with the policies, the outcomes were less clear.

To be sure, all of this was not just the result of doctrinal exhaustion; 1947 was a horrendous year, with food, fuel and convertibility crises for Attlee and his colleagues to wrestle with. Arguably, the government never recovered its sense of direction and momentum. But, in sum, it did mean that the Labour government was now out of fresh ideas. In a great burst of energy, in their first few years in power, Attlee and his colleagues passed the measures they had set out to introduce. There were no more crusades to launch, no enticing battles to fight, no dragons left to slay. Perhaps it is little surprise if they had exhausted their doctrines; Attlee and most of his colleagues were products of the structures of authority in Britain and had little desire to modify them more than they had already. But, for whatever reason, the Attlee government suffered that sense of deflation that often follows brilliant achievement in all walks of life. There were no more worlds to conquer; and plenty of Labourites wept over that fact, while others – including Attlee and Morrison – simply scratched their heads. Ever since the Attlee government, Labour has struggled to work out 'what next?' and craft a compelling vision of the future. Wilson plumped for 'White Heat' and Blair for the 'personalisation' of public services. But solutions to this problem have certainly proved hard to come by, and all have lacked the raw emotional appeal of those aspirations satisfied between 1945 and 1948.

Equally important as a disinclination to go further was the fact that Attlee and his colleagues were physically exhausted, if not broken, by their experiences. Most of the government's senior figures had been in office continually since May 1940. A decade spent dealing, on a daily basis, with total war, its aftermath, and an ambitious legislative programme took its toll. There were few opportunities to recharge. The pressure was unrelenting as one crisis followed another. The senior figures were ageing and often in poor health. The vitality of formidable figures like Attlee, Bevin, Cripps and Morrison ebbed away – and with it the vitality of the government. By 1948, their best days were behind them: Bevin died in harness in 1951, Cripps a year later, having been compelled to retire in 1950, while Attlee and Morrison suffered bouts of illness and hospitalisation. This issue of physical and mental decline has to be important to any persuasive account of the decline and fall of the Attlee government. John Charmley's view that the ministry was 'exhausted in mind, body and manifesto commitments' sums it up

(Charmley, 2008: 158). The crusading army of 1945 was reduced to a host of walking wounded by the end of the decade. Small wonder, then, that they were in no mood for new legislative offensives.

As a result, Labour's appeal to the public in the 1950 and 1951 elections was lacking in freshness and clarity. In both election campaigns Attlee largely opted to fight on the record of his government, combining this with suggestions that the Conservatives could not be trusted with the welfare state and the economy. But the socialist mind is one that demands constant forward movement and can rarely be satisfied; and it was precisely this crusading zeal that was lacking when the party submitted itself to the judgement of the electors. The party's manifesto for the 1950 election stood in stark contrast to the sheer scope of *Let Us Face the Future*, and the election saw Labour's majority in the Commons collapse to just six. It was certainly a curious result. The party's share of the vote remained 3 per cent higher than that of the Conservatives, but the proportion of non-manual workers voting Labour had declined by 10 per cent since 1945 (from 55 per cent to 47 per cent) – a clear warning of the dissatisfaction with austerity.

Its drastically reduced majority after the 1950 election left the government hanging on to 'office without authority or power', as Dalton put it. He thought it was difficult to see 'how we can improve our position', feeling 'events moving against us' (Pimlott, 1986: 471). Gaitskell thought that defeat next time was not certain, however, 'if we play our cards right' and 'if we can avoid giving unnecessary offence and quietly improve the economic position' (Williams, 1983: 167–8). The second Attlee government certainly had few legislative achievements to its name, and Attlee discovered no new sense of purpose for his administration. But in the short term it was able to carry on, winning votes in parliament despite Conservative harassment, remaining popular in the polls, and presiding in the first half of 1950 over an improving economic situation (with the balance of payments moving into surplus, the announcement that Britain would make no further calls on Marshall Aid, production and exports strong, and 'points' rationing and petrol rationing ending). 'It looks as though those bastards can stay in as long as they like', Churchill complained at one stage (Morgan, 1984: 412). It was 'an entirely unforeseen external development' (Jefferys, 1993: 25) – the outbreak of the Korean War in June 1950 – that, we can see with hindsight, marked the beginning of the end for the Attlee government, the massive rearmament programme it triggered placing serious strains on both the Labour Party and the national finances.

Another factor is that the government had – rather spectacularly – failed to play the redistribution game effectively. Although Edmund Dell (1999: 206) argues 'this was not a cost which would have had to be paid by a more successful government', most historians and participants in the Attlee government acknowledge its importance. The 1945 boundaries probably favoured Labour, but the 1948 redrawing of constituency boundaries played into Conservative hands, taking seats from Labour heartlands and rebalancing them to the more suburban areas. Those suburban seats were likely to prove more amenable to the Conservatives' message, and certainly did so in the context of austerity. The Nuffield election studies for the 1950 and 1951 contests found that the redistribution of seats offered the Conservatives an advantage of about 35 seats and 500,000 votes, accounting for between one-quarter and one-half of Labour's losses (Nicholas, 1951: 329–33; Butler, 1952: 243). In many cases, as Attlee acknowledged, the impact of redistribution was to transfer Labour voters from marginal constituencies to solid Labour seats, so that the party got bigger majorities in its strongholds and safe seats but lost out in the marginals. Of the 60 largest majorities in 1950, 50 were in Labour-held seats. 'We suffered from being too moral over that', Attlee later admitted (Williams, 1961: 229). Herbert Morrison's biographers talk of Labour's 'masochistic honesty' in implementing the boundary changes (Donoughue and Jones, 1973: 453). Labour polled 800,000 more votes than the Conservatives in 1950, a lead in votes, it has been calculated, which would have given the latter an overall majority of 65–70 seats – the redistribution of seats and the more 'efficient' distribution of the Conservative vote helping to explain that discrepancy. If the 1950 election had been fought on the old boundaries, it has been suggested that Labour would have won with a comfortable majority of about 60 (Williams, 1982: 151; McKibben, 2010: 171–2).

Attlee himself has to bear some responsibility for the government's problems. He had largely failed as leader of the opposition between 1935 and 1939, and was only rescued by the opportunities of war (Crowcroft, 2011). The cunning, ruthless political operator of 1940–47 was in decline, his inadequacies and limitations more apparent. As Kenneth Morgan put it, he had invaluable qualities for running a government with an agreed programme when things were going well, but performed less well in crises that demanded energy, grip and ideas (Morgan, 1984: 351). Nor was he politically skilled on economic issues, the Achilles' heel of the government. Peter Hennessey notes that Attlee's lack of grasp of the British economy and economic diplomacy was 'a serious weakness' (Hennessy, 2000: 160). The presentational, campaigning and communication aspects of politics had always been Attlee's weakest areas. He was best at managing (and controlling) those around him, not at 'the vision thing'. As leader and prime minister it was his responsibility to instil a sense of purpose in his government, or at least find someone who could. Attlee had always relied on Morrison for that, but 'consolidation' was hardly a war cry fit to rouse the troops. His example shows that a prime minister does not necessarily have to give a strong policy lead or provide ideas and a vision for a government to be successful, provided that the Cabinet and the party have a sense of purpose and remain united – but that was not the case by 1950–51.

It was the February 1950 general election, not the October 1951 one, that destroyed the huge Labour majority won in 1945. Labour lost 78 seats while the Conservatives gained 88, Attlee's majority in the House of Commons slumping to just six. As Edmund Dell (1999: 209) has pointed out, 'this was before the Korean war and before any Cabinet resignations had divided the party.' The 1950 election has been described as 'astonishingly ill-timed' (Marquand, 2008: 146), and Attlee, as prime minister, must carry the ultimate responsibility for that, though there had been a number of Cabinet discussions and ministerial exchanges about the next election from mid-1949 onwards. From May 1949 Bevan had been pressing for an early election as opposed to hanging on until 1950. Labour MPs, he believed, 'will be getting nervy and demoralised and there will be no more really interesting legislation. We shall be marking time, and lose our power of manoeuvre' (Pimlott, 1986: 448). Gaitskell thought that either November 1949 or June 1950 would be the best dates, but not the period in between (Williams, 1983: 151–4). Morrison, who feared the party machine was not yet tuned up, initially sat on the fence, but then came out in favour of delay (Donoughue and Jones, 1973: 448–9). But a crucial influence was Cripps, who refused (with threats of resignation) to produce a pre-election budget, the mixture of his moralism, personal strain, poor political judgement and fears for sterling leaving the prime minister with no choice but to go to the polls at a rather unpropitious time. Polls in May 1950, after petrol had been de-rationed, suggest that if the election had been held later Labour might have won with a majority of 40 or 50 seats in the House of Commons, a secure enough platform for the government to carry on longer than it in fact did in 1950–51 (Jay, 1980: 192–3).

Attlee can also be faulted for the poor timing of the October 1951 general election that finally evicted Labour from office. The prime minister's innate conservatism and sense of propriety led him to conclude that the political uncertainty in the country had to be resolved before

King George VI set off on a planned Commonwealth tour of six months' duration. Attlee had already forced the King to postpone the tour once (keeping him in the country for the 1949 Festival of Britain so as to maximise the financial opportunities accruing from the aura of monarchy) and thus decided that the election would have to take place in late 1951. (In the event, illness prevented the King from going on his tour and he died in February 1952.) Other ministers backed an autumn election, but Morrison and Gaitskell were not confident about the prospects of defeating the Conservatives again, and both advised soldiering on into 1952 in the hope that something – an economic recovery – would come up. But Attlee made the decision not to do so, and called the election even though the state of the economy and the opinion polls (with the Conservatives enjoying an 11 per cent lead in September 1951) were not favourable. This was clearly an error; quite apart from the election, someone with Attlee's political antennae should have known that, once out of office, the splits in the party would develop into outright factional conflict. Writing in 1963, Richard Crossman blamed the prime minister for the election results: 'if only Mr Attlee had held on, instead of appealing to the country in the trough of the crisis, he would have reaped the benefit of the 1951 recovery' (Crossman, 1966: 151–2).

Party unity and discipline were coming under increasing strain towards the end of the government – as highlighted by the Gaitskell/Bevan split and Cabinet resignations – but internal party problems had not until then damaged the party's capacity to govern. Compared with other periods of Labour government, for most of the Attlee government the party was broadly united and relations with the unions were stable and supportive. Bevan, in fact, told the 1950 party conference that over the previous five years the party had achieved 'a greater degree of unity' than he had ever known, and the reason for that was 'we achieved it in activity. We are always better when we are getting on with the job.' Party solidarity was related, therefore, to the sense that the government was moving forward, and as it stalled in its final phase that loyalty and party support came under strain (Campbell, 1987: 215).

On the whole, the parliamentary Labour Party 'presented few problems of management for the government down to 1951' (Morgan, 1984: 59). The Liaison Committee worked well as a bridge between ministers and MPs, standing orders were suspended, and Morrison set up 17 specialist policy groups to keep backbenchers busy (though this experiment was not a success in the case of the foreign affairs group, which clashed with Bevin). There was some dissent and periodic rebellions by varying groups of MPs – mostly on foreign policy and defence issues – but no sustained and organised internal opposition endangering the government's majority or significant parliamentary revolt, even from the 'Keep Left' group. Party discipline had been a problem for MacDonald, but, as Morgan (1984: 59) noted, the Attlee government had little difficulty keeping the loyalty of its backbenchers on domestic issues down to and well beyond the 1950 election. The wafer thin majority after 1950 actually assisted party management, as backbench critics felt constrained to toe the party line in the face of increased Conservative pressure, though tensions were building up and some of Bevan's supporters started to snipe and mount attacks after his resignation in 1951.

In contrast to the damage they caused to the Wilson and Callaghan governments, relations between the government, the party and the unions were also generally good and close in this period. Lewis Minkin, the historian of the party–union relationship, labels these 'the years of stability' and 'fundamental unity' in the party–union alliance, based on a 'tight alliance' between the key union bosses (who were at this time on the right of the party) and the parliamentary leadership, and on a broad sense of union and working-class satisfaction with the achievements and record of the government, though there was increasing discontent with the wages freeze by the end of the government (Minkin, 1980: 24; 1991: 77). Jonathan Schneer also noted the 'overwhelming loyalty' of the unions: 'during 1945–51 the majority of trade unions gave the Attlee government massive, unswerving and crucial backing' (Schneer, 1988: 134). The union block vote was put firmly behind the leadership at the party conference, a body that gave little real trouble – Morgan (1984: 73) calling it 'docile and impotent' – though a straw in the wind was the way in which places on the National Executive Committee constituency section increasingly fell to left-wingers from 1948 onwards. The Left was a more significant grass-roots presence in the constituency parties, some unions and the Parliamentary Labour Party than sometimes thought – and its criticism of and disaffection with government policies and decisions grew, particularly after 1949 – but it was never an organised force in this period (Schneer, 1988). Rank and file party membership increased after 1945, the union affiliated membership almost doubling to 4.9 million and individual membership in the constituency parties increasing from 487,000 in 1945 to a peak of over 900,000. Party finances and the party organisation were solid enough, though Labour had a smaller membership than the Conservatives, fewer election agents around the country, and a smaller and less professional headquarters staff (Nicholas, 1951: 24, 28; Butler, 1952: 22–3, 25, 27, 29, 30).

Despite this relative general stability within the Labour Party as a whole, the latter stages of the Attlee government did see an outbreak of serious fratricidal strife among senior members of the ministry (Crowcroft, 2008). It boiled down to a struggle for political ascendancy between the two leading lights of the 'next generation': Bevan and Gaitskell. Bevan, widely perceived as the architect of the new National Health Service in his role as minister of health, saw himself as having a claim to authority and future power in the Labour movement – especially when Attlee's generation left the scene. He had not, as a minister, encouraged left-wing backbench revolts against the government or dissent at the party conference, calling for solidarity, loyalty and discipline in the party (Morgan, 2011: 218–19). But he deeply resented the emergence of the middle-class Gaitskell as a major figure in the government. As the Korean war placed grave burdens on the country's finances in the second half of 1950 (in August, it was decided to boost annual defence spending to £950 million, an increase of £210 million; in November, the Cabinet raised this £3.6 billion over three years; and in December the decision was taken to increase spending still further), relations between the two men began to break down. Crucial to this was the appointment of Gaitskell as chancellor of the exchequer in October, when Cripps was compelled to retire. Bevan was furious, believing that Cripps had intended him to have the job. He insisted that the post should have gone to someone 'who had some standing in the movement' (in other words, himself), and rapidly started to 'behave very badly and alienate' his colleagues (Pimlott, 1986: 490, 498).

Gaitskell's appointment had, therefore, seemingly impeded the rise of the ambitious Bevan. It was not something that he ever forgave. Within weeks of Gaitskell's move to the Treasury Bevan was considering resigning, ostensibly over the issue of defence spending (Foot, 1975: 308). Crucially, though, Bevan's drive towards martyrdom on the issue of rearmament only began after he had been snubbed and Gaitskell awarded 'his' job. Relations became truly poisonous in subsequent months, as the new chancellor sought to raise money for defence spending by capping the costs of Bevan's NHS. Bevan was driven into a rage and began to oppose Gaitskell in Cabinet with venom. The issue at stake was deeply personal – Bevan's petulance was always to the fore, and it would be naïve to think that, even given Gaitskell's stubborn and inflexible nature, the chancellor did not relish the opportunity to drive a rival out of office through provocative policies. Though Michael Foot and Philip Williams painted the struggle as an ideological conflict over the future of British socialism, and Kenneth Morgan (1984: 443) likewise thought it 'calumny' to see the feud in terms of personal advancement, in reality it was always about who was on top, and who was not.

In January 1951, a United Nations resolution introduced by the United States condemning China as an aggressor in Korea was the occasion for further rancour between the two men. As perhaps the most instinctively Atlanticist Cabinet minister, Gaitskell believed that Britain must support the resolution. But Bevan wanted to oppose it. He was developing a marked tendency to discover antipathy for any policy that Gaitskell supported. This was to see Bevan make some truly remarkable intellectual leaps in the next five years of party civil war, but in early 1951 Gaitskell was hardly likely to countenance capitulation to his rival as their rows over defence spending continued to rage; he thus exerted considerable pressure upon the Cabinet and ensured British support for the United States position (Williams, 1983: 229–33). Bevan was furious at having been bested yet again. A suitable pretext for revolt immediately arrived, when Gaitskell took the decision to increase defence spending to £4.7 billion over three years – up almost a third on what the Cabinet had previously agreed. The state of crisis persisted until March, when Gaitskell again rubbed salt in the wound by seeking to raise money through imposing charges on certain NHS services – spectacles and false teeth. Gaitskell won acquiescence from the Cabinet for this, leaving Bevan looking positively 'evil' in meetings (Pimlott, 1986: 514–15). The Welshman finally exploded in March 1951 when Herbert Morrison got the Foreign Office in the wake of Bevin's retirement. For the second time in six months, Bevan felt himself to have been snubbed for the two most senior posts in the government besides the premiership. Publicly threatening resignation if NHS charges were introduced, he lambasted Gaitskell as a 'second Snowden', and, after the Cabinet chose to rebuff his protests and endorse Gaitskell's budget, quit the government altogether in April 1951 (*The Times*, 4 April 1951; Pimlott, 1986: 521–2). Curiously – and this might be thought important – Bevan's resignation letter made no mention of rearmament or foreign policy. Having taken his bat and ball home, at a PLP meeting he then launched into a tirade that Dalton likened to Oswald Mosley and 'seemed to be on the edge of a nervous breakdown' (Pimlott, 1986: 538–9). The civil war that was to rack the Labour Party until Attlee retired and Gaitskell replaced him in December 1955 had begun.

The crisis could probably have been avoided: the argument centred on only £23 million of NHS spending; Attlee was away ill at a crucial time and did not exert himself to find a compromise; and experience soon showed that Gaitskell had got his budget sums wrong (the Churchill government later scaling down rearmament spending). Yet, while the long-term consequences were momentous, and the feuding within Cabinet hardly helped even in the short term, it must also be questioned how far the Bevan–Gaitskell rivalry directly contributed to the fall of the government. Party meetings thereafter were spiteful and bad-tempered, but the *public* conflict only renewed itself after the 1951 general election, when Labour was back in Opposition. The contest was unquestionably vicious, but was not played out on the public stage while Labour was still in government.

The Conservatives and the propaganda battle

For their part, the Conservatives did not stand still after their crushing defeat in 1945. Far from it: the party worked hard to recover its hold on the political situation and, in a series of presentational and policy shifts, was able to gradually reconnect with important strands of public opinion. To be sure, this was slow going; the recovery was only partially complete by the time of the 1951 general election – Labour performed strongly even in going down to defeat – but it was just enough to nudge the Conservatives over the finishing line ahead of their opponents. Labour's defeat can thus only be understood in the context of the wider party-political competition. The Conservative leaders quickly discerned in Attlee's Britain the opportunity to reframe the battle for public support and polarise it around wholly new issues. The main issue enabling this polarisation was that of living standards.

Living standards – encompassing issues including austerity, consumption and rationing – were high on the political agenda throughout the entire life of the Attlee government. The crisis of consumption and living standards began less than a year after the 1945 election. In February 1946, dried egg (a dietary staple) was withdrawn from rations in order to reduce dollar imports. This decision resulted in a public outcry. Press coverage focused on the problems this posed for the housewife, with emotive headlines such as 'Families almost under-nourished' and 'Britain's women unite in revolt against food cuts' (*Daily Telegraph*, 8 February 1946; *Daily Mail*, 8 February 1946). In July 1946, this situation became one of real toxicity when bread rationing was introduced for the first time (something avoided even during the war). There were large-scale media campaigns against the measure. In the autumn of 1947, this was followed by fresh import cuts, resulting in reduced rations. In the November 1947 local elections, there was a clear swing towards the Conservatives; the Attlee government had been warned that the public was unwilling to tolerate deprivation. And, though shortages became less pressing from 1948 onwards, rising prices became a similarly pressing problem in everyday life. Living standards thus remained fixed high atop the political agenda. Though this was – until relatively recently – neglected by historians keen to focus on nationalisation and other aspects of socialist policy, the reality is that the quality of everyday life was of far greater concern to the public than party or ideological dogmas (Zweiniger-Bargielowska, 2000). And living standards were squeezed very hard indeed in post-war Britain as austerity took hold. As a result, the Conservative Party calculated that popular dissatisfaction with living standards could be turned into the site of a major – and profitable – propaganda battle with the Attlee government. It is impossible to grasp the fall of the Labour ministry without considering the efforts of the Conservative Party to fracture its electoral base and dislodge it from power.

But the first, and necessary, task was to ensure that the Conservatives could actually win a hearing from the public. The party had borne the blame for the 1930s and the war, and – as if that were not bad enough – in the 1945 election the Conservatives appeared unresponsive to the unfocused, temporary but powerful desire for a new beginning. Improving the party's image by bringing its appeal up to date was crucial. Of course, the Conservative Party has frequently proven flexible in adapting to changing political, social and economic conditions, and the years following 1945 saw the party prove to be rather fleet of foot.

Much of this, of course, can be attributed to the fact that in doctrinal terms the ascendant Conservative leadership was by no means inimical to a policy based on welfarism and a mixed economy. In 1945, Churchill was unfairly caricatured as an enemy of such policies, and it remains a popular image almost 70 years on. But it is bogus. Despite the hysteria over his resistance to parts of the Beveridge report, Churchill accepted 16 of its 23 recommendations and gave a broader commitment to what he called 'Beveridge-type' reforms. And men like Butler (architect of the 1944 Education Act), Anthony Eden and Harold Macmillan (author of *The Third Way* in 1938) similarly understood that, in order to successfully compete, political parties now had to promise certain things. The Conservatives were simply reclaiming ground that Attlee had elbowed them off six years earlier. More to the point, the reality is that no political party has done more to advance collectivism in Britain than the Conservative Party, no matter how much its activists and opponents alike bemoan that fact (Greenleaf, 1983). Therefore, the presentational shift after 1945 was hardly a wrenching one; it was wholly traditional (and perhaps predicable) that, in the 1947 *Industrial Charter*, the party explicitly committed itself to 'central direction of the economy' and a policy of full employment. That was, after all, where the votes were.

R. A. Butler was the main driving force in this bid to remake the Conservative Party's public image. 'Power is the first goal of party politics, the *sine qua non* of political effectiveness', he recalled when describing the reorientation of the party (Butler, 1971: 127). As chairman of the Conservative Research Department from 1945 to 1964, and as chairman of the Advisory Committee on Policy and Political Education, Butler sought to ensure that his party caught up with Labour. He worked alongside figures like Oliver Lyttelton, Iain Macleod, Harold Macmillan, David Maxwell Fyfe, Enoch Powell and Oliver Stanley – a formidable combination of political minds. In 1945 Labour had polemically depicted the Conservatives as the traditional enemies of social reform; but, as it was difficult to substantiate this charge when set against the record of the party, it is unsurprising that Butler's first priority was to combat it. What *was* true was that public language in Britain had changed because of the war, and in 1945 the Conservatives struggled to react to this as skilfully as the Labour Party. This was another problem that Butler worked to remedy. He therefore set about bringing the party's 'modes of expression' up to date (Butler, 1971: 127). Butler felt that the 'propaganda victory' had gone to Labour months before the 1945 election due to the endless pamphlets rolled out by Herbert Morrison, and he thus patterned his own efforts on those of the wartime home secretary.

As the brains behind the *Industrial Charter*, Butler pledged in a speech in March 1946 that 'modern Conservatism' necessitated 'strong central guidance over the operation of the economy' (Butler, 1971: 133–4). The *Charter* has been described as 'the most important post-war policy document produced by the Conservatives', because, while substantively it was largely a continuation of the economic thinking of the 1930s National governments, nevertheless it was strikingly modern in tone (Lindsay and Harrington, 1974: 151, 154). In the pamphlet *Fundamental Issues*, Butler declared that, due to the complexity of modern economic life, 'the state will have to be the grand arbiter between competing interests' (Butler, 1946: 7). Elsewhere, Butler argued that government was needed to 'redress injustice' and he endorsed 'planning' to that end on behalf of the party (Butler, 1947: 4–6). He and Macmillan said that 'A good Tory in history has never been afraid of the use of the state', and that 'Toryism has always been a form of paternal socialism' (Greenleaf, 1983: 199). In the *Industrial Charter, The Agricultural Charter, Right Road for Britain* and *10 Points of Conservative Policy* the party combined its anti-collectivist pledges with broad support for Attlee's welfare state. While some Conservatives inevitably thought this all very 'pink', the approach was in the ascendancy from 1946 onwards (Butler, 1971: 143–4). Butler described the party's position as halfway 'between Manchester and Moscow' (Charmley, 2008: 156). The purpose was to give the public 'positive' reasons for voting Conservative (such as a pledge to greatly expand the construction of houses – Britain still being a million units short by 1950), and to ensure that the party spoke a comparable language to its enemy. In this, Butler succeeded; and the outcome was, as John Charmley (2008) puts it, a New Model Toryism. By the 1950 general election, the Conservative Party appeared up to date once again.

But, as suggested above, the reason that all of this struck a chord with the public was that there existed widespread discontent with everyday life. Propaganda will only find purchase where it connects to actual experience. In the case of post-war Britain, there existed ample raw material to mine. There was no return to normality and, unsurprisingly, the Labour government got much of the blame. There were successive economic crises, living standards continued to be squeezed long after the guns fell silent, consumer products of all kinds were subject to rationing and control (sometimes more stringent than during the war itself), shortages were prevalent and there was relative deprivation throughout the country. Life was drab and austere. This was not what *Let Us Face the Future* had promised; the public having been seduced by the idea of a New Jerusalem, the reality was a disappointment.

What the Conservative Party did was to couple its new policy of vocal commitment to welfarism with another, dual, strategy: exploitation of this disillusionment. Specifically, the Conservatives recognised an opportunity to win back key voter groups who had partially abandoned them in 1945. Under Butler's guidance, the party thus forged a new coalition of voters based on the issue of living standards. And the middle classes were central to this.

Middle-class living standards had fallen significantly under the Attlee government. The staples of their lifestyle – ample food and clothes, access to consumer products, entertainment, luxuries like motor cars, travel and perhaps domestic service – were all squeezed very considerably. Middle-class protein and calorie intake was reduced sharply during the war and failed to recover thereafter. The middle classes were buffeted by the simultaneous gales of rising prices, high taxation, labour shortages, rationing and controls. Savings were eroded and their lives disrupted in significant ways. It is true that the working classes were also hit by shortages, but in general terms this was offset by full employment. The middle classes suffered disproportionately in Attlee's Britain. In early 1950, Gaitskell confided to his diary that the people in the middle felt they had 'suffered considerable economic disadvantage by our actions' (Williams, 1983: 167). Ina Zweiniger-Bargielowska (1994: 180) labels this phenomenon 'the plight of the middle classes', and it was perhaps natural that Labour's inroads into middle-class areas in the South of England, the Home Counties and around London in particular – made in 1945 and crucial to the outcome of that election – were left vulnerable.

The public frequently struggled to understand why there were continued shortages years after the end of the war. While they had been willing to make sacrifices for the war effort, there was bafflement as to why such measures were necessary once the war was over. The people did not share Labour's ardour for the socialist project – indeed, as Steven Fielding (1991) has argued, had probably *never* shared it – and proved to be far more interested in the food on their tables. Food shortages were always high on the political agenda in the late 1940s. Britons were an increasingly hedonistic lot, and that did not align with the problems and priorities of the Attlee government. Rationing and controls had an immediate impact on everyday life; there were more than 25,000 controls in all (Zweiniger-Bargielowska, 1994) and opinion polls regularly showed that rationing was the key domestic issue in the minds of the voters (Gallup, 1976: 135, 148, 160, 165). People wanted to *consume* things again, as they had in the 1930s. Harold Wilson's 'bonfire of controls' was a political response to the fact that, by late 1948, criticism of the government on the issue was at fever pitch. Doing what any sensible opposition does, the Conservative Party aligned itself with this public mood. Ina Zweiniger-Bargielowska (2000: 204) has identified party politics from the late 1940s onwards as coming to represent nothing less than a 'battle over consumption', in which living standards became the key issue and Labour's evident failure to deliver the goods could be contrasted with a positive Conservative appeal to do better.

But the middle classes were not the only targets. Much of the burden of managing households under the difficult conditions of the post-war years fell on women specifically. Wives were usually in charge of the domestic sphere, and it is therefore no surprise that women were more antagonised by the Labour government than men. In its propaganda, the Conservative Party therefore sought to align itself with this female discontent. A pamphlet, *A True Balance*, was aimed at female voters, as was a short magazine, *Home Truths*. This found traction in a social context of inadequate access to even basic essentials like eggs, fat, meat and bread; and, in early 1951, the meat ration was reduced to its lowest ever level – six years after the end of the war. In 1952, an internal Labour report suggested that the 1951 election was lost 'in the queue at the butcher's or the grocer's' (Willets, 2005: 188). Indeed, the election saw a large swing to the Conservatives among women. This was crucial in determining the outcome.

Life in Attlee's Britain was frequently felt to be 'illiberal and restrictive of personal choice' (Morgan, 1990: 104). This was, after all, the era of Douglas Jay's boast that 'the gentleman in Whitehall really does know better what is good for people than the people know themselves' – a statement that seemed to sum up Labour's lack of empathy (Jay, 1947: 258). Gallup found that on every domestic issue bar employment the Conservatives were viewed more positively than Labour. That had electoral consequences. As Morgan comments, austerity 'had taken hold of the public consciousness like a malignant disease' (Morgan, 1990: 76). The Conservatives depicted the problems of post-war Britain as being an inevitable product of socialist mismanagement of the economy rather than – as Labour maintained – simply a consequence of the war. One Conservative slogan offered a sardonic invitation to 'shiver with Shinwell and starve with Strachey' in reference to a shortage of fish and coal (Charmley, 2008: 157). This was one example of many wherein the Conservative Party utilised the rhetoric of austerity to both reinforce and profit from the public's misgivings about Labour. Butler combined Conservative promises on welfare with pledges to dismantle restrictions on consumer products, get rid of controls, and permit people to run their own lives again. They waged this battle in the 1950, 1951 and 1955 elections. The Conservatives thus developed and propagated 'an aggressive redefinition of socialism' – based on 'bureaucracy, red tape, taxation and, above all, a vindictive austerity' (McKibben, 2010: 164). It is striking that, in *10 Points of Conservative Policy*, the number one pledge was 'individual freedom'. That demonstrates the public mood that the Conservatives sought to tap into. It was potentially a rich resource – and so it proved. The political system became highly polarised, and – if the turnout of 84 per cent in 1950 and 82.5 per cent in 1951, the highest ever recorded in the age of mass democracy, is any indication – the public were similarly polarised.

So effective was the party in this that David Willets (2005) and Zweiniger-Bargielowska (1994 and 2000) have both depicted it as the architect of its own return to power, the decisive winner of the propaganda battle with the government. As Ross McKibbin puts it, the

Conservatives were able to fight on two slogans: 'the welfare state is safe in our hands *and* we will set the people free' (McKibben, 2010: 167). It must be acknowledged that the Conservative Party did not actually win a by-election seat between 1945 and 1951. Butler pointed out that 'despite the inexorable rise in the cost of living, increasing burdens of direct and indirect taxation, intensification of physical controls, restrictions and rationing...and above all the series of recurring economic and financial crises ...the government's stock in the country remained obstinately high' (Butler, 1971: 132). That said, there were clear and often large swings towards the party at by-elections, and the Conservatives also did well in local elections (Zweiniger-Bargielowska, 1994: 183–5). Labour lost control of major cities, including Birmingham, Glasgow, Manchester and Newcastle. As noted earlier, the Conservative Party's recovery was incomplete in 1951, and significant sections of the public continued to stick by Labour, but, given that the general election was such a close-run thing, the Conservative strategy of exploiting popular disaffection was almost certainly central to Labour's defeat. It seems that the new Conservative coalition of voters was *just* broad enough to deliver Churchill the keys to Downing Street.

After Labour's fall from office, Attlee once privately suggested that Labour had taken austerity measures too far:

> when we saw the real state the country was in at the end of the war, the finances, the economy, the railways, the housing stock, we all went into a blue funk. Scared the pants off us, as the Americans would say. Austerity and more austerity seemed the only way out... [W]ere we too heavy on the brake? Yes, I think we got it wrong there.
>
> (Addison, 2010: 23)

However, popular discontent needs to be seen in the context of the economic situation faced by the Attlee government, and the economic policies it pursued.

Labour's economic inheritance in 1945 had been horrendous. The cost of the Second World War was colossal, depriving Britain of around a quarter of its wealth. In focusing on armaments production, the Churchill coalition had been compelled to give up much of Britain's export sector; but, as the country still required imports, a huge balance of payments crisis loomed at the end of the war. The country had also been dependent on the Lend-Lease policy with the United States. Thus, when Lend-Lease was suddenly terminated following the Japanese surrender in August 1945, Britain was fatally exposed. In August 1945, foreseeing a 'financial Dunkirk', Keynes had argued that Britain would require an unrelenting focus on restoring exports and drastic reductions in overseas expenditure on imports in order to resolve the crisis.

The economic statistics tell a story of painful economic reconstruction and recovery. The Attlee government saw increased industrial production (by one-third between 1946 and 1951), growth in exports, and – in contrast to the aftermath of the First World War and the experience of the 1920s and 1930s – full employment (below 2 per cent). Between 1946 and 1952 exports grew by a total of 77 per cent while imports increased by only 15 per cent; the increase in gross domestic fixed capital formation (investment) over the period was 58 per cent, while consumers' expenditure increased by barely 6 per cent overall (Cairncross, 1985: 24). The growth in exports absorbed nearly three-quarters of the growth in Gross Domestic Product under Attlee, mostly going into improving the balance of payments. It was in many ways, as Addison (2010: 12) says, a creditable performance, but ultimately a big political price was paid because of the way in which consumer spending was held down for the sake of exports and investment, and because of the economic crises that punctuated the life of the government – in 1947 (the fuel crisis and then the convertibility crisis), 1949 (devaluation) and 1950–51 (the effects of the outbreak of the Korean war and the excessive rearmament programme). In an environment of austerity and relative deprivation, Labour's record was simply not good enough in the eyes of key sections of the electorate. The Conservatives after 1951 were to reap the benefits of Labour's economic achievements in the 1940s, against a more favourable economic background (Pearce, 1994: 43).

The Liberals: The decisive factor?

A final force at work in Labour's ejection from office was the Liberal Party. Attlee later recalled that, even before the 1951 election, he was sure that the outcome would turn 'on the way Liberal electors cast their vote' (Attlee, 1954: 208). Whereas in 1950 the Liberals had put up 475 candidates, in 1951 they could only manage 109. Even in 1950 they captured only nine seats (this fell to six in 1951), but the point is that the Liberals still won a sizeable number of votes: 2.6 million in 1950 (9.1 per cent). With the Liberals unable to field so many candidates in 1951, their vote collapsed to just 730,000 (2.6 per cent).

Most constituencies lacked a Liberal candidate, and that made the question of how Liberal supporters would cast their vote a matter of great significance. The evidence indicates that this made a crucial

Table 4.1   The general election of 1951

Party	Votes won	MPs elected	Share of vote (%)
Conservative	13,717,538 (1950 12,502,567)	321 (1950 299)	48 (1950 43.5)
	(1945 9,577,667)	(1945 213)	(1945 39.8)
Labour	13,948,605 (1950 13,266,592)	295 (1950 315)	48.8 (1950 46.1)
	(1945 11, 632,191)	(1945 393)	(1945 48.3)
Liberal	730,556 (1950 2,621,548)	6 (1950 9)	2.5 (1950 9.1)
	(1945 2,197,191)	(1945 12)	(1945 9.1)
Others	198,969 (1950 381,964)	3 (1950 2)	0.7 (1950 1.3)
	(1945 674,863)	(1945 22)	(1945 2.8)

Note: Figures for 1945 and 1950 in brackets.
Source: Craig, 1987.

difference to the outcome of the election (Table 4.1). Backing for the Conservatives increased to 13.7 million in 1951, up from 12.5 million the year before. In terms of share of the vote, that translated into an increase from 43.5 per cent to 48 per cent. The Conservatives were highly energetic in cultivating the Liberal voter: a 1949 market research study commissioned by the party concluded that the typical Liberal supporter was near-identical to the classic 'floating voter', and the Conservatives set about trying to win their support (Conservative Party Archives: CRD, 2/21/1, 'The floating vote', 6 December 1949). Large-scale press advertising was supplemented by direct mailing of millions of leaflets (stressing that the Conservative Party was the spiritual home for supporters of Gladstone and Lloyd George) to likely Liberal voters, and Conservative activists targeted them for doorstep work. The Conservatives exploited the issue of austerity and the collapse of the Liberals to capture middle-class floating voters, attract those who had previously supported the Liberals, and thus win back seats in suburban areas. While Labour secured large majority in its heartlands, the Conservatives won smaller – but ultimately sufficient – majorities elsewhere. It was a strategy that worked well.

Given how robust Labour's own vote proved, for all the Conservatives' efforts, the collapse of the Liberals was perhaps the decisive factor in forcing Attlee from office. Labour's poll increased by 700,000 votes in 1951, and its share of the vote grew from 46.1 per cent to 48.8 per cent. Morgan (1984: 486) argued that 'had it not been for the much reduced tally of Liberal candidates, Churchill would not have won at all. By a six-to-four proportion, Liberals voted Conservative in seats where there was no Liberal candidate.' In important respects Labour did not 'lose' the election, outperforming its opponents by 230,000 votes in all; it was surely only the lack of Liberal candidates that enabled the Conservatives to win in sufficient constituencies. The Liberal swing to the Conservatives, not a falling away of Labour's own support, may have been the key to a result in 1951 that has been well described as a 'psephological anomaly' (Pearce, 1997: 137).

References

Addison, P. (2010), *No Turning Back* (Oxford: Oxford University Press).
Anderson, P. (1992), *English Questions* (London: Verso Books).
Attlee, C. R. (1954), *As It Happened* (London: Odhams Press).
Butler, D. (1952), *The British General Election of 1951* (London: Macmillan).
Butler, R. A. (1946), *Fundamental Issues* (London: Conservative Party).
Butler, R. A. (1947), *About the Industrial Charter* (London: Conservative Party).
Butler, R. A. (1971), *The Art of the Possible* (London: Hamish Hamilton).
Cairncross, A. (1985), *Years of Recovery: British Economic Policy 1945–51* (London: Methuen).
Campbell, J. (1987), *Nye Bevan and the Mirage of British Socialism* (London: Weidenfeld and Nicolson).
Charmley, J. (2008), *A History of Conservative Politics since 1830* (Basingstoke: Palgrave Macmillan).
Coates, D. (1975), *The Labour Party and the Struggle for Socialism* (Cambridge: Cambridge University Press).
Craig, F. W. S. (1987), *British Electoral Facts 1832–1987* (Aldershot: Dartmouth).
Crossman, R. (1966), 'The Lessons of 1945', in Anderson, P. and Blackburn, R. (eds), *Towards Socialism* (New York: Cornell University Press).
Crowcroft, R. (2008), 'The "High Politics" of Labour Party Factionalism, 1950–5', *Historical Research*, Vol. 81, No. 214, 679–709.
Crowcroft, R. (2011), *Attlee's War: World War II and the Making of a Labour Leader* (London: I. B. Tauris).
Dell, E. (1999), *A Strange Eventful History: Democratic Socialism in Britain* (London: HarperCollins).
Donoughue, B. and Jones, G. W. (1973), *Herbert Morrison: Portrait of a Politician* (London: Weidenfeld and Nicolson).
Fielding, S. (1991), ' "Don't know and Don't Care": Popular Political Attitudes in Labour's Britain, 1945–51', in Tiratsoo, N. (ed.), *The Attlee Years* (London: Continuum).
Foot, M. (1975), *Aneurin Bevan 1945–1960* (London: Paladin).
Gallup, G. H. (1976), *The Gallup International Public Opinion Polls: Great Britain, 1937–1975*, Vol. 1 (New York: Random House).
Greenleaf, W. H. (1983), *The British Political Tradition, Volume Two: The Ideological Heritage* (London: Routledge).
Hennessy, P. (2000), *The Prime Minister: The Office and its Holders since 1945* (London: Penguin).
Jay, D. (1947), *The Socialist Case* (London: Faber and Faber).
Jay, D. (1980), *Change and Fortune: A Political Record* (London: Hutchinson).

Jefferys, K. (1993), *The Labour Party Since 1945* (London: Macmillan).

Lindsay, T. F. and Harrington, M. (1974), *The Conservative Party 1918–1970* (London: Macmillan).

Macmillan, H. (1969), *Tides of Fortune 1945–1955* (London: Macmillan).

Marquand, D. (2008), *Britain Since 1918: The Strange Career of British Democracy* (London: Weidenfeld and Nicolson).

McKibben, R. (2010), *Parties and People: England 1914–1951* (Oxford: Oxford University Press).

Miliband, R. (1961), *Parliamentary Socialism* (London: The Merlin Press).

Minkin, L. (1980), *The Labour Party Conference* (Manchester: Manchester University Press).

Minkin, L. (1991), *The Contentious Alliance* (Edinburgh: Edinburgh University Press).

Morgan, K. (1984), *Labour in Power 1945–51* (Oxford: Oxford University Press).

Morgan, K. (1990), *The People's Peace* (Oxford: Oxford University Press).

Morgan, K. (2011), *Ages of Reform* (London: I. B. Tauris).

Nicholas, H. G. (1951), *The British General Election of 1950* (London: Macmillan).

Pearce, R. (1994), *Attlee's Labour Governments 1945–51* (London: Routledge).

Pearce, R. (1997), *Attlee* (London: Longman).

Pimlott, B. (ed.) (1986) *The Political Diary of Hugh Dalton, 1918–40, 1945–60* (London: Jonathan Cape).

Schneer, J. (1988), *Labour's Conscience: The Labour Left 1945–51* (London: Routledge).

Whiting, R. (2000), *The Labour Party and Taxation: Party Identity and Political Purpose in Twentieth-Century Britain* (Cambridge: Cambridge University Press).

Willets, D. (2005), 'The New Conservatism? 1945–1951', in Ball, S. and Seldon, A. (eds), *Recovering Power: The Conservatives in Opposition since 1867* (Basingstoke: Palgrave).

Williams, F. (1961), *A Prime Minister Remembers: The War and Post-war Memoirs of the Rt Hon Earl Attlee* (London: Heinemann).

Williams, P. (1982), *Hugh Gaitskell* (Oxford: Oxford University Press).

Williams, P. (ed.) (1983), *The Diary of Hugh Gaitskell 1945–1956* (London: Jonathan Cape).

Zweiniger-Bargielowska, I. (1994), 'Rationing, Austerity and the Conservative Party Recovery after 1945', *Historical Journal*, Vol. 37, No. 1, 173–97.

Zweiniger-Bargielowska, I. (2000), *Austerity in Britain: Rationing, Controls, and Consumption* (Oxford: Oxford University Press).

5
The Fall of the Wilson Government, 1970

Peter Dorey

> There are just four days to go and so far it has been one of the
> easiest campaigns I've known...that the mood is on our side
> and that people are good-humouredly willing to accept another
> six years of Labour Government...at this particular moment, as
> in the spring of ''66, the British elector feels good. The country
> isn't in the mood for Cassandra [Edward Heath] prophesying
> doom, nor does the electorate want Heath's reconstructed, reac-
> tionary Toryism of free enterprise and anti-trade unionism.
>
> (Crossman, 1977: 944–5, diary entry for 14 June 1970)

> I sensed an undercurrent of detachment among our own
> activists and Party audiences. As early as 13 June, I was writing
> in my diary: 'I wish there weren't another five days before the
> Election! I don't believe those poll figures ...I have a haunting
> feeling there is a silent majority sitting behind its lace curtains,
> waiting to come out and vote Tory'.
>
> (Castle, 1990: 407)

The Labour government's defeat in the June 1970 general election was
a considerable surprise to many commentators, because, according to
Gallup Polls, the party had enjoyed a 49–42 per cent lead over the
Conservatives through May and the first half of June. The same opinion polls had shown that Labour's leader, Harold Wilson, enjoyed a
much higher approval rating than his Conservative counterpart, Edward
Heath; their respective approval ratings were 49–28 per cent in May and
51–28 per cent in June. In the context of such figures, the proportion of
people expecting a Labour victory increased from 56 per cent in May to
68 per cent in June, while those envisaging a Conservative victory fell
from 26 per cent to a mere 13 per cent.

Table 5.1   The 1970 general election

Party	Votes won	MPs elected	Share of vote (%)
Conservative	13,145,123 (11,418,433)	330 (253)	46.4 (41.9)
Labour	12,179,341 (13,064,951)	287 (363)	43.0 (47.9)
Liberal	2,117,035 (2,327,533)	6 (12)	7.5 (8.5)
Others	906,346 (452,689)	7 (2)	3.1 (1.7)

Note: Figures for 1966 in brackets.
Source: Butler and Butler, 1994: 217.

Yet, as Table 5.1 illustrates, when the general election was held on 18 June 1970, the Conservatives defeated the incumbent Labour government by 13,145,123 votes to 12,179,341, winning 330 seats (out of 630) on a 4.7 per cent swing, and thereby securing a parliamentary majority of 30 seats. Labour's tally of seats fell from 363 (won in 1966) to 287, while its share of the vote declined from 47.9 per cent to 43 per cent.

It should be noted that, although the Conservatives had won 253 seats in 1966, they entered the 1970 general election campaign with 263 seats, due to by-election victories in the intervening four years, while Labour's tally fell from 363 to 346 during the same period. This meant that, by 1970, the Conservatives 'only' trailed Labour by 83 seats compared with 110 seats in 1966.

To understand why Labour lost in June 1970, in spite of its poll leads during the two months immediately preceding the general election, it is essential to examine the party's record in government from 1964, and particularly the problems it encountered after being re-elected in 1966. As a more detailed analysis of the results later in this chapter will suggest, Labour's defeat in the 1970 general election owed much to three particular factors: first, abstentions by many erstwhile Labour supporters in June 1970; second, higher turnout by Conservative voters, who had themselves apparently abstained in 1964 and/or 1966, but who rallied to their party in June 1970; third, the impact of the Liberal Party on Labour's support in many constituencies.

Labour's trials and tribulations in office

The Labour government elected in 1964 was committed to an ambitious National Plan which envisaged an average rate of growth of 4 per cent per annum, which in turn was to deliver the economic expansion on which many of Labour's other policy objectives and pledges were dependent, particularly those pertaining to social policies. It was a quintessentially social democratic or 'revisionist' approach (Drucker, 1979: 44–9; Foote, 1985; Chapters 9–11; Jones, 1996: Chapters 2–4) melded with the Fabianesque faith in the ability of experts and technocrats to plan and build the 'good society' largely though efficient and benign administration (Thompson, 2006, see also Foote, 1985: 27–30). Certainly, the first half of the 1960s was a period when: 'Technocratic approaches to economic problems appeared to be at their zenith' (Harris, 2000: 36).

Furthermore, much of the Labour leadership assumed that a judicious blend of economic planning and technological progress would deliver sufficient steady growth and prosperity to transcend the traditional left–right fissures in the parliamentary Labour Party (PLP), and thus avoid the old doctrinal disputes over nationalisation or higher taxation of the rich (Dorey, 2012). As one commentator observed, 'The revisionists won over the majority of the party to the concept of public control of the economy by Keynesian ... measures ... rather than the public ownership of major sectors of manufacturing industry' (Hatfield, 1978: 19).

Another advantage intended by making the National Plan the fulcrum of achieving steady economic growth was that it would obviate the need for incomes policies, which were invariably invoked to secure wage restraint. The trade unions resented such initiatives, partly because they were strongly wedded to 'free collective bargaining', and partly because incomes policies were predicated on the assumption that various economic problems, most notably inflation, derived from ordinary workers 'selfishly' obtaining 'excessive' wage increases; large salaries or high levels of profit at the top were rarely, if ever, subject to such curbs or restraint.

In this context, the National Plan envisaged, not a traditional incomes policy, but a 'policy for incomes', whose objective was '*not* to keep increases down to a minimum, but [to allow increases] up to the maximum possible ... not wage restraint', but a policy which 'should allow real wages to rise' (Labour Party Archives, RD.433/March 1963, emphasis in original). This point was reiterated by Wilson himself when he declared that 'a planned growth of incomes' would be 'the condition of sustained growth ... because a pledge of sustained growth is a condition of that policy', and 'we are willing to create the conditions in which it can be established' (Wilson, 1964: 29).

Yet, from the moment the Labour Party entered office in October 1964, it was beset by serious economic difficulties which resulted in the abandonment, dilution or postponement of sundry other objectives and policies pledged prior to the election. Initially, in 1964 and 1965, the Labour government could claim that its main hindrance was the precariousness of its parliamentary position, having won the October 1964 election with a majority of only four seats – which was narrowed further when the party lost a January 1965 by-election in East London – but various economic indicators already provided an ominous portent, and instantly raised doubts about the efficacy of the National Plan and the assumptions on which it had been based. For example, upon entering office in October 1964, Labour was confronted with a £800 million balance of payments deficit (equivalent to about £12 billion in 2012), to which the Cabinet responded with the first of a series of deflationary measures.

Worse was to follow, though. Ostensibly, the Labour government ought to have been in a stronger position, having been re-elected in the March 1966 general election with a comfortable parliamentary majority of 97 seats. It could even claim that it now had a proper mandate for its programme of ostensibly radical economic and social reform. Yet financiers and others in the business community have rarely paid much heed to parliament or (professed) electoral mandates when pursuing profit and other forms of capital accumulation. Indeed, the very fact that Labour had obtained a comfortable parliamentary majority in March 1966 itself caused considerable consternation among 'the City' and international financiers, who feared that the government would now feel confident enough to embark upon a programme of more radical reforms. If there had previously been apprehension that Labour's narrow parliamentary majority would result in weak or indecisive government, then the increased and comfortable majority prompted nervousness about what an emboldened Labour government might seek to do. Either way, as an editorial entitled 'Labour Men, Tory Measures' in *The Economist* (31 July 1965: 127) observed, 'when orthodox policies are pursued by a left-wing government, they do not attract the same return in financial confidence as exactly the same policies pursued by the Tories.'

Consequently, the Labour government repeatedly struggled to secure the confidence of either domestic or international business communities, almost regardless of the measures it took to tackle Britain's serious economic problems during the 1960s. Initially, ministers relied on orthodox deflationary measures to reduce consumer spending on imports and, *inter alia*, reduce the balance of payments deficit, while also curbing public expenditure and thus deferring or reducing sundry planned increases in the 'social wage' or welfare provision. Clearly, such measures constituted a *de facto* abandonment of the National Plan;

indeed, rather than planning the economy, the Labour government found itself increasingly responding to economic events largely beyond its control. The confidence of 1964 was superseded by almost permanent crisis management.

Moreover, deflation was intended to obviate recourse to devaluation (of the pound), which some Treasury officials and a few senior ministers favoured, but which Harold Wilson himself was resolved to avoid. Initially, Wilson's stance prevailed, but when increasingly stringent deflationary policies and statutory wage restraint failed to improve Britain's balance of payments and, *inter alia*, assure overseas investors of the efficacy of the Labour government's economic strategy, the ensuing run on the pound during the autumn of 1967 made devaluation virtually unavoidable. Thus it was that, on 18 November 1967, the pound was devalued from $2.80 to $2.40, a measure which Wilson only acceded to with much reluctance and regret, having finally been persuaded that there was no feasible alternative.

Yet, despite having previously pursued deflation as an alternative to devaluation, it henceforth became necessary to persevere with deflationary economic policies (with all that these implied for previously pledged improvements in social provision and the 'planned growth of incomes') in order to ensure that devaluation proved a success. One consequence of this was 'to move productive capacity from the home consumption to the exporting sectors of the economy – there would, in other words, have to be a restriction on the domestic standard of living' (Butler and Pinto-Duschinsky, 1971: 25).

Not surprisingly, continued wage restraint and cuts in public expenditure (which often actually meant postponed or lower-than-planned increases) meant that the Labour government found itself increasingly at odds with the trade unions. Although the unions and ministers alike initially assumed that recourse to incomes policy was a temporary expedient to address unexpectedly unfavourable economic circumstances, the pursuit of wage restraint became a permanent feature of the Labour government's economic strategy (see Dorey, 2006a), as the Cabinet repeatedly sought to convince the City and international financiers that it could curb inflation and cut Britain's balance of payments deficits. Moreover, the incomes policies increasingly became statutory or more stringent, and thus wholly different in character from the 'planned growth of incomes' originally pledged in 1963–64.

Not surprisingly, the deflationary measures adopted increasingly antagonised the trade unions and alienated many of the workers who had voted for Labour in 1964 and/or 1966. This manifested itself in two particular, and ominous, ways. First, initial trade union acquiescence with voluntary incomes policy – largely on the aforementioned assumption that this was a short-term, temporary measure – was replaced by increasing resentment and resistance when ministers invoked subsequent, sometimes statutory, incomes policies. This was evident in the increased industrial militancy and strike activity which occurred in the latter half of the 1960s, which simultaneously exacerbated the anxieties of the business community and increasingly incensed ministers.

Indeed, a strike by the National Union of Seamen in May 1966 seriously affected the shipping of exports, while causing further consternation to industrialists and financiers, who harboured doubts about the Labour government's determination or ability to 'get a grip'. An evidently rattled Wilson publicly denounced the seamen's strike, and alleged that it had been fomented by Communists whose ultimate motives were political, rather than being concerned with wages. One prominent left-wing Labour MP, Eric Heffer, subsequently claimed that, in responding to the seamen's strike in such a manner, 'The government had done itself a great deal of harm and laid the basis for defeat in 1970', for it heralded 'the beginning of conflict with the trade unions and an example of how Labour governments can turn friends into enemies' (Heffer, 1991: 123).

The second manifestation of the damage to Labour's popularity deriving from the government's deflationary measures and pay curbs was the party's ratings in the opinion polls from 1966 onwards, coupled with a succession of by-election defeats. For example, whereas Labour enjoyed a 5.7 per cent lead over the Conservatives in 1966, just two years later the Conservatives had secured an 18.2 per cent lead over Labour, and this narrowed only very slightly the following year (Butler and Butler, 1994: 237, 252–3).

This loss of popularity resulted in a series of by-election defeats during these four years. Indeed, 15 of the 16 seats in which there was a by-election had been held or won by Labour in 1966, but every one of them was lost in the subsequent by-elections; 12 to the Conservatives and one each to the Liberal Party, Plaid Cymru and the Scottish National Party. The only by-election which Labour did not lose during this four-year period was in a Northern Ireland constituency in which the incumbent MP was an Ulster Unionist.

The Labour government's response to the marked increase in strike activity, and concomitant breaches of the Cabinet's incomes policies, was to propose placing industrial relations in an explicit legal framework, thereby replacing the *voluntarist* system which had prevailed hitherto, and to which the unions had been wedded (in tandem with their commitment to free collective bargaining). This new approach was presaged in a 1969 White Paper entitled *In Place of Strife*, but the planned comprehensive legislation was to be preceded by a short Industrial Relations Bill which would grant the Secretary of State for Employment and Productivity (Barbara Castle) statutory powers to intervene in certain types of industrial action, particularly unofficial strikes, with fines to be imposed on trade unions that persevered with such action following ministerial intervention and orders to desist.

Such was the opposition among many Labour MPs, particularly those who were sponsored by trade unions, that in March 1969, following a parliamentary debate on *In Place of Strife*, over 50 of them voted against it, while 40 abstained. Yet in proceeding with the Industrial Relations Bill, in lieu of more comprehensive legislation based on the 25 proposals enshrined in the White Paper, Wilson insisted that it was:

> an essential Bill. Essential to our economic recovery. Essential to the balance of payments. Essential to full employment. It is an essential component of ensuring the economic success of the Government. It is on that economic success that the recovery of the nation...depends...the passage of this Bill is essential to its [the Labour Government's] continuance in Office. There can be no going back on that....
>
> (Wilson, 1971: 643)

However, the opposition within the PLP remained such that the government's Chief Whip, Bob Mellish, warned the Cabinet that the 'short' Industrial Relations Bill was unlikely to gain sufficient support in the House of Commons. Indeed, by June 1969, several Cabinet ministers were also harbouring grave doubts about the wisdom of the Bill (NA CAB 128/44 Part 1, CC (69) 26th Conclusions 9 June 1969; NA CAB 128/44 Part 1, CC (69) 28th Conclusions 17 June 1969). Finally acknowledging his and Castle's isolation on this issue, Wilson announced the abandonment of industrial relations legislation, in return for a 'solemn and binding undertaking' by the Trade Union Congress's General Council that it would itself 'intervene in serious unconstitutional stoppages' (House of Commons Debates, 5th series, 19 June 1969, col. 700) (see Dorey, 2006b, for a full discussion of this episode).

It must also be emphasised that the economic difficulties which the Labour government grappled with throughout the 1966–70 period also had an understandably detrimental impact on various social policies to which the party had been committed, yet which consequently had to be abandoned, diluted or postponed. For example, it had pledged to raise the school leaving age from 15 to 16, the primary purpose being to improve the educational attainment and career prospects of working-class children, who tended to leave school at 15, while middle-class pupils stayed on and consequently attained (better) educational qualifications.

However, because of the costs which would have accrued from raising the school leaving age in the midst of a period of deflation and public expenditure curbs, the reform was deferred until 1972–73, a decision which Tony Benn described as 'disgraceful' (Benn, 1988: 17, diary entry for 15 January 1968), and which George Brown deemed to be 'one of the greatest betrayals a Labour Government, so overwhelmingly composed of University graduates, could make of the less privileged people who, after all, had elected it' (Brown, 1971: 175, see Dorey, 2008a, for a full account of this decision).

Another education policy which was abandoned due largely to financial stringencies was the planned building of several new universities, mainly in northern towns such as Blackpool, Burnley, Darlington, Doncaster, Carlisle, Halifax and Southport (Labour Party Archives, RD.368/December 1962). It was envisaged that a larger number of universities would not only increase places for students from working-class backgrounds, but also enable more students to go to a local university, and thereby live at home; this would, of course, make higher education cheaper for them. Instead, though, the 1964–70 Labour government opted to increase student places at existing universities (acknowledging that this would entail larger lectures and seminars), while also expanding polytechnic education to enhance 'vocational' qualifications. Meanwhile, having abolished National Health Service prescription charges in 1965, the Labour government reintroduced them in 1968.

Disunity and disagreement within the PLP

The intra-party divisions over ideological orientation and policies to which Labour had traditionally been prone became more pronounced and visible during the government's second (1966–70) term of office. The optimism that ministers would have derived from Labour's comfortable re-election in March 1966 proved very short-lived, as the rapidly deteriorating economic situation and increasing trade union resistance compelled the Cabinet to invoke a number of unpalatable measures, as noted above, which placed an immense strain on party unity. However, intra-party divisions were not solely due to policy decisions deriving from the Cabinet's response to devaluation, vitally important though these were, because other non-economic policies, such as House of Lords reform and sundry social policies or reforms, also prompted disagreements within the PLP, and these, in turn, exacerbated the image of a governing party riven by dissent and disunity.

This doubtless further demoralised many of Labour's supporters, while also raising serious doubts in the minds of 'floating voters' about Labour's fitness to govern. After all, it is widely acknowledged that voters generally dislike or distrust political parties or governments which are clearly divided, and thus distracted from providing effective political leadership and policy-making in office.

Naturally, much of the disunity within the PLP occurred along ideological lines, with the left condemning austerity measures which would invariably impose the greatest hardships and sacrifices on the working class in general, and the poor in particular, even though these people were not the ones who had caused the financial crisis. As ever, though, the Labour leadership's response to a capitalist crisis was to demand sacrifices of many of its own supporters, in order to address the concerns and demands of capital and the international money markets – or those whom Harold Wilson contemptuously referred to as 'the gnomes of Zurich'. In so doing, ministers incurred the wrath of those Labour MPs angered by their leadership's attacks on the wages and welfare of the industrial working class, and the concomitant betrayal of socialism which this was deemed to signify.

Policies pertaining to wage restraint and industrial relations reform also highlighted intra-party divisions deriving from relationships with the trade unions, with those Labour MPs and ministers either sponsored by a union, or with a pre-parliamentary background in trade unionism (such as James Callaghan), proving to be the strongest opponents of measures to curb workers' pay or impose statutory curbs on the trade unions. Many of these MPs and ministers were by no means on the left (certainly not Callaghan) of the PLP, but, on issues such as statutory incomes policies and/or industrial relations legislation, their opposition matched and reinforced that emanating from the left.

However, a third demarcation became discernible within the PLP from the mid-1960s onwards, deriving from a demographic or socio-educational distinction between the party's (generally) older 'proletarian' MPs and the increasing number of rather younger, often university-educated, middle-class MPs who became more prevalent during the 1960s (see Dorey, 2006c, for an account of the compositional changes in the PLP during this decade). This particular compositional change itself yielded two main sources of disagreement, one of which was related to social reform, while the other was concerned with the role of the PLP in policy-making in general.

The first of these divisions arose from Labour's 'permissive' legislation during this period, when abortion, divorce and homosexuality were all liberalised or legalised. These reforms were generally strongly supported by Labour's younger, university-educated and/or more intellectual MPs and ministers, and seemingly reflected Anthony Crosland's call, in his seminal 1956 book *The Future of Socialism*, for socialists to shift their focus from economic regulation and bureaucratic statism, and instead campaign for more social libertarianism and quality-of-life issues:

> We need not only higher exports and old-age pensions, but more open-air cafes ... later closing-hours for public houses ... Total abstinence and a good filing-system are not now the right sign-posts to the socialist Utopia ... [We need to address] the more serious question of socially-imposed restrictions on the individual's private life and liberty ... the divorce laws, licensing laws, prehistoric (and flagrantly unfair) abortion laws, obsolete penalties for sexual abnormality, the illiterate censorship of books and plays and remaining restrictions on the equal rights of women ... these are intolerable, and should be highly offensive to socialists, in whose blood there should always run a trace of the anarchist and the libertarian, and not too much of the prig and the prude.
>
> (Crosland, 1956: 355–6)

However, many of Labour's older or more working-class MPs were unenthusiastic, if not openly critical, in their attitudes towards liberal social reform and libertarian sexual politics, reflecting either their own disapproval or/and the anticipated hostility of their constituents. Thus did some Labour MPs warn that the electorate might start viewing Labour as 'the Party that cared more about the "odd people" in society, such as murderers and homosexuals and the like, rather than the ordinary, hardworking members of the community' (Labour Party Archives, Minutes of a PLP meeting, 12 May 1965).

Such views were reiterated when the legislation to legalise homosexuality was enacted during the 1966–67 parliamentary session, whereupon two of the government's whips, George Lawson and Walter Harrison (MPs for Motherwell and Wakefield respectively) were prominent among those Labour MPs who 'objected fiercely that it [the Sexual

Offences (No.2) Bill] was turning our own working-class support against us' (Crossman, 1976: 171–2, diary entry for 19 December 1966). Similarly, Kevin McNamara claimed that many of his fellow Labour MPs were opposed to the Bill, believing that the government had already gone too far in legislating on issues which 'had no bearing on our Socialist programme', and which would 'do us no good in the country', yet ministers were pursuing it at the expense of more pressing matters (Labour Party Archives, Minutes of PLP meeting, 29 June 1967).

Nor was the Cabinet happy about the legalisation of homosexuality, with the then Foreign Secretary, George Brown, insisting that 'society ought to have higher standards', and warning that: 'This is how Rome came down.' If the Bill was passed, he envisaged 'a totally disorganised, indecent and unpleasant society', and claimed that: 'We've gone too damned far on sex already' (quoted in Castle, 1990: 54, diary entry for 11 February 1966). Elsewhere, Richard Crossman recorded that 'working class people in the north jeer at their Members at the weekend.... It has gone down very badly that the Labour Party should be associated with such a Bill' (Crossman, 1976: 407, diary entry for 3 July 1967). Meanwhile, the Chair of the PLP, Manny Shinwell, 'stalked the [House of Commons] tea rooms' trying to mobilise Labour MPs to vote against the Bill, and 'making known, as ever, his contempt for the intellectuals who would bring disastrous opprobrium upon the Labour government' (Abse, 1973: 149).

By contrast, it tended to be Labour's more middle-class, university-educated MPs and ministers who were most 'liberal' on social issues and sexual politics, and who favoured legislation to outlaw sundry forms of repression or discrimination. This socio-educational division within the PLP seemed to endorse Seymour Martin Lipset's arguments about working-class authoritarianism, the prevalence of which 'has posed a tragic dilemma for those intellectuals of the democratic Left who once believed the proletariat to be a force for liberty...equality and social progress' (Lipset, 1960: 97).

Meanwhile, the second source of division arising from demographic and socio-educational changes in the PLP's composition from the mid-1960s onwards concerned the aspirations of many of the newer and younger cohort of Labour MPs, many of whom wanted to play a more active role in shaping their government's policies, rather than remaining passive backbenchers herded hither and thither by the party whips (see Anderson, 1968; Dalyell, 1989: 150–1). As such, some of these Labour MPs were less deferential towards the party leadership than their predecessors, and demanded to be taken more seriously; they were not willing to be treated as mere lobby fodder, and complained that some of their ministerial colleagues failed to display 'a spirit of comradeship' in their dealings with backbench Labour MPs (NA PREM 13/1055, Shinwell to Wilson, 14 November 1966).

It was partly to pacify these newer, younger, often more educated Labour MPs that a few experimental select committees were established in the latter half of the 1960s, although these could readily be viewed as a wily Wilsonian ruse to give these backbenchers something to do, lest the devil made work for their idle hands (NA PREM 13/1053, Wilson to Bowden, 21 November 1964; Wilson to Crossman, 6 April 1966).

Not surprisingly, some older or/and more senior Labour parliamentarians looked askance at these allegedly disrespectful upstarts and young (wo)men in a hurry, who seemingly expected to shape government policy as soon as they entered the House of Commons, rather than working their way up the ministerial hierarchy over the course of a political career (Dorey, 2008b: 63–4, 74–5; Dorey and Honeyman, 2010: 158–63). Certainly, one senior minister, Michael Stewart, was irked at the apparent impudence of some younger Labour MPs, who, he claimed, 'should be thankful that as a socialist government, we want to keep the Executive strong, not to strengthen parliamentary control', a declaration for which he was 'applauded by many people round the [Cabinet] table' (Crossman, 1976: 130, diary entry for 17 November 1966).

Revived and credible conservative opposition

In 1964, Harold Wilson had depicted himself as a politically young and dynamic leader offering technocratic modernisation and institutional reform, primarily in order to reinvigorate the British economy. In so doing, he had contrasted himself with an ageing, seemingly tired Conservative leadership which seemed devoid of ideas or inspiration, and which seemed increasingly out of touch with modern Britain.

By 1970, the situation seemed to have reversed, for it was now Wilson and his Labour government which seemed politically exhausted and bereft of ideas, whereas the Conservatives were now pledging modernisation and institutional reform, under the relatively youthful (certainly in comparison to his party's previous leaders) leadership of Edward Heath. At least, back in 1964, the Conservatives could attribute their tiredness and need for renewal to having been in government for 13 years; in 1970, Labour seemed almost moribund after only six years in office, although, of course, they had presided over much more difficult economic circumstances than their political predecessors, as well as a less cohesive parliamentary party, which itself repeatedly vexed the leadership.

Having been elected Conservative leader in July 1965 (the first time that the party had actually elected its leader), Heath had presided over an extensive review of the party's policies (see Patten, 1980: 15–7; Ramsden, 1980: Chapter 9; 1996: 23–8), with many of the ensuing policies being endorsed at a special meeting of Heath's shadow Cabinet, held at the Selsdon Park Hotel (in Surrey) in January 1970. They then formed the basis of the Conservative Party's election manifesto a few months later. The policy review heralded the Conservative Party's commitment to restoring 'the market' by reducing state intervention in the economy, whereupon unprofitable firms and loss-making industries – 'lame ducks' – would no longer be rescued by government via public take-over or subsidy, but, instead, would be left to go bankrupt. This was intended to provide companies and industries with a major spur to become more competitive and profitable, and, *inter alia*, reinvigorate the British economy overall; it would be leaner, but fitter.

However, while the Selsdon Park conference committed the next Conservative government to greater freedom in the economic sphere, it simultaneously committed it to imposing greater authority and discipline in the social sphere; a freer economy, a stronger state. In particular, a much tougher stance was to be adopted *vis-à-vis* law and order, immigration and social policy, with the welfare state and its recipients to be subjected to greater 'selectivity' in the allocation of resources and entitlement for benefits. This stronger discipline was also to be applied to the trade unions, whose activities were to be placed in a clear legal framework, ostensibly to ensure they behaved in a more 'responsible' manner.

With characteristically acerbic wit, Harold Wilson coined the term 'Selsdon Man', the implication being that the policies being canvassed by the Conservative opposition were prehistoric, and apparently presaged a break with the 'progressive' post-war consensus in favour of reversion to an earlier mode of free market capitalism and rugged self-help individualism.

However, it was not only Conservative policies which had seemingly been modernised by June 1970; the party had also adopted somewhat younger, relatively more socially representative, parliamentary candidates. This owed much to a 1965 initiative presided over by the then party chairman, Edward Du Cann, whereby Conservative Central Office redrafted its list of prospective parliamentary candidates with the objective of securing the selection of younger, more 'representative' candidates. In so doing, it seemed to be responding to complaints from some of its own supporters about the type of people who seemingly dominated the higher echelons of the party, and who thus conveyed the out-of-touch image which the Conservatives had acquired. One such complaint was conveyed in a trenchant letter sent to Central Office, in December 1963, from an industrialist describing himself as a lifelong Conservative, claiming that:

> We are sick of seeing old-looking men dressed in flat caps and bedraggled tweeds strolling with a 12-bore [shot-gun]. For God's sake, what is your campaign manager doing? These photographs of Macmillan's ghost with Home's face date about 1912...these tired old men...[and] the Etonians, their 19th century appearances and their 18th century platitudes...We are looking for a 1963 leader.
>
> (Quoted in Ramsden, 1980: 225–6)

Apparently in response to such criticisms, half of the candidates who fought the 1966 general election for the Conservative Party were subsequently de-selected or persuaded to stand down, in order to make way for a new generation of Conservative candidates who supposedly reflected and represented a more meritocratic Britain. Furthermore, it was some of these new, younger Conservative candidates who were most critical of the consensual, steady-as-she-goes approach of the 1951–64 Conservative governments, and who, therefore, warmly welcomed the more radical approach heralded by the party's policy review. This perspective was evident in (Conservative MP) Timothy Raison's assertion that 'it is not the One Nation Spirit that we need today, but willingness to risk the tension that may arise from greater readiness to root out...weaknesses' (Raison, 1965: 15). Yet even some of the party's more senior MPs and former ministers acknowledged the need for change by the mid-1960s, with Reginald Bevins (1965: 150) asserting that it 'must search its own soul. It must decide its principles anew. The principles of Disraeli, or even of 1951, will no longer do'.

Where did Labour's former support go in 1970?

As is invariably the case in political science, there is no single or simple answer as to why Labour lost the 1970 general election but, rather, several factors whose combined and cumulative impact contributed to Labour's defeat. Political phenomena are almost always multicausal in origin, and so can rarely, if ever, be explicated by just one factor or key event. As such, understanding why the Labour Party lost the 1970 general election behoves us to consider a range of endogenous and exogenous factors, but, before we do so, more detailed examination of the 1970 general election result is warranted, because this may provide some preliminary clues as to *where* Labour's former support went, before we contemplate *why*.

In June 1970, the Conservatives won 1,726,690 votes more than in 1966, whereas Labour lost 885,610 votes from 1966. It immediately becomes evident that the Conservative victory was not simply attributable to disillusioned Labour voters switching to the Conservatives. Even if these 885,610 Labour votes had all been transferred directly to the Conservatives, this would still beg the question of where the other Conservative 841,080 votes were acquired from.

One answer seems to be that 1,081,192 more people voted in 1970 than in 1966, the total electorate having increased from almost 36 million in 1966 to more than 39 million in 1970. The larger electorate was due to the 1969 reduction in the voting age, from 21 to 18, which naturally boosted the pool of potential voters. This also helps explain the apparent discrepancy between a higher numerical turn-out in 1970 and a lower proportional turn-out; in 1966 the total electorate was 35.96 million people, of whom 27.26 million actually voted, representing a 75.8 per cent turn-out, whereas by 1970 the total electorate had increased to 39.34 million, so that the 28.34 million who actually voted constituted a 72 per cent turn-out.

However, it is not clear to what extent the higher turn-out in June 1970 was actually due to the increased size of the electorate, and how much was because of Conservative voters who had abstained in 1966, but who rallied to their party in 1970. In June 1970, the Conservatives won 68 seats from the Labour Party; these gains were not confined to any specific region of Britain, but derived from constituencies the length and breadth of the country, ranging from Aberdeen down to Southampton, and from Falmouth and Camborne across to Norfolk. However, in many of these 68 seats, the Conservative candidate's victory derived from an increase in support which was greater than Labour's loss of support. In other words, as we noted above, the increase in the Conservatives' vote was double the loss of Labour's votes from 1966. This means that the Conservatives' victory in June 1970 cannot be attributed simply to Labour switchers; they must have attracted extra support from other sources. For example, in Bebington (Merseyside), the Labour candidate polled just ten votes fewer than in 1966 (30,545 down to 30,535), whereas the Conservative vote increased from 28,208 to 31,260. Similarly, in Bedfordshire South, the Labour vote fell by 1,442, while the Conservative vote increased by 7,776.

Moreover, in a few constituencies, the Labour vote actually increased slightly in 1970, but this increase was significantly outstripped by the increase in the Conservative vote. To give just one example of this particular phenomenon, in the High Peak (Derbyshire) constituency, the Labour vote increased from 16,938 to 18,054, but the Conservative vote rose from 16,124 to 19,558, with the total number of votes cast rising from 41,052 to 44,731. In most of the 68 seats which the Conservatives won from Labour in June 1970, the turn-out was notably higher than it had been in 1966. That said, it is not clear whether the increased number of votes cast in 1970 was due to the larger electorate deriving from the lowering of the voting age in 1969 from 21 to 18, or reflected a greater propensity by Conservative supporters actually to vote for their party, whereas a sizeable number of erstwhile Labour voters abstained. Probably it was a combination of both, although, if the Conservatives' success was partly attributable to the new voters in the 18–21 age cohort, it would rather undermine the assumption that young people are/were more left-wing than older people – otherwise, the lowering of the voting age ought to have benefitted Labour rather more.

Thirteen of the seats which the Conservatives won from the Labour Party were constituencies in which the Liberals fielded candidates in the 1970 general election, not having done so in 1966. There certainly seemed to be a close statistical correlation between the votes won by the Liberal Party in many of these seats and the loss of votes suffered by Labour, which then provided the Conservative candidate with a simple plurality of votes. For example, in Brighton Kemptown, Labour's vote declined by 3,831, while the Liberal candidate attracted 3,833 votes – just two more than Labour lost. This enabled the Conservative candidate to win the seat with a 'majority' of 3,103, even though the Conservatives only polled 103 more votes than in 1966. Similarly, in Stockport North, the Liberals won 4,022 votes (not having contested the seat in 1966), whereas the Labour candidate polled 4,330 fewer votes than in 1966. This enabled the Conservative candidate to win by a margin of 871 votes, even though the party polled only 130 votes more than in 1966. Again, the Labour Party clearly suffered as a consequence of the Liberal Party's intervention. Moreover, in Conway, the Conservative vote itself fell from 17,622 (in 1966) to 16,927, but the party still won the seat, because Labour's vote dropped from 18,203 to 16,024 (a loss of 2,179 votes), while the Liberal candidate polled 2,626.

The Conservative Party also won seven seats from Labour where the Liberals did *not* field a candidate in 1970, having done so in 1966. The impact of this Liberal 'withdrawal' can be gleaned from, for example, Billericay, where turn-out increased from 85,971 to 91,484, Labour's vote actually rose from 40,013 to 43,765, but the Conservatives' support increased from 38,371 votes to 47,719; a 9,348 increase, which strongly suggests that the Conservative Party was the main beneficiary of the Liberals' failure to contest the seat in 1970, the latter having won 7,587 votes in 1966. Similarly, in Stretford, Labour polled just 125 fewer votes than in 1966, whereas the Conservatives gained 7,255 votes, evidently the prime beneficiaries of the fact that the Liberals did not field a candidate in 1970, having won 6,382 votes in 1966.

Why did Labour lose support in 1970?

Although the above statistical analysis offers significant clues about *where* Labour's support went in June 1970, and *how* the Conservatives were the prime beneficiaries, we still need to consider *why* the opinion poll leads enjoyed by Labour during May and much of June were not sustained, and thus failed to deliver the electoral victory which many in the party, and the media, had so confidently predicted.

As already intimated, there is no clear or definitive answer; instead, we need to consider the combined and cumulative impact of several factors pertaining to Labour's record in office since being re-elected in March 1966. In this regard, the record of the 1966–70 Labour government, as discussed in the first half of this chapter, certainly provides a number of clues about the party's loss of support on polling day in June 1970. However, one or two factors during the latter part of the election campaign also weakened Labour's apparent support in a fatal manner.

One thing to note straight away is that the significant poll leads enjoyed by Labour in sundry opinion polls during May and the first half of June 1970 were largely an aberration, because, the party had consistently trailed the Conservatives in the polls, often by substantial margins, throughout the previous two years. As such, the fact that Labour suddenly attained a 7 per cent poll lead in May and the first two weeks of June 1970 was almost certainly attributable to electoral volatility and ephemeral short-term factors, rather than a genuine and sustainable revival of party support. After all, if a political party's negative opinion poll rating becomes a seven-point lead in just a matter of weeks, then, unless the dramatic increase in support derives from a major crisis or scandal suddenly affecting its main political opponent, it is highly likely to dissipate with equal rapidity. A sudden and significant surge in public popularity is likely to prove 'soft', and thus extremely unreliable (as the Liberal Democrats' leader, Nick Clegg, discovered in the 2010 general election).

To have won the 1970 general election, therefore, Labour would, among other things, have needed to have enjoyed a rather longer, and somewhat slower or more gradual, recovery in the opinion polls, because this would probably have provided a more solid and consistent basis of electoral support than that which so suddenly evaporated in the last 48 hours or so of the 1970 general election.

Certainly, a major feature of the June 1970 general election was the extent to which many erstwhile Labour voters abstained, rather than directly switching to the Conservatives; too many of Labour's potential or professed supporters simply stayed at home, rather than actually going to their local polling booth and voting Conservative – they were sitters, rather than switchers. After all, in many of the seats won by the Conservatives, their increase in votes was considerably greater than the decrease in Labour's votes. As one commentary on the 1970 election results observed: 'The absolute fall in the Labour vote by more than three-quarters of a million is best interpreted as a positive decision by Labour voters to abstain' (Rose, 1970: 31).

Furthermore, it seems that many of those erstwhile Labour voters who abstained only decided to do so in the last 48 hours or so of the campaign, which would help to explain why the opinion polls predicted a Labour victory throughout the campaign; the decision by many hitherto Labour supporters not to vote was made too late to be registered in the plethora of opinion polls about voting intentions. One Labour backbencher, Ian Mikardo, was alerted to this phenomenon when canvassing in his Poplar (East London) constituency:

> What I heard on the doorsteps was not that a lot of people who had voted Labour in 1966 were going to vote Tory or Liberal in 1970, but that a lot of people who had voted Labour in 1966 were, in 1970, not going to vote at all.

After the election, Mikardo managed to locate 116 of these abstainers (who had voted Labour in 1966), and asked them whom they had voted for instead on 18 June; two had voted Liberal and three had voted Conservative, but the other 111 simply had not voted. When Mikardo then enquired why they had abstained, the standard response was that 'they couldn't see much, if any, difference between what the Labour Government had done in the last four years and what a Conservative Government would have done' (Mikardo, 1988: 181, 182).

Richard Crossman, having previously exuded confidence to the point of hubris (as symbolised by his quote at the beginning of this chapter), realised that Labour was in trouble a few hours before polling finished on 18 June: 'it was obvious that something was going very badly wrong; The poll was only just over 50, 52, 55 per cent, even in our safest, biggest wards, and by 9 o'clock, it was only 60 per cent' (Crossman, 1977: 949, diary entry for 18 June 1970). The next day, Crossman ruminated on Labour's apparent last minute loss of support, and concluded that doubts about the underlying state of the economy, accruing from 'the endless repetitive reminders [by the Conservatives] of rising prices, broken promises, unfavourable trade figures, all took their toll'. Crucially, Crossman averred that, although some former Labour voters had probably switched to the Conservative Party, most of the 4.7 per cent swing to the Conservatives 'was the result of Labour abstentions' (Crossman, 1977: 949, diary entry for 19 June 1977).

Crossman acknowledged that 'the only relevant lesson of the election is that three months was too brief a period of convalescence from the self-inflicted wounds of nearly six years' (Crossman, 1970: 2), a judgement fully shared by Roy Hattersley (1970: 10–11). Crossman's conclusions about why Labour had lost were shared by one of his Cabinet colleagues, Michael Stewart. The former Foreign Secretary recalled that: 'It was not till 6.00 pm on polling day, back in Fulham, that I saw what was happening; that is when one can see whether Labour voters are coming out in sufficient numbers. They were not.' Stewart's explanation for much of this abstention among former Labour voters was that:

> the disappointment of our own supporters during the successive financial crises and Government economies had left wounds which had not yet healed, and the rebuff to the Government over *In Place of Strife* was too recent. The trade figures for May were disappointing.... In common with nearly everyone else, I did not realise the strength of these factors at the time. Buoyed up by opinion polls.... I expected victory.
>
> (Stewart, 1980: 254)

An identical conclusion was drawn by Harold Wilson himself, who acknowledged that: 'the improvement in our economic position ... had

not erased all the scars from the tough things we had to do to get to
that strong position' (Wilson, 1971: 790). Many years later, Denis Healey
(Defence Secretary at the time of the 1970 general election), reflected
that: 'The Wilson Government of 1966–70 was not regarded as a success
even by the Labour movement' (Healey, 1990: 345).

Similar views were expressed at a meeting of the PLP a month after
the election, with John Mendelson insisting that the election had not
been lost during the campaign itself, but two years earlier 'when the
Government had made mistakes and ignored the feeling of the Party in
the country'. Similarly, John Mackintosh argued that the election had
been lost in 1966–69, adding that Labour ought to have devalued earlier
than November 1967 (presumably to have allowed more time for an
economic recovery to establish itself and thereby win back lost support)
(Labour Party Archives, Minutes of a meeting of the PLP, 15 July 1970).

Perhaps not surprisingly, the Left (particularly the Tribune Group and
its eponymous weekly paper) also blamed the economic policies of the
1966–70 Labour governments for the party's fate in June 1970. According to the then editor of *Tribune*: 'The major factor in the defeat was
the policy which the Government had pursued in Office', and which
'above all else, characterised the future prospects of future Labour Governments as bleak indeed' (Clements, 1970: 1). From elsewhere in the
party came criticism that Labour's social liberalism had been pursued at
the expense of bread-and-butter issues affecting 'ordinary' people; those
who would, several years later, be deemed 'the silent majority'. This perspective was trenchantly expressed by a Labour supporter in a letter to
the *New Statesman* (of which Richard Crossman had just become editor),
in which it was claimed that:

> The man [*sic*] in the street is not interested in homosexual law reform,
> in easier abortions, in easier divorce, in liberation of women, in the
> ending of capital punishment [the death penalty] – mere sop to the
> intellectuals. What we want is an improvement in the lot of the poor,
> the sick and the underprivileged. And it is here that Labour have lost
> the confidence of the British people.
>
> (*New Statesman*, 26 June 1970: 7)

The notion that Labour suffered from abstentions among many of its
erstwhile supporters, and that much of this loss of support was largely
attributable to dissatisfaction with the government's performance and
policies since 1966 (rather than Labour voters being attracted to the
alternative seemingly offered by Edward Heath and the Conservatives),

has been endorsed by various other accounts and analyses of the 1970 general election result. For example, the Gallup polling company conducted some post-election analysis which indicated that, of respondents who declared (during the campaign) their intention to vote Labour, only 77 per cent actually did so; 'most of the rest did not vote.' These findings were published in *The Daily Telegraph* (10 July 1970) under a headline declaring that the 'Tories won election in last two days.' Yet, important though they are, these factors alone do not fully account for Labour's defeat in the June 1970 election, although we will discount the suggestion that the despondency induced by England's defeat by West Germany, in a World Cup quarter-final match four days before the general election, was a contributory factor in weakening support for Labour (Keating, 2010).

It had also been commonly assumed that the expansion of the total electorate due to the 1969 lowering of the voting age from 21 to 18, thereby adding at least 2.5 million voters to the electoral register at the time, would benefit Labour, due to the assumption that younger people were more left-wing than older voters. Moreover, the late 1960s had witnessed the emergence of a New Left and counter-culture social movements among sections of the urban young and university-educated, this manifesting itself via issues pertaining to sexual politics and sexual liberation, anti-racism and anti-American sentiment deriving from the Vietnam War. Yet the anticipated surge in youth support for Labour singularly failed to materialise on 18 June 1970.

One reason seems to be that up to a third of 18–21-year-olds had not registered to vote, and this 'self-disqualification was apparently highest among working-class youngsters – i.e., among those most likely to have voted Labour' (Abrams, 1970: 320). Yet what is not clear is how those 'youngsters' who were on the electoral register actually voted, or how many of them did vote. Nonetheless, it is evident that the lowering of the voting age in 1969 did not benefit Labour in the manner which many had anticipated. It may have been that, at least for some of those 18–21-year-olds who were part of the New Left, Harold Wilson's Labour Party/government was seen as part of the establishment or status quo, regardless of the socially liberal or 'permissive' reforms enacted between 1964 and 1970. If so, this could be a further reason why the expansion of the electorate in 1969 did not yield electoral dividends for Labour the following year.

Another issue pertaining to turn-out which affected Labour rather more than the Conservatives was the proportional decline in the number of men who voted in June 1970 compared with women. The proportion of men who voted in 1970 was virtually 10 per cent lower than in 1964, whereas the decline in the proportion of women voting during this period was 5.6 per cent. As Labour's support was usually higher among men than women, the scale of this decline provides a further possible explanation for Labour's loss of support in June 1970 (Electoral Commission, 2004: 9).

One further factor which has variously been cited to account for at least some of the decline in Labour's vote is that of summer holidays, for a June general election was a highly unusual phenomenon. Indeed, 1970 was the first occasion when such an election was held in June, and, as such, it coincided with 'Wakes Week' in the Potteries (centred on and around Stoke-on-Trent), when many firms and factories closed simultaneously. Consequently, many workers in this area took their summer holidays at the same time, rather than annual leave being 'staggered' over the whole summer as would ordinarily be the case (although some Lancashire towns also had Wakes Weeks, albeit usually in July).

It has been suggested that approximately 750,000 people were on holiday on polling day in June 1970 (Abrams, 1970: 320), and, while some of these would doubtless have been middle-class Conservative voters, it has been noted that in 'the Potteries' conurbation turn-out was about 20 per cent lower than in 1966 (Butler and Pinto-Duschinsky, 1971: 341). This particularly affected Labour's support in a few constituencies. For example, in Stoke-on-Trent Central, turn-out fell from 39,178 votes in 1966 to 29,985 in 1970, while Labour's support fell from 26,653 to 18,758. Similarly, in Stoke-on-Trent South, turn-out was more than 10,000 lower in 1970, with Labour's support down by 6,610 votes.

Finally, there were a couple of economic factors in the latter part of the election campaign itself which seemed to erode Labour's support at the last minute, and which occurred too late to be registered by most of the opinion polls. One of these was the 15 June publication of unfavourable balance of payments figures for May. Ordinarily voters would not pay too much attention to such specific economic criteria – it is not usually ascribed importance as an issue of electoral saliency – but, on this occasion, the figures lent credence to a core theme of the Conservatives' election campaign, namely, not only that Labour had a poor record of economic management during the previous four years (and consequently failed to 'deliver' on various other electoral pledges made in 1964 and 1966), but also that Labour's 1970 claims that the economy was now recovering strongly were specious.

The figures for May's balance of payments seemed to vindicate this argument, and, according to opinion polls, prompted a steady increase in the number of voters who trusted the Conservatives on the question of which party would provide the most competent economic management; from 43 per cent to 49 per cent between 11 and 17 June, while the proportion endorsing Labour on this issue fell to 40 per cent (Teer and Spence, 1973: 199). The second economic factor which seemed to erode Labour's support at the end of the campaign was the increase in inflation which manifested itself during May and June. Indeed, with official figures showing an increase in inflation during the spring of 1970, the former Governor of the Bank of England, Lord Cromer, claimed (on a BBC *Panorama* programme broadcast on 1 June) that 'there's no question that any government that comes into power is going to find a very much more difficult financial situation than...in 1964', a claim that was elaborated upon a few days later in an article in *The Times* (Butler and Pinto-Duschinsky, 1971: 155).

Not surprisingly, such warnings lent further credence to the Conservatives' criticism of Labour's economic record and the concomitant allegation that the economy was not recovering as robustly as ministers were trying to claim; far from it. Thus it was that, when a mid-June opinion poll asked voters: 'Which party would do the best job of solving the cost of living problem?', the proportion citing the Conservatives rose from 42 per cent in mid-May to 48 per cent, whereas those opting for Labour fell from 38 per cent to 28 per cent (Teer and Spence, 1973: 200).

The atrophy of Labour's extra-parliamentary organisation

One final problem which might well have hindered Labour's performance in the 1970 general election was the poor state of the party's organisation in many constituencies, which, according to Butler and Pinto-Duschinsky (1971: Chapter 2), seriously affected the party's ability to campaign effectively. True, a more professional and better-resourced party infrastructure would probably not have prevented the Conservatives' victory, but Labour's extra-parliamentary organisational and financial weaknesses certainly impeded the party's ability to conduct a more effective and energetic election campaign in May–June 1970, and, as such, may have contributed towards Labour's defeat. In this context, the observation by one of Wilson's erstwhile ministerial colleagues that: 'There were 19 constituencies where the Conservative majority was less than 1,000...In fact, 10,000 votes more and we should have had 307 seats against the Tories' 311' (MS. Wilson c.1410, Greenwood to Wilson, 22 June 1970) acquires particular significance.

According to Butler and Pinto-Duschinsky's in-depth study of the 1970 general election, Labour's grass-roots campaign suffered from a marked decline in the party's extra-parliamentary organisation following the 1966 election victory, to the extent that there was 'insufficient time to improve matters before the end of the parliament'. To give just one example, the number of full-time constituency agents declined from 204 in 1966 to 146 by early 1970 (Butler and Pinto-Duschinsky, 1971: 47). They cite several factors which account for this increasingly moribund Labour Party machine beyond Westminster, including Harold Wilson's concern that a stronger extra-parliamentary party might actually embarrass the parliamentary leadership by demanding a greater input into policy-making and/or calling for 'unrealistic' or electorally damaging policies. Wilson was also deemed to harbour 'a very simple view of the electorate. It was subject to tendencies and moods, which were more important in determining voting its disposition than were... governmental actions [or] some sudden propaganda activity from the party headquarters' (Butler and Pinto-Duschinsky, 1971: 47).

In addition to Wilson's own apparent lack of concern about ensuring a more professional extra-parliamentary party organisation and campaigning capacity, Butler and Pinto-Duschinsky highlight another set of factors which further depleted Labour's grass-roots organisation of staff and resources, namely, that various measures enacted by the 1966–70 Labour government, in response to the economic crises it faced, seriously demoralised some of its grass-roots members, to the extent that the number of constituency Labour parties with more than 2,000 members fell from 68 in 1966 to 23 in 1969 (Butler and Pinto-Duschinsky, 1971: 54).

Coupled with the decline in the number of full-time agents, the effect was to deprive the Labour Party of sufficient staff 'on the ground' who could establish or maintain links with local voters and other party members. Moreover, it is claimed that, for much of 1968 and 1969, many Labour agents and canvassers experienced 'a great reluctance to go from door to door, because [they] were so likely to encounter abuse' (Butler and Pinto-Duschinsky, 1971: 267). This atrophy arguably further damaged the Labour Party in the 1970 election, when it struggled to match the resources of a rejuvenated Conservative Party.

One particular constituency where the apparent atrophy of the local Labour Party was deemed to have contributed significantly to the incumbent Labour MP's defeat in June 1970 was Cannock. Here, Jennie Lee had been returned in 1966 with a lead over the Conservative candidate of more than 11,000 votes, but in 1970 the Conservatives won

Cannock with a swing of 10.7 per cent, well over double the national average. Various factors contributed to Lee's defeat, including a feeling among some of Cannock's working-class voters – and local party members – that she had grown aloof from them, and was more interested in socialising in London (she had been minister for the Arts in the 1966–70 Labour government) than she was in keeping in touch with local constituents and their day-to-day concerns.

However, one of the factors also cited by her biographer was that declining respect for their 'remote' MP was reflected in, and in turn reinforced, the virtual collapse of the local Labour Party organisation in Cannock: 'A good campaign might have pulled it back for her', but in Cannock 'the mood was sour, and Jennie had no full-time staff to help her.' The few party workers 'had neither the energy nor the inclination to do a proper canvass', and, as a consequence, failed to engage with voters on the doorstep who were being courted by the Conservatives. Then, after the polls had closed, Lee's agent 'could not find enough people for the count' (Hollis, 1997: 374–8).

The scale of atrophy of the Labour Party machine in Cannock, along with the apparent personal animosity which had developed towards the incumbent MP, was exceptional, but in sundry other Labour seats, too, the run-down constituency parties seem to have struggled to wage an effective campaign. On this particular point, Rita Hinden, the editor of *Socialist Commentary*, criticised Transport House (Labour's HQ) for presiding over a 'faulty' Labour Party organisation, alleging that: 'The leadership of the Party showed no interest in remedying this fatal weakness, and the National Executive [Committee – NEC] seemed adamantly resistant to organisational reform' (Hinden, 1970: 1).

This clearly undermined Labour's ability to retain or regain the support of former Labour voters who had been alienated or felt betrayed by various policies enacted – or reneged upon – by 'their' ministers in the latter half of the 1960s. Of course, the Conservatives are almost always better resourced than Labour, but it does seem that in the 1970 election campaign Labour suffered even more than usual from a depleted local membership and weak national organisation. Indeed, it may be that the many serious problems which the Labour leadership grappled with at national level during the latter half of the 1960s prevented it from paying sufficient heed to what was happening to the extra-parliamentary Labour Party at local level.

Meanwhile, Butler and Pinto-Duschinsky identify one other factor which further impeded Labour's ability to conduct an effective election campaign in 1970, namely, Wilson's failure to communicate to the wider party his intention to call a general election in June. As a consequence of this, the already enfeebled Labour Party machine was caught somewhat unawares when Wilson announced the date of the poll.

There are two main explanations as to why he failed to indicate his intention to call a June election. The first is simply that he had originally intended either to wait until the autumn, or even go the full term until 1971, but had then changed his mind in response to the 7 per cent opinion poll lead which Labour had secured in May 1970, after trailing the Conservatives by considerable margins throughout the previous two years. Wilson might have also interpreted this lead as a reflection that voters were confident about the apparent economic recovery after three years of austerity, and were therefore willing to grant the Labour government another term in office.

Certainly, some senior officials at Transport House had been preparing for an autumn general election, as indicated by a March 1970 Campaign Committee paper (authored by a David Kingsley) simply entitled 'If...', which opened with the warning that: 'If there is an election in October...we have only six months left of our campaign', whereupon the paper proposed a detailed publicity campaign to be conducted throughout the rest of spring and over the summer. It also suggested that a conference of Labour MPs should be held in June, before Parliament's summer recess (MS. Wilson c.1393, DJK [David Kingsley], 'If...', 23 March 1970).

However, Butler and Pinto-Duschinsky suggest a second explanation as to why Wilson failed to indicate his intention to call a June 1970 election, namely, his concern that if he conveyed his plans to his ministerial colleagues there would probably be leaks to the press, which would in turn alert the Conservatives that a general election was imminent. Of course, by trying to keep his political opponents in the dark concerning the date of the general election, Wilson simultaneously kept the Labour Party in the dark too, and thereby left it ill prepared when the campaign was formally launched. Indeed, according to Butler and Pinto-Duschinsky (1971: 61), such was the lack of awareness of Wilson's intentions among the wider Labour Party that Transport House spent part of spring 1970 preparing a summer advertising campaign, perhaps reflecting an assumption that Wilson would call the election in the autumn, or even wait until spring 1971.

By early May, however, when speculation was rapidly increasing that Wilson was about to call a June election, Ron Hayward (who had been appointed Labour's national agent the previous year, and became General Secretary of the Labour Party in 1972) was warning that, if there was an election in June, 'it will be very much a "Do-It-Yourself" campaign' (quoted in Butler and Pinto-Duschinsky, 1971: 61). Certainly, in the context of the depletion of the grass-roots membership and the atrophy of the extra-parliamentary organisation, Wilson's failure to alert the wider party to his intention to call a June election merely compounded Labour's problems in conducting an effective and professional election campaign; the wider party was often unprepared and under-resourced.

Conclusion

In June 1970, the Labour government 'was forced to fight the general election on a record of [economic] failure', although it is suggested that 'the surprising thing, in view of their lack of policy success, was that they did not lose more heavily than they did' (Cronin, 1984: 189–90). Meanwhile, in his classic study of the history of the Labour Party, Pelling noted that: 'The main reason for the government's unpopularity during most of its term lay in the failure of its economic policies' (Pelling, 1985: 140). Then, as today, the electorate's perceptions about economic competence play a crucial part in shaping party preferences, at least among those voters who are not die-hard supporters of one particular party (and who thus symbolised the phenomenon of 'partisan alignment', which has actually declined steadily since 1970).

After all, virtually from the time it was elected in October 1964, the Labour government was beset by serious economic problems which were to prove deeply damaging to many of the objectives and plans devised in opposition. Not surprisingly, the cumulative impact of abandoning, diluting or postponing sundry policy pledges, and the consequent tensions this caused within the parliamentary Labour Party, served to damage the government's image and political credibility beyond Westminster, ultimately leading to a fatal loss of popular support among erstwhile Labour voters in the June 1970 general election.

It was of little comfort to Labour that many of the economic problems which it encountered were not of its own making, for the need to tackle inherited difficulties had a deeply damaging impact on Labour's manifesto commitments, many of which were inextricably linked to the attainment of high rates of economic growth. Right from the outset, the 1964–70 Labour governments spent much of their time engaged in crisis management and reacting to external pressures, yet it was Labour that bore much of the blame in the 1970 election – just as Labour governments were deemed culpable for economic crises in 1979 and 2010, even if and when the origins or underlying causes of those crises resided overseas in the wider international economic system.

This should not be too surprising to political scientists, for the electorate is generally concerned with the visible and directly experienced consequences of governmental policies, rather than underlying causes (which are themselves subject to ideological dispute and contestation) of problems which underpin or prompt those policies. In effect, when a Labour government presides over unfavourable economic circumstances, and thus enacts unpopular decisions, it is easier for many voters to blame that government (or a visible institution or section of society, such as the trade unions, immigrants, the 'bloated' public sector or the EU, for example) than the much less visible, and thus vague, international financial markets, currency speculators, bond markets and 'the City'. All too often, Labour is blamed for the crises and contradictions inherent in capitalism, whereupon many voters turn to the Conservatives – who then blame their increasingly unpopular decisions on 'the mess' left by the 'incompetent' or 'reckless' previous Labour government.

References

Abrams, M. (1970), 'The Opinion Polls and the 1970 British General Election', *The Public Opinion Quarterly*, Vol. 34, No. 3, 317–24.

Abse, L. (1973), *Private Member* (London: MacDonald).

Anderson, D. (1968), 'Parliament and the Executive', in Lapping, B. and Radice, G. (eds), *More Power to the People: Young Fabian Essays on Democracy in Britain* (London: Longman).

Benn, T. (1988), *Office Without Power: Diaries 1968–72* (London: Hutchinson).

Bevins, R. (1965), *The Greasy Pole* (London: Hodder and Stoughton).

Brown, G. (1971), *In My Way* (London: Book Club Associates).

Butler, D. and Butler, G. (1994), *British Politics Facts, 1900–1994* (Basingstoke: Macmillan).

Butler, D. and Pinto-Duschinsky, M. (1971), *The British General Election of 1970* (London: Macmillan).

Castle, B. (1990), *The Castle Diaries, 1964–76* (London: Papermac/Macmillan).

Clements, R. (1970), 'Editorial: Why It Happened – and What We Are Going to Do', *Tribune*, 26 June.

Cronin, J. (1984), *Labour and Society in Britain 1918–1979* (London: Batsford Academic).

Crosland, A. (1956), *The Future of Socialism* (London: Jonathan Cape).

Crossman, R. (1970), 'Editorial: Labour After Defeat', *New Statesman*, 10 July.

Crossman, R. (1976), *The Diaries of a Cabinet Minister, Volume Two: Lord President of the Council and Leader of the House of Commons, 1966–68* (London: Hamish Hamilton/Jonathan Cape).

Crossman, R. (1977), *The Diaries of a Cabinet Minister, Volume Three: Secretary of State for Social Services 1968–70* (London: Hamish Hamilton/ Jonathan Cape).

Dalyell, T. (1989), *Dick Crossman: A Portrait* (London: Weidenfeld and Nicolson).

Dorey, P. (2006a), 'From a Policy for Incomes to Incomes Policies', in Dorey, P. (ed.), *The Labour Governments, 1964–1970* (London: Routledge).

Dorey, P. (2006b), 'Industrial Relations Imbroglio', in Dorey, P. (ed.), *The Labour Governments, 1964–1970* (London: Routledge).

Dorey, P. (2006c), 'The Social Background of Labour MPs Elected in 1964 and 1966', in Dorey, P. (ed.), *The Labour Governments, 1964–1970* (London: Routledge).

Dorey, P. (2008a), ' "It Really was Rather Disgraceful. Still, that is Politics": The 1967–68 Decision to Defer the Raising of the School Leaving Age', *Public Policy and Administration*, Vol. 23, No. 4, 391–407.

Dorey, P. (2008b), *The Labour Party and Constitutional Reform: A History of Constitutional Conservatism* (London: Routledge).

Dorey, P. (2012), 'Harold Wilson, 1963–4 and 1970–4', in Heppell, T. (ed.), *Leaders of the Opposition from Churchill to Cameron* (Basingstoke: Palgrave).

Dorey, P. and Honeyman, V. (2010), 'Ahead of his Time: Richard Crossman and House of Commons Reform in the 1960s', *British Politics*, Vol. 5, No. 2, 149–78.

Drucker, H. (1979), *Doctrine and Ethos in the Labour Party* (London: George Allen and Unwin).

The Electoral Commission (2004), *Gender and Political Participation* (London: The Electoral Commission).

Foote, G. (1985), *The Labour Party's Political Thought: A History* (Beckenham: Croom Helm).

Harris, J. (2000), 'Labour's Political and Social Thought', in Tanner, D., Thane, P. and Tiratsoo, N. (eds), *Labour's First Century* (Cambridge: Cambridge University Press).

Hatfield, M. (1978), *The House the Left Built: Inside Labour Policy Making 1970–1975* (London: Gollancz).

Hattersley, R. (1970), 'Could Labour Have Won?', *New Statesman*, 31 July.

Healey, D. (1990), *The Time of My Life* (Harmondsworth: Penguin).

Heffer, E. (1991), *Never a Yes Man: The Life and Politics of an Adopted Liverpudlian* (London: Verso).

Hinden, R. (1970), 'Editorial: Not without Comfort', *Socialist Commentary*, 18 July.

Hollis, P. (1997), *Jennie Lee: A Life* (Oxford: Oxford University Press).

Jones, T. (1996), *Remaking the Labour Party: From Gaitskell to Blair* (London: Routledge).

Keating, F. (2010), 'The World Cup Defeat that Lost an Election', *The Guardian*, 21 April (http://www.guardian.co.uk/football/blog/2010/apr/21/world-cup-1970-harold-wilson?, accessed 30 November 2011).

Lipset, S. M. (1960), *Political Man* (London: Heinemann).

Mikardo, I. (1988), *Back-Bencher* (London: Weidenfeld and Nicolson).

Patten, C. (1980), 'Policy Making in Opposition', in Layton-Henry, Z. (ed.), *Conservative Party Politics* (London: Macmillan).

Pelling, H. (1985), *A Short History of the Labour Party* (Basingstoke: Macmillan).

Raison, T. (1965), *Conflict and Conservatism* (London: Conservative Political Centre).

Ramsden, J. (1980), *The Making of Conservative Party Policy* (London: Longman).

Ramsden, J. (1996), 'The Prime Minister and the Making of Policy', in Ball, S. and Seldon, A. (eds), *The Heath Government 1970–74* (Harlow: Longman).

Rose, R. (1970), 'Voting Trends Surveyed', in *The Times, Guide to the House of Commons 1970* (London: Times Newspapers Ltd).

Stewart, M. (1980), *Life and Labour: An Autobiography* (London: Sidgwick and Jackson).

Teer, F. and Spence, J. D. (1973), *Political Opinion Polls* (London: Hutchison).

Thompson, N. (2006), 'The Fabian Political Economy of Harold Wilson', in Dorey, P. (ed.), *The Labour Governments, 1964–1970* (London: Routledge).

Wilson, H. (1964), *The New Britain: Labour's Plan Outlined by Harold Wilson* (Harmondsworth: Penguin).

Wilson, H. (1971), *The Labour Government, 1964–1970: A Personal Record* (London: Weidenfeld and Nicolson/Michael Joseph).

6
The Fall of the Callaghan Government, 1979

John Shepherd

On 28 March 1979 James Callaghan's beleaguered Labour government faced a crucial vote of no confidence in a packed House of Commons. During one of the most dramatic nights at Westminster, the minority administration was defeated in a knife-edge vote (311 votes to 310) by a motley coalition of Conservatives, Liberals, Unionists and Scottish Nationalists. In 1979 Labour's Energy Secretary, Tony Benn, noted in his diary: 'That's the end of a memorable day in British politics, the first time for 54 years that any government has been defeated on a vote of confidence.' Not since Ramsay MacDonald's first short-lived ministry that lasted only 287 days in 1924 had a government been dismissed in similar circumstances (Benn, 1991: 478; Shepherd and Laybourn, 2006: 161–84).

In the frenetic atmosphere at Westminster, Callaghan made a short parliamentary statement: 'Mr Speaker. Now that House of Commons has declared itself, we shall take our case to the country' (Parliamentary Debates, 28 March 1979, col. 590). As at the 1945 landslide victory, when Callaghan first entered parliament, Labour MPs sang 'The Red Flag' (Parliamentary Debates, 28 March 1979, col. 589). However, on 4 May 1979 Margaret Thatcher entered 10 Downing Street as Britain's first woman prime minister, the beginning of 18 years of unbroken Conservative rule. After five years in government, the May 1979 General Election defeat was a decidedly critical setback in the history of the Labour Party that resulted in 18 years out of power. It was also followed by bitter post-mortems over the party's downfall and fratricidal internal strife about the party's future.

This chapter focuses on the various political and electoral circumstances that played a significant part in the eventual downfall of the Callaghan government over the vote of no confidence on 28 March

1974. It also attempts to place these factors in a wider context by exploring why the minority Labour governments of 1974–79 had survived in difficult political and economic conditions for virtually five years. In the end it was the Callaghan Labour government that lost the 1979 election; Mrs Thatcher and the Conservatives won it largely by default. The manifold causes of Labour's 1979 defeat are also examined – including the breakdown of Labour's social contract with the unions and the impact of the notorious 'winter of discontent', as well as more long-term factors, such as Labour's dwindling electoral support in the 1970s.

Minority government

From February 1974 to March 1979, over the course of two parliaments, the Wilson and Callaghan governments displayed extraordinary durability in the face of the most serious global capitalist crisis since the Second World War, as well as recurrent economic and political difficulties at home. Following the 1973 Arab–Israeli War, the Organization of Petroleum Exporting Countries (OPEC) imposed an export embargo and quadrupled the price of oil. The troubled world economy was hit by soaring inflation and economic recession. In Britain, unparalleled inflation peaked at 27 per cent in August 1975, while investment and manufacturing output declined and unemployment was on an upward trend to 1 million and more (Ferguson et al., 2010: 1–21).

Altogether, despite being in a minority at Westminster for nearly five years (except for six months with a very slim majority), the two Labour administrations survived longer than some governments with a majority. In reality, defeat for the Callaghan government could have occurred far earlier than 28 March 1979, when the crucial no confidence vote was lost by the smallest of margins. Yet the Wilson and Callaghan administrations were handicapped by surviving in office for five years of increasing economic difficulties and international pressures after the post-war boom (late 1940 to 1973) of full employment and Keynesian management had ended. In the October 1974 election, after six months of minority government, Harold Wilson returned to Downing Street. With 319 MPs in the new parliament, Labour held a lead of 42 over the Conservatives in the House of Commons, but only an overall majority of three against all the combined opposition parties. Twenty years before, the vast majority of the electorate had voted Labour or Conservative. Now the presence of minority parties at Westminster demonstrated that the two main parties had lost their ascendancy. This new parliamentary grouping of three Plaid Cymru, 11 Scottish Nationalists and 12 MPs from Northern Ireland, as well as 13 Liberals, could hold the balance of power, as was clearly revealed on the night of 28 March 1979. However, as Philip Norton has shown, this was not always the case. On certain parliamentary measures, Labour might gain support in the division lobbies of the Liberals, as well as Welsh and Scottish Nationalists, who often possessed more in common with Labour than with their Conservative opponents. At the same time, some Irish members were not always the most frequent of attendees at Westminster.

During their time in government, the parliamentary existence of the Wilson and Callaghan governments was always vulnerable, due to deaths and defections of MPs, as well as by-election losses. Between 1974 and 1979 13 Labour MPs died, mainly from heart attacks. Two Scottish Labour MPs, Jim Sillars and John Robertson, defected in 1976 to the newly formed Scottish Labour Party, though afterwards they generally voted with their former party. In all, from October 1974 to March 1979 the Wilson and Callaghan governments suffered 42 defeats in the Commons (and 347 in the Lords), which made life very difficult. Yet only 19 losses could be directly attributable to opposition parties combining together against the government (Norton, 2004: 192–8). However, for Labour's team of hard-working party whips, and for the Labour leadership at Downing Street, day-to-day life at Westminster was dominated by constant 'wheeling and dealing' with minority parties, as well as dissenters in their own ranks. Important votes had to be secured to progress legislative programmes and to maintain a minority Labour administration in office (Ashton, 2000: 177–9; Norton, 2004: 198–201).

At Westminster, Labour faced its hardest test when Mrs Thatcher put down a vote of no confidence for 23 March 1977 with the support of the other parties. The government was forced in a great hurry to cobble together an arrangement with one of the minor parliamentary parties, or face certain defeat followed by a general election. After preliminary soundings, the Lib–Lab Pact was negotiated between the prime minister and David Steel, the new leader of 13 Liberal MPs. The agreement established a consultative committee on departmental legislation, regular meetings between the Chancellor of the Exchequer, Denis Healey, and John Pardoe, the Liberal economic spokesman, as well as talks between other government ministers and Liberal MPs. At an emergency Cabinet on the day of the motion of no confidence, Callaghan explained that the pact also included direct elections to the European parliament and a renewed commitment to Welsh and Scottish devolution. The minority Labour government was guaranteed vital support on motions of no confidence, while leaving the Liberals free on other issues. The Cabinet backed the pact by 20–4; the vote of confidence was defeated by 322 votes to 298.

Kenneth O. Morgan has written that the Lib–Lab pact, renewed in July for the new parliamentary year, 'was an event of considerable political significance'. Though not a formal coalition, it gave the Callaghan administration an important period of relative parliamentary stability for its economic proposals until the summer of 1978. Yet, two years after the genesis of the Lib–Lab pact, the Callaghan government could not survive another more fatal Westminster crisis (Michie and Hoggart, 1978: 9–40, 173–83; Steel, 1980: 26–42, 152–7; Bartram, 1981: 140–65; Morgan, 1997: 566–70; 573, 578). As David Owen has rightly revealed, a less noticed arrangement in March 1977 – the informal Unionist Labour pact that endured until 1979 – was arranged with James Molyneaux, the Leader of the Ulster Unionists, and Enoch Powell, by Michael Foot and James Callaghan in return for an all-party conference to review Northern Ireland parliamentary representation. This new understanding, which provided general support until the end of the parliament, produced three Ulster Unionist abstentions on the night the Callaghan government survived Mrs Thatcher's motion of no confidence by 322–298 (Donoughue, 2008 : 166–72; Owen, 1992: 286–90).

While this well-practised form of parliamentary horse trading at Westminster kept the Callaghan administration in office for three years, a unique combination of political and personal factors eventually caused its fatal breakdown and led to the downfall of the Callaghan government in March 1979. By the 1979 election Labour had 13 fewer seats than when it gained its slender overall majority of three in October 1974. Of the 30 by-elections during the 1974–79 parliament, there were 13 Labour victories, 16 Conservative and 1 Liberal. Yet Labour did not take a single seat from its opponents, but lost a total of seven seats (six Conservative gains and one Liberal gain), starting on 26 June 1975 with Greenwich and Woolwich to the Conservatives, and Liverpool Edge Hill constituency to the Liberals on the eve of the 1979 election. Within six months of taking office in April 1976, the Callaghan government on 4 November lost two out of three crucial by-elections on the same day. Only Newcastle upon Tyne (Central) was held narrowly, but Walsall (North) and Workington were lost to the Conservatives. In 1977 the Conservatives also took Birmingham, Stechford from Labour on 31 March, followed on 28 April by the Labour stronghold of Ashfield, both with very large swings. By March 1979 the Callaghan government was in a minority of 17.

Maintaining party discipline was imperative as part of Labour's survival at Westminster. However, while the vociferous Tribune Group co-ordinated its 89 left-wing Labour MPs in voting on a range of issues and was often a thorn in the side of the Labour administrations, only on relatively rare occasions did it endanger the party's parliamentary survival. As few as six out of 23 defeats could be directly accredited to this parliamentary faction. Shortly before Harold Wilson's unexpected retirement, Tribunites helped to vote down Labour's Public Expenditure White Paper on 10 March 1976, forcing the government to table a life-saving vote of confidence the next day. During the 1974–79 parliaments a majority of the Tribune Group MPs voted against their government 40 times or more. All 27 Labour MPs with a similar voting record on 70 or more occasions were members of the Tribune Group (for further details, see Norton, 1980). More serious were the occasions when opposition to the Wilson and Callaghan governments by Labour dissidents came from different parts of the parliamentary Labour Party. Of 23 defeats inflicted on the Callaghan government by Labour rebels, six were by left-wing MPs, two by right-wing MPs. In particular, dissension within Labour ranks over the controversial issue of devolution was rife during 1976, in 1978 and again in 1979, when it eventually triggered the downfall of the Callaghan government (Norton, 2004: 196–8).

Social contract

Between 1974 and 1979 the social contract was a central plank in the economic and industrial policy of the Wilson and Callaghan Labour governments. Fashioned by the Labour–Trade Union Liaison Committee, it offered a fresh alliance between the party and the unions after the fierce opposition in the trade union and labour movement to Barbara Castle's White Paper *In Place of Strife* (1969), of which Callaghan was a leading adversary in Cabinet. At the same time, the breakdown of the social contract was also a highly significant milestone on the pathway to the fall of the Callaghan administration. When Jim Callaghan, a former active trade unionist and previously assistant secretary to Douglas (later Lord) Houghton at the Inland Revenue Staff Federation, became prime minister in April 1976, he inherited Wilson's economic policy and Labour's social contract, which underlined its major claim to be the only party capable of working successfully with the unions in the troubled 1970s. On the government side, the social contract had promised a legislative programme on industrial relations and industrial democracy (mostly passed between 1974 and 1976, including the repeal of the Heath government's Industrial Relations Act), as well as radical economic measures for full employment, increased social expenditure and a policy of wealth redistribution. The undertakings from the unions were less defined – voluntary wage restraint at best, instead of an overt commitment to an incomes policy (Taylor, 1993: 222–62; Dorey, 2001: 142–5).

During these years unparalleled double-digit inflation in Britain soared to around 27 per cent in August 1975. Other economic indicators, including investment and output, dipped sharply, except for an ominous upward trend in unemployment. Yet the Trades Union Congress and its member unions from 1976–78 delivered nearly three years of voluntary wage restraint that were instrumental in contributing to the reduction of the rate of inflation to around 8 per cent by the middle of 1978. At this time, the principal architect of the social contract on the union side was Jack Jones, general secretary of the Transport and General Workers' Union (T & G WU) and a key figure on the Labour–TUC Liaison Committee in industrial and economic policy-making. Although opposed to incomes policies, he accepted in the mid-1970s that inflationary wage settlements should be offset by voluntary wage restraint (Jones, 1986: 295–302). His retirement in 1978 shortly before the beginning of the 'Winter of Discontent', as well that of his ally Hugh Scanlon, general secretary of the Amalgamated Union of Engineering Workers, removed the two leading trade union leaders from the political scene. As allies of a government in difficulties with the unions they were a considerable loss, particularly as their successors were not of the same experience or stature (Dorey, 2001: 149–58; Callaghan, 2006: 416–17).

In 1976 a major sterling crisis forced the Callaghan government to negotiate a £2.3 billion loan from the International Monetary Fund (IMF) in order to defend the pound. The IMF terms required £5,000 million cuts in public expenditure on social welfare, health, housing and education. As Tony Benn has observed, the IMF expenditure cuts imposed on Britain were another significant milestone on the pathway to the 'Winter of Discontent'. Effectively, the IMF crisis killed the social contract, which afterwards operated solely as an incomes policy – in effect, out and out wage restraint (interview with Tony Benn, 26 June 2011). The August 1977 Stage III set a maximum ceiling of 10 per cent for wage increases (until July 1978), though a number of groups in the private sector, such as British Oxygen, oil tanker drivers and the road haulage industry, alongside various groups in the public services, secured more substantial settlements – a portent of what was to come.

However, Callaghan, who was utterly determined to finally squeeze inflation out of the system, took a highly personal decision to impose an unrealistic figure of a 5 per cent norm for the fourth round (1978–79) of the government's incomes policy. It was a severe tightening of the pay policy imposed at a time when the rate of inflation was almost double and living standards were commonly perceived to be falling. Union leaders firmly opposed the new 5 per cent limit. The popular Jack Jones had been shouted down by angry delegates at the biennial T & G WU conference in 1977 on the Isle of Man in appealing for a further year of wage restraint to keep a Labour government in office. Roy Hattersley, Cabinet Secretary of State for Prices, has pointed out that co-operation between the government and the unions finally broke down in the summer of 1978. The unions believed that higher real wages could be achieved by a return to free collective bargaining, while in their view the IMF settlement represented the end of higher levels of public expenditure and improved public services, as envisaged originally in Labour's social contract. At the TUC Annual Conference in Brighton in September 1978, a broad range of the major unions overwhelmingly voted for the National Union of Mineworkers's motion for 'a return to normal and responsible collective bargaining' and the National Union of Public Employees (NUPE) resolution for a national minimum wage for the low-paid. A month later, the Annual Labour Party Conference at Blackpool voted overwhelmingly – 4,017,000–1,924,000 – against phase four of the government's incomes policy and for a return to free collective bargaining (Hattersley, 2009: 16–18).

Callaghan defers 1978 general election

The 18 months from the IMF crisis of 1976 to the autumn of 1978 witnessed relative economic improvement in Britain. The main indicators – particularly the reduction in the rate of inflation, a strengthening pound, improved currency reserves and exports – moved in the Callaghan government's favour. In addition, there was the prospect of Britain's North Sea Oil that had just begun to flow (Morgan, 2007: 303–5). With these blue skies, the prime minister was widely expected to call a general election in the autumn. His chief political adviser, Tom (now Lord) McNally, was briefing the press that the polling day would be on 5 October 1978 (interview with Lord McNally, 23 June 2007). Joel Barnett, Chief Secretary to the Treasury, recalled that ministerial approval for the unenforceable 5 per cent pay norm had been gained relatively easily, as an autumn election seemed certain (interview with Lord Barnett, 22 June 2010; Hattersley, 2009: 17–22).

On 11 October 1977 the Prime Minister had hinted to Bernard Donoughue that they should plan for the next election 'in the autumn

1978 or the summer of 1979'. He added: 'but of course we might be forced into one earlier' (Donoughue, 2008: 245). Twelve months later, Callaghan's stock as Prime Minister had also risen with Britain's economic recovery. In October 1976, his Ruskin Speech on improving standards in schools promised new horizons in education. He acted as a mediator in international affairs between the United States and Europe (especially Helmut Schmidt, the German chancellor) and assisted President Carter to broker the Camp David Agreement (September 1978) between Egypt and Israel (Morgan, 1997: 608–9, 753). Expectations of a general election were high, not only within Labour circles but also across the country. On 5 September Callaghan's address to the TUC conference in Brighton famously included a ditty (wrongly ascribed to 'Marie Lloyd'). Donoughue noted: 'tremendous Press for the PM ... Great send off for an election campaign- assuming there is one' (Donoughue, 2008: 336–7). However, trade union leaders felt misled or even betrayed (interview with Brendan Barber, 4 August 2008). On 7 September, Callaghan astonished his Cabinet and his political advisors, who had been kept in the dark, with his announcement that there would be no autumn election. The Prime Minister apparently had made his decision alone at his Sussex farm in mid-August after studying constituency material and polling data from Bob Worcester that indicated an autumn election would produce no clear Labour majority (interview with Robert Worcester, 27 June 2011). Callaghan's decision to defer the general election, which he announced that evening in a broadcast on national television, has been considered his 'greatest tactical mistake' (Taylor, 2008: 28). It the Prime Minister's judgement into question and was another stepping stone on the route to the demise of the Labour government.

Whether or not Callaghan would have won a general election in the autumn of 1978 is one of the great 'if onlys' of late twentieth-century Labour history. The future Labour leader, Neil Kinnock, then a vociferous backbench MP, urged Callaghan and Foot not to delay, since Labour would be at the mercy of the minority parties, especially the nationalists, with Scottish and Welsh referendums scheduled to be held on 1 March 1979 (interview with Lord Kinnock, 2 November 2011). However, a number of Callaghan's Cabinet colleagues, particularly his deputy, Michael Foot, and the Home Secretary, Merlyn Rees, as well as some of the Labour whips, backed Callaghan's decision to put off the election (Morgan, 1997: 637–42). The Prime Minister's decision to defer the general election – and the way it was mishandled – haunted the last six months of the Labour administration. In particular, the government was compelled to enter another parliamentary term with a largely unworkable pay policy and the advent of a difficult winter of industrial trouble (Donoughue, 2008: 355–61, 366–8).

The 'Winter of Discontent'

In September 1978 the nine-week Ford strike, for higher wages and a shorter working week, began. In the end the highly profitable American Ford company settled the unions' claim at 17 per cent, over three times the government's norm. Callaghan called the settlement 'the bellwether of the flock'. It was the pacesetter for a host of inflationary wage claims in both the private and the public sectors during what became dubbed as the British 'Winter of Discontent'. While the government was the main employer in the public services, its attempt to get parliamentary approval for sanctions against private firms in breach of the pay policy was narrowly defeated on the 12 December 1978 by the opposition parties and a revolt of Tribune MPs against their own government. Callaghan had refused to make the issue of sanctions a vote of confidence to bring the Tribune MPs in line. Although on the following day Callaghan tabled a vote of confidence, which was won with Scottish Nationalist support, his government had lost the power to impose sanctions. In David Owen's view, 'sanctions were like a finger in the dyke; once removed the whole edifice of restraint collapsed. Before we knew where we were the Winter of Discontent descended on us....' Though he didn't keep a diary, he made a special note that 12 December 1978 was the day he knew Labour had lost the 1979 election (Owen, 1992: 382–5; 2011: 30–3).

Two months before the crucial vote of no confidence on 28 March 1979, Owen advised Callaghan that June was his preferred date to go to the country, as he was not confident of a Labour victory in March. 'I would be very surprised if we could win in March/April – the wounds and sores of our present industrial trouble will still be too new', he confided (Owen to Callaghan, 26 January 1979, Owen Papers, D 709, 2/71/7). As a leading member of the Labour Cabinet, the Foreign Secretary, also a medical doctor, fully realised the pressures of high politics at Westminster, including the constant need to cobble together votes at Westminster to keep a minority administration in existence. Six months before his 1979 election defeat, on 19 September 1978, James Callaghan had scribbled on his notepad in Cabinet: 'I have been written off more times than I care to remember.' The Prime Minister listed various crises when his parliamentary opponents, and a hostile press, had unsuccessfully predicted the downfall of his administration and his political demise. Callaghan scribbled down five occasions when his critics 'wrote him off': March 1976 (an autumn election predicted); October 1976 Labour Party Annual Conference ('my best and last speech as PM'); March 1977 (before the Lib–Lab Pact) would be forced to call a general election; after the Lib–Lab Pact agreed (an election forecast for October 1977); and attempts by the media and his Tory opponents to fix the general election date in the autumn of 1978. His notes demonstrate his determination to remain in power: 'neither the press nor the Tory Party will fix it [the date of the next general election]' (James Callaghan, 'PM's Notes for Future Policy Initiatives Meeting', 19 September 1978, TNA PREM 16/1667). However, Owen noted that

> the government was beginning to look tired and was running out of steam. We were facing an increasingly confident Margaret Thatcher and a Conservative Party which had rediscovered the will to win. I had by chance witnessed this one particular incident (not declaring a vote of confidence on 12 December 1978), but Jim (Callaghan), Michael (Foot) and Denis (Healey) had been facing similar issues since 1974. The whole process of maintaining a majority in the House of Commons and beating back inflation was beginning to wear them out.
>
> (interview with Lord Owen, 16 November 2011)

After Labour's demoralising 1979 defeat, a dejected Callaghan acknowledged that 'memories of the winter [strikes] have been too great for many people and undoubtedly that handicapped us ... I have a feeling that people voted *against* last winter, rather than *for* the Conservative proposals' (Clark, 1979: 26). Callaghan's verdict that the industrial anarchy caused by the unions was the main reason for Labour's downfall has been largely shared by many of his Cabinet colleagues and political advisors (Shore, 1993: 117–19; Donoughue, 2008: 428, 505; Williams, 2009: 249–50). However, the left-wing Labour MP Michael Meacher, who had served as a junior minister in the Wilson and Callaghan governments, asked a blunt question in 1979: 'was it really the Winter of Discontent that lost Labour the election?' Remarkably, in his view, little attention had been given to the *causes* (emphasis added) of the widespread industrial unrest between September 1978 and March 1979, which he attributed primarily to the government's inflexible and stringent 5 per cent pay policy at a time when inflation was around 10 per cent and living standards had been falling (Meacher, 1979).

Thirty years on, however, the graphic events of the Winter of Discontent have remained deeply etched in the national psyche. Iconic images of widespread industrial turmoil appeared almost daily in the press and on television screens, particularly in January and February 1979. Mountains of refuse remained uncollected. In the heart of London's theatre land, Leicester Square became 'Fester Square'; once rats supposedly appeared. Elsewhere, there were stories of militant left-wing shop stewards preventing hospital admissions, anti-cancer drugs left on the Hull dockside, and panic buying as a national road haulage strike emptied supermarket shelves. On 22 January 1979 1.5 million workers – the largest number since the 1926 General Strike – stopped work during a 'National Day of Action' (Wrigley, 1996: 210–16; Beckett, 2010: 464–97; Sandbrook, 2012: 715–50). Most powerful were the pictures of chained cemetery gates at the Springwood Crematorium in Allerton, Liverpool, shut by the Merseyside gravediggers and crematorium workers' strike. A hysterical tabloid press screamed: 'Now they won't let us bury our dead!' It was 'manna from heaven' for the opposition leader, Mrs Thatcher, and her Conservative colleagues. Future Conservative election broadcasts regularly dug up images of the 'Winter of Discontent' and the new prime minister never campaigned without stories of the industrial mayhem during Labour's last months in office (Thomas, 2007). As late as 2008, one newspaper carried the front page banner headline 'Echoes of the Winter of Discontent... bodies not buried' (*The Mail on Sunday*, 12 October 2008).

Conservative opposition

At the 1985 Conservative Party Conference at Blackpool, Mrs Thatcher, who had replaced the former leader, Edward Heath, ten years before, asked her audience and the nation: 'Do you remember the Labour Britain of 1979? It was a Britain in which union leaders held their members and our country to ransom... a Britain that was known as the sick man of Europe' (Thatcher, 1989: 109). It was a highly characteristic speech to the party faithful by Margaret Thatcher, Britain's first woman prime minister, who won three successive general elections in 1979, 1983 and 1987 to serve as the longest peacetime premier in the twentieth century. How far was a revived and credible opposition under the leadership of Margaret Thatcher an important contributory factor in the downfall of the Callaghan government? Dennis Kavanagh has demonstrated that Thatcher was an inexperienced and cautious new leader of the opposition from 1975 to 1979, who had only stood for the leadership after Sir Keith Joseph declined to do so. During these years in opposition, there was little evidence of ground-breaking Thatcherite policies, or the public endorsement, associated with her three administrations in the 1980s. As the new party leader, her first Cabinet continued to include Heath loyalists, making for a moderate administration.

Key changes were made to some effect in the party organisation, including the appointment of former Conservative minister Lord Thorneycroft as party chairman and Gordon Reece as Director of Publicity. Reece was influential in the selection of the Saatchi & Saatchi advertising agency, and specific attention was given to targeting the readers of the *Daily Mail* and the *Sun* in preparation for the general election. However, in terms of personal approval ratings, the shrewd old hand Callaghan outpaced the relative newcomer Thatcher – even securing a 20 per cent margin in one election campaign poll – as well as generally producing more imposing performances at Westminster (Kavanagh, 2005; Campbell, 2007).

Thatcher's attitude towards the unions had been cautious and moderate. The more genial Jim Prior held the important employment and industrial portfolio from 1975 to 1983 in dealing with the unions (minutes, 51st Meeting Leaders Steering Committee, 1978, LSC 78/51st mtg, Margaret Thatcher Foundation). While Thatcher valued the new right-wing think-tanks, particularly the Centre for Policy Studies, for their neo-liberal ideas, she retained a circumspect stance towards the 'Stepping Stones' report by John Hoskyns and Norman Strauss with an alternative union strategy that identified the unions as the primary obstacle to government action on achieving fundamental economic reform in Britain. However, the advent of the 'Winter of Discontent', particularly the industrial unrest in the arctic winter of January–February, transformed Conservative fortunes and heartened their leader's fighting qualities. The media coverage, especially the tabloid press, portrayed Britain as under siege from the unions and almost 'as ungovernable as Chile'. In particular, the secondary picketing during the national road haulage strike provided the strategic opportunity for Thatcher to adopt a more aggressive stance in the national interest against a failing government. After an impressive performance in the Commons debate on industrial unrest on 16 January – which even the Prime Minister publicly acknowledged – Thatcher's television broadcast the following day broke new ground in seemingly abandoning party politics to offer the government support for urgent union reform (*Parliamentary Debates*, 16 January 1979, vol. 960, cols. 1524–34, 1541; Campbell, 2007: 420–3).

In many people's eyes, particularly in her own party, Thatcher was beginning to articulate popular concerns. At last the leader of the opposition began to emerge as a 'prime minister in waiting'. The polls indicated Labour was ahead of their Conservative opponents by about four percentage points in November–December 1978; by February this margin was transformed into a commanding Conservative lead of 19 points. While Labour was able to close this gap to some extent during the remaining weeks before the election, it was probably not completely recoverable.

Hostile media coverage

On 22 January 1979, Tony Benn noted in his diary: 'the press is just full of crises, anarchy, chaos and disruption – bitterly hostile to the trade union movement' (Benn, 1991: 443). Any explanation of the downfall of the Callaghan government has to consider the part increasingly played by a hostile press, especially the tabloid newspapers.

James Callaghan returned to Britain on 10 January 1979 after attending an international summit with French president Giscard D'Estaing, US President Jimmy Carter and German chancellor Helmut Schmidt (mainly about the second round of US–Soviet strategic arms limitation talks – SALT II) on the sun-drenched French Caribbean island of Guadeloupe. The temperature was –7°C at Heathrow, and lower elsewhere. Snowbound Britain was in the grip of the worst winter in post-war years and in the midst of industrial chaos: strikes, go-slows. The next day, the *Sun* newspaper famously carried a front-page banner headline 'Crisis? What Crisis?' It famously misquoted the prime minister's reply to a reporter's question at a hastily summoned airport press conference. Unfortunately, it also confirmed popular perceptions of a sun-tanned prime minister totally out of touch with the escalating industrial and political drama during his absence abroad. In fact, while briefly away at a summit of international importance, Callaghan was in detailed communication daily with events at home, as shown by his stream of telegraphic communications (see, for example, 'Tanker Drivers and Road Haulage Disputes', Private Office telegram no.62 (confidential), T. Lankester to P. Wood, Prime Minister's Party, 9 January 1979. TNA PREM 16/2124).

From January to March 1979, the industrial disorder during the 'Winter of Discontent' reached its peak with a nationwide road haulage strike and widespread strikes by public sector workers. On 22 January 1979, a 'National Day of Action' brought 1.5 million public service workers – the largest number since the 1926 General Strike – on strike with demonstrations on the streets of London, Cardiff, Edinburgh, Belfast and elsewhere to campaign for a national minimum wage of £60 per week and a 35 hour working week, as public sector workers extended their industrial action.

Media reporting of the 'Winter of Discontent' created enduring popular myths that powerful militant unions had paralysed Britain by striking to get colossal and inflationary pay claims, showing a total disregard for the general public. Larry Lamb, editor of the *Sun*, which had changed its allegiance to the Conservatives in early 1978, was credited with having devised the 'Winter of Discontent' phrase (derived from the opening couplet of William Shakespeare's *Richard III*). In 1979 the TUC's Media Working Group published a detailed booklet on the different ways trade unionists and their actions in the 'Winter of Discontent' had often been misleadingly portrayed by the press, radio and television during the industrial unrest. Very little media coverage was given to the causes of industrial action or the grievances of those forced to take industrial action (TUC, 1979).

Colin Hay has given particular attention in his eclectic interpretation of the 'Winter of Discontent', and, in demystifying the mythology associated with it, to the politicised media coverage in creating a 'manufactured or constructed crisis' in the British state. According to Hay, this was also enabled by 'the existence of an alternative paradigm – Thatcherism – capable of providing such a construction'. The Conservatives and their allies in the press became highly effective in interpreting the various episodes of the 'Winter of Discontent' in terms of the popular perceptions and experiences of the strikes and shortages as evidence of a more wide-ranging crisis in the British state that required a radical neo-liberal political solution. In this way, the Winter of Discontent was emblematic of the transition from post-war Keynesianism to monetarism in late twentieth-century British history (Hay, 1996, 2009, 2010).

Devolution and downfall

After three years battling unparalleled inflation, surviving the IMF crisis, the deaths of MPs, by-election losses, parliamentary defeats, the breakdown of the social contract and the industrial confrontations of the 'Winter of Discontent', why was the Callaghan government finally brought down so narrowly by a vote of no confidence?

On 1 March 1979 the Scottish and Welsh referendums on devolution were held. During 1974–79, devolution had been a constant and controversial problem as the Wilson and Callaghan governments endeavoured to respond to the rise of the Scottish Nationalist Party and Plaid Cymru in British politics. Eventually in 1978 two separate devolution acts for Wales and Scotland had been passed, but contained a critical amendment by the hostile opponent of Scottish devolution, Labour MP George Cunningham. What became known as 'the Cunningham amendment' required the 'Yes' vote in the referendums on devolution to constitute at least 40 per cent of the total electorate in each country. After referendum campaigns in Wales and Scotland in 1979, which took place against the background of the winter industrial unrest, devolution was rejected massively in Wales, with only 11.9 per cent of the electorate in favour. By contrast, in Scotland, the 'Yes' vote was smaller than expected at 32.8 per cent, compared with the 'No' vote of 30.8 per cent (with 36.4 per cent not voting). Nevertheless, the government was compelled to withdraw the devolution legislation for Wales and Scotland, since the 'Yes' votes did not meet the Cunningham amendment (Harvie, 1981: 162–5; Wood, 1989: 126–9; Morgan, 1997: 628–32). As Michael Foot, the most pro-devolution member in the Callaghan Cabinet, remembered: 'it was truly the results of the Referendum which led to the government's defeat within the same month of March' (for the abortive Foot–Callaghan negotiations (1–26 March 1979) following the results of the referendums, see 'How the Government Fell: A few brief notes', Michael Foot Papers MF/C11/1).

The balance of power was now held by a grouping of smaller parties. The Liberals, who had ended their Lib–Lab pact with the Callaghan government in the summer of 1978, sought an early election. After the failure of the devolution referendums, the Scottish Nationalist MPs now openly opposed the government and put down a vote of no confidence. Even so, the denouement of the Callaghan government might have been avoided, before Mrs Thatcher finally tabled the fatal vote of no confidence for 28 March. From 4 to 26 March various delaying schemes were discussed by Foot and Callaghan, as well as in Cabinet, about Foot's proposal to table a government motion for talks with the other parties to be completed by the end of April. However, with the prime minister's indecision, all came to naught. Mrs Thatcher put down a vote of no confidence for 28 March once confident of the Scottish Nationalist support.

Why did Labour lose the vote of confidence on 28 March? During the last days before the vote of no confidence it appeared Labour would lose by two or three votes. According to Donoughue, the Prime Minister wavered at first, even stopping his whips and ministers from bartering for votes until persuaded forcefully by his key advisors to alter course (Donoughue, 2008: 467–70). Fourteen years later, Austin Mitchell, Labour MP for Grimsby at the 1977 by-election, brought to mind the fall of the Labour government as a 'night to remember' – in febrile terms reminiscent of the sinking of the Titanic. He wrote:

> Every string was being pulled. Rumours abounded. Clement Freud (Liberal) was to be offered the passage of his Freedom of Information Bill and would miss his train back from Liverpool. The Welsh Nationalists would support us in return for help with the disabled miners. The Unionists would stay home. The press were describing Jim Callaghan as some Tammany tyrant.
>
> (Mitchell, 1993)

Roy Hattersley later recalled that on the evening of the vote of no confidence in the House of Commons he didn't realise at the time he was witnessing 'the last rites of "Old Labour", the party of nationalisation, redistributive income and trade union power'. His role on the day included guarding two Unionist MPs – John Carson and James McCusker – to secure their votes with a promise to tackle inflation in Ulster (interview with Roy Hattersley, 25 June 2009). Yet, Callaghan turned down outright a possible deal with Enoch Powell for Ulster Unionist MPs' abstentions for a gas pipeline to Northern Ireland – probably another sign of fatigue and lack of willingness to continue the travails of minority government. The two Irish Catholic MPs Gerry Fitt and Frank Maguire, who usually supported the Labour government, had flown from Belfast to London to abstain. In the debate, Fitt explained his utter disillusionment with the government minister Roy Mason's conduct of Irish policy. Both Irish members abstained, under threats from the IRA not to support the Labour government.

In retrospect, Mitchell also recognised that the Callaghan government 'had been skating on thin ice for so long that few of us realised there was no ice left'. The administration's survival had owed much to the work of the Labour whips' team at Westminster. 'We also ascribed miraculous powers to those presiding genii of British politics [Michael] Cocks and Walter Harrison Chief Whip and Deputy Chief Whip], a double act who had become legends in their own time. Surely they could pull another body out of the hat?' However, this was not possible. Sir Alfred Broughton, the long-serving Labour MP for the Yorkshire constituency of Batley and Morley, was mortally ill and remained at home. Desperate last-minute attempts to persuade Maguire not to abstain, and keep the Callaghan administration in office, were of no avail. Afterwards, at a sombre party in the Whips' Office, there were bitter recriminations between the Chief Whip, Michael Cocks, and Bernard (now Lord) Donoughue about the Prime Minister's intransigence over possible deals on offer that would have secured victory (Donoughue, 2009: 470–3).

With the date of the election fixed for 3 May, Callaghan had purposely arranged for an unusually long campaign lasting over five weeks in the hope that memories of the industrial unrest during the winter months would largely fade. In 1979, by general consent, Labour generally ran an effective campaign centred on the personality of the Prime Minister. In reality, Labour's chances of electoral victory were doomed from the outset, as Callaghan's Chief Political Advisor, Tom McNally, later freely acknowledged (interview with Lord McNally, 23 July 2007). From the start the Conservatives enjoyed an average lead of 11.9 percentage points over Labour. In theory, it was not an impossible gap to close, since this margin had shrunk to only four points by the penultimate week. However, in the final week the Conservative lead had increased to seven points.

The Conservatives scored over Labour on the main election issues, particularly those for which the electors felt confident their party had believable and workable proposals or possessed a very sound record. In a BBC Gallup survey, conducted on the eve of polling, the issues most frequently mentioned in 1979 were prices, unemployment, taxes, strikes, and law and order. While Labour led the Conservatives on prices (+13) and unemployment (+15), the Conservatives scored far higher on taxes (+61) and law and order (+72) and as well as Labour on strikes (+15). Moreover, many electors supported Labour's objectives of securing a 5 per cent rate of inflation within three years and an enduring pact with the unions on wages. Understandably, polling revealed there was considerable doubt in electors' minds after the 'Winter of Discontent'. Palpably, these proposals were not solely within a Labour government's gift, whereas the Conservative proposals on income tax reduction were measures well within the control of a new administration's jurisdiction (Leonard, 1981: 95–116).

In terms of personalities, Callaghan had put his imprint not only on Labour's election manifesto, but also on the election campaign itself. As a highly skilled politician who had held all four major offices of state, Callaghan had led the inexperienced Mrs Thatcher in the personal approval ratings ever since becoming prime minister in April 1976. The avuncular and patriotic 'Sunny Jim' proved Labour's ace in his party's election pack. But in 1979 it was not sufficient to win the election, in which issues counted more than personalities. Memories of the 1976 IMF crisis, and an apparently bankrupt Labour government forced to apply for the biggest financial bail-out ever, may have receded. In retrospect, Callaghan had skilfully kept his Cabinet together without any resignations. However, the prime minister with his finger normally on the political pulse had lost his sure touch on fatal occasions in the final months of his premiership. The general election had been deferred in the autumn of 1978 when, arguably, it was Labour's best chance to be returned to office. Callaghan's clear-cut pay policy to reduce the scourge of unprecedented inflation won union co-operation for a while. But the history of post-war incomes policies in Britain demonstrated they were short-lived. During the Callaghan government the inflexible 5 per cent pay limit was dogmatically upheld and led directly to the industrial turmoil of the 'Winter of Discontent'. The prime minister's nonchalant performance at the Heathrow press conference on returning from Guadeloupe in January 1979 was disastrous for a politician with matchless experience of handling the media. In the end the stress and fatigue of minority government became apparent in his crucial indecision on 28 March, when Labour could and should have won the vital vote of confidence.

During the final week MORI reported a 3 per cent Tory lead. Bob Worcester declared he was a 'boomerang-backlash-bandwagon' man. He claimed the public would 'boomerang' against the possibility of an 80–100 seat Tory majority; would 'backlash' against a possible Labour win after all, and finally reverse in the final days of the campaign. 'In the event, I think that's exactly what happened', the MORI chief reported. On polling day, the vast majority of the polls had the result almost correct. MORI's final two polls were within 1 per cent of the share of the vote of all three parties. MORI's last poll, published in the London *Evening Standard*, predicted the outcome of the 1979 election in terms of the share of the votes cast almost precisely: Conservatives 45 per cent; Labour 37 per cent (Market & Opinion Research International, *British Public Opinion: General Election 1979. Final Report*, 1979: i–iv).

After five years of largely minority government since February 1974, the 1979 election produced the first clear and decisive result since Edward Heath's unexpected win in 1970 (Table 6.1). The general swing to the Conservatives of 5.2 per cent was a post-war record, although there continued to be a long-term trend of deviant variations between, and within, different regions in Britain. In general terms, the Conservatives owed their victory to the more affluent constituencies in the South

Table 6.1   The general election of 1979

Party	Votes won	MPs elected	Share of vote (%)
Conservative	13,679,923 (10,464,817)	339 (277)	43.9 (35.8)
Labour	11,532,218 (11,457,879)	269 (319)	37.0 (39.2)
Liberal	4,313,804 (5,346,752)	11 (13)	13.8 (18.3)
Others	1,676,453 (1,920,528)	16 (26)	5.3 (6.7)

Note: Figures for October 1974 in brackets.
Source: Butler and Kavanagh, 1980.

and Midlands, while Labour had been pushed back to its industrial heartlands in Scotland, the North of England and Wales.

In the new parliament there were 339 Conservatives MPs to Labour's 269 – a Conservative lead of 70. Mrs Thatcher enjoyed an overall majority of 43 over the combined opposition parties, which was a comfortable result for a full-term parliament. The Conservatives had secured 2 million more votes than Labour (around 7 per cent), which was the biggest switch of votes between two parties since 1935. However, on a turnout of 76 per cent, the Conservative share of the vote in 1979 (43.9 per cent) was significantly less than the Conservative victories in 1951 (48 per cent), 1955 (49.7 per cent) or 1959 (49.3 per cent). In terms of the numbers and percentages of votes cast, the Conservatives secured 13.7 million votes (43.9 per cent of the poll) while Labour had 11.5 million votes (39.2 per cent). In numerical terms Labour had recorded close to the number of votes in the February 1974 and October 1974 general elections, but its share of the poll had slumped to 36.9 per cent. Above all, Labour had failed again to secure even 40 per cent at the polls for the third time. In this respect, it was the worst Labour performance since the debacle of the 1931 general election. Despite the fact that 56 per cent of voters in 1979 did not choose a Conservative candidate, the 1979 general election could be seen as a prime example of a government losing an election rather than the opposition winning it (Crewe, 1979: 249).

For Bob Worcester, founder of MORI in 1969 and James Callaghan's chief pollster, the strategic battleground that determined the outcome of the 1979 election was the skilled working class (the C2s) forming a third of the electorate. In 1979 Mrs Thatcher made a highly significant inroad into Labour's traditional core support and secured a greater swing among the C2s (11.5 per cent) – almost double the overall national swing (6.5 per cent). As a result, the two major parties had equal backing (41–41 per cent) among skilled workers, whereas in the February

1974 and October 1974 elections the Conservatives had been trailing by sizeable margins of 19 per cent and 23 per cent. In 1979, among the C2 women voters, Mrs Thatcher had secured a commanding 12 per cent lead among the 25–34-year-olds (despite the Labour government transferring the family allowance to the child benefit allowance paid directly to the mother).

There were other noticeable changes among the British electorate between 1974 and 1979. Mrs Thatcher was highly successful in capturing the support of the younger, mainly first-time voters (18–24-year-olds – traditionally often Labour voters). Among this group, Conservative support virtually doubled (from 24 per cent to 42 per cent), particularly among middle-class (ABC1) women and skilled working-class (C2) men. The Liberal vote dropped from 5.3 million (18.3 per cent) in October 1974 to 4.3 million (13.8 per cent) in May 1979, particularly among younger voters. The collapse of the Liberal vote contributed towards Mrs Thatcher's working majority in the new parliament.

However, according to MORI, in 1979 Labour still retained the allegiance of one group of traditional Labour voters – middle-aged (35–54-year-old) unskilled working-class (DE) men. This group were the electoral bedrock of Labour support, as evidenced by a colossal 29 per cent lead over the Conservatives (56–27 per cent). However, among women in this group, there was only a small gap between the two parties (41 per cent voted Labour and 38 per cent Conservative), probably attributable to Mrs Thatcher's flagship policy of council home sales to tenants. Finally, MORI polling revealed that in the 1979 election trade unionists formed 30 per cent of the electorate (compared with 26 per cent in 1974) at a time of peak union membership of over 13 million. Mrs Thatcher, who had only been Conservative Party leader for four years, was successful in attracting a third (33 per cent) of the trade unionists' votes, whereas in 1974 fewer than a quarter of trade unionists had been Conservative voters (Crewe, 1979: 249–51; Worcester, 1979: 1–7; Sandbrook, 2012: 801–2).

In part, the 1979 Nuffield College election study readily supported Mrs Thatcher's view that her party had secured a decisive victory over all rival parties to end the electoral uncertainty from 1974. However, it challenged whether the outcome represented a permanent realignment in British politics in terms of a deep-seated shift in votes or political ideas. Traditional Labour voters, disenchanted with the party's policies, had been deserting its ranks at elections for more than a decade. The 1979 election revealed the extent to which Mrs Thatcher was able to carve a swathe into Labour's support among skilled workers with her appeal of tax cuts. Many voters (including a significant number of trade unionists) had been wary of growing trade union militancy since the 1960s. Paradoxically, due to its historic alliance with the trade union movement, polling evidence revealed that Labour was still perceived as the party to handle the unions. During the 1979 election, those polled also highlighted unemployment and prices among their chief concerns (Butler and Kavanagh, 1980: 338–40).

More recently, the Labour governments of 1974–79 have received a more favourable press with the availability of a range of political archives and publication of new detailed biographies and other studies. In particular, Kenneth O. Morgan, James Callaghan's renowned biographer, has drawn significant attention to his achievements in international and domestic politics in a long career that included all four highest offices of state. In terms of Labour's 1979 defeat, he gave particular attention to the reality of Labour's diminishing support among its traditional voters: '[Labour] must connect with its political and industrial base. The decay of that base, the fundamental tensions within Keir Hardie's old Labour alliance at a time of a global capitalist crisis left the [Callaghan] government bereft' (Morgan, 2007: 307).

In 1979 psephologists and political commentators all drew attention to Labour's dwindling electoral support, made apparent by the election result. Peter Kellner's verdict was that 'Labour had suffered not merely a defeat but a disaster' at the hands of the electors on 3 May. The party had achieved its lowest share of the poll since 1931. What is more, the corrosion among its core voters was so extensive that he questioned whether the party might ever regain a working majority at Westminster again.

What was unmistakably apparent was the clear-cut North–South divide in the regional voting patterns (based on the Mersey–Humber Line) with Labour bedrock support largely concentrated in the party's heartlands of the industrial North, as well as Scotland and Wales. By contrast, the victorious Conservatives dominated the more affluent Midlands and South. This was not a new occurrence, but an electoral trend that by 1979 had become even more pronounced. In 1979, Labour, with 151 MPs (to the Conservatives on 75), did almost as well in the North as in the 1945 Attlee landslide victory (when it had secured 165 to the Conservatives on 72), whereas in the South Labour's lead of 100 seats over the Conservatives in 1945 (Labour 228 to the Conservatives 128) had been transformed into a thumping Tory majority of 146 (Labour 118 to the Conservatives 264) by 1979 (Kellner, 1979: 80). As Kellner put it:

> Defined by either geography or class, Labour has been forced back
> into its hinterland – the North and the semi and unskilled working
> class – and out of the rich pastures of the Midlands and the south of
> skilled workers and their families.
>
> (Kellner, 1979: 80)

The Conservatives had being making inroads into Labour's traditional
areas of support. The swing to the Tories in May 1979 was the highest among working-class voters, especially C2 skilled workers and DE
semi-skilled and unskilled workers (including trade union members and
first-time voters). Two statistics were particularly apposite concerning
Labour's lost voters. In 1979 trade union membership had soared to a
peak at over 13 million, with a significant part of this expansion in the
Midlands and the South among skilled and white-collar workers. In the
same year over 30 per cent of trade unionists voted Conservative, a compelling advance on the 25 per cent at the 1974 elections (Butler and
Kavanagh, 1980).

With his distaste for the media, Tony Benn turned down invitations to
participate in any of the media post-mortem programmes, but at the ex-
Cabinet's first meeting he persisted on raising the question of Labour's
1979 election defeat so forcefully that Callaghan retorted: 'I'll tell you
what happened. We lost the election because people didn't get their
dustbins emptied, because commuters were angry about train disruption
and because of too much trade union power. That's all there is to it'
(Benn, 1991: 493–4, 499). On 4 May, on leaving 10 Downing Street for
the last time, Callaghan had declared: 'the people wanted a change.'
The only former trade union official to become Prime Minister in Britain
added: 'the unions did it: people could not forget and would not forgive
what they had to suffer from the unions last winter' (Donoughue, 2008:
503). In his memoirs, Callaghan recalled the industrial action taken by
public sector workers, and its adverse effects on the public, which he
characterised as a contagion spreading to different industries and public
services. In graphic and condemnatory terms he wrote:

> Even with the passage of time I find it painful to write about some
> of the excesses that took place. One of the most notorious was
> the refusal of the Liverpool grave diggers to bury the dead ... Such
> heartlessness and cold-blooded indifference to the feelings of fam-
> ilies at the moments of intense grief rightly aroused deep revul-
> sion ... My own anger increased when I learned that the Home
> Secretary Merlyn Rees had called upon Alan Fisher, the General

Secretary of NUPE, to use his influence to get the grave-diggers to
go back to work.

(Callaghan, 2006: 537)

As an insider at 10 Downing Street, Donoughue was even more explicit,
bitterly placing the blame on Alan Fisher (NUPE) and Moss Evans T & G
WU). The next day at his local polling station Donoughue observed the
behaviour of a 'trickle of old ladies':

They had not come to vote FOR anybody. They had come to vote
AGAINST Alan Fisher and Moss Evans and every trade union thug
who stood in a picket line barring the way to the hospital and
graveyard that they feared might be their destination tomorrow.

(Donoughue, 2009: 498)

In retrospect, Denis Healey also conceded the 'Winter of Discontent'
had been the major factor in Labour's loss of office. He observed that
'All the evidence suggested we had lost the election mainly because the
"Winter of Discontent" had destroyed the nation's confidence in the
Labour Party's ability to work with the unions.' However, the primary
cause of the 'Winter of Discontent' was not the built-up grievances of
ordinary workers, but 'local trade union activists' angered by three years
of incomes policies negotiated with their trade union leaders: 'they felt
like Othello when he had to give up soldiering; that their occupation
had gone' (Healey, 1991: 467). Following Labour's 1979 election defeat,
Ron Hayward, in his Chairman's Address, opened the annual party conference with a blistering attack on the Labour leadership for ignoring
the grass roots of the party. He blamed Labour's loss of office squarely
on James Callaghan and his ministers. He declared:

A year ago the TUC Conference almost unanimously rejected the
rigid and inflexible 5 per cent wage ceiling. The Labour Party Conference a month later voted equally solidly. But the cabinet majority
took no notice. Hence the troubles of January and February (the 'winter of discontent') [*Applause*]. And that's why Mrs Thatcher is in No.10
Downing Street at the moment [*Applause*].

(Labour Party, *Report of the Seventy Eighth Annual
Conference of the Labour Party*, 1979: 167–8)

It was a speech that was echoed by others participating in the debate.
Ron Thomas, former MP Bristol North West, argued that the Callaghan

government, in adopting Treasury orthodox policies, had failed to deal with the problems and crises of British capitalism in the 1970s. He added that:

> despite the decision of Labour Party Conference and the TUC a small group in the Cabinet decided that they knew best, and they insisted on the 5 per cent policy. Those of us who stood against it were called the rebels. They were the rebels. They were the rebels who refused to accept Conference decisions.
>
> (Labour Party, *Report of the Seventy Eighth Annual Conference of the Labour Party*, 1979: 167–8)

Shortly after polling day, Anthony King examined the gulf between Labour's policies and traditional Labour voters as a principal cause for the party's defeat. Moreover, he confirmed that this rift had been a long-term trend for more than a decade, though somewhat obscured by Labour being in government for five years. With the exception of 1970 (43 per cent), not since 1935 had Labour failed to secure 40 per cent of the total vote in a general election. Yet, a year before the 1979 election, NOP's regular monthly survey had put Labour ahead of its opponents by 4.5 per cent. In early November 1978 MORI had the two main parties neck and neck. However, as already noted, by early February 1979 there had been a remarkable reversal of fortunes. The Conservatives led by a staggering 19 per cent. The industrial anarchy had destroyed, or gravely undermined, Labour's claim to be the party that could govern with the unions. Poll evidence always confirmed support for Labour's policies on the welfare state and the NHS, but since the 1960s there had been a decline by Labour 'identifiers' (voters who indisputably perceive themselves as Labour supporters) in Labour policies on nationalisation, close links with trade unions and even more public expenditure on social services. In 1979 Anthony King summed up:

> put simply, the message of all the available evidence is that the British people deeply resent trade union power, increasingly dislike having to pay ever higher levels of government spending (except on a few of the basic social services) and not least are profoundly suspicious of nationalisation and government intervention in the economy generally. Labour's misfortune is that these are precisely the causes that the Party has stood for over the years ... If it wants to reverse the defeat

of last Thursday, the Labour Party will have to start showing a greater
respect for the opinions of the British people.

(King, 1979)

Jim Callaghan concluded his memoirs, which ended with Labour's
defeat in 1979, by reflecting that 'it was a miracle we had governed
for as long and effectively as we had and carried out as much of our
programme.' In addition, he was on record as stating: 'I let the country down.' How to judge the balance of factors that contributed to the
downfall of the Callaghan government in 1979 will remain a matter of
some debate. Undoubtedly, foremost of the 'external' pressures and difficulties, largely beyond the government's control, was the global oil crisis
in the 1970s. This created the scourge of unprecedented double-digit
inflation that Callaghan strove to eliminate with an extended incomes
policy. By contrast, 'internal' factors, more within the government's
management, were probably more significant: the decision (badly han-
dled) to defer the general election in 1978; an inflexible 5 per cent
pay norm without trade union support; and the disastrous Heathrow
press conference were among the most crucial. Donoughue's diary provides adequate testimony to the indecision and failings of the Callaghan
administration in endeavouring to cope with the industrial anarchy of
the 'Winter of Discontent'. At one point the government appeared to
be at a standstill, like a becalmed ocean liner. At the end, the defeat on
the vote of no confidence – the first since 1924 – by a single vote could
have been avoided. Instead, it revealed the indecision at the heart of
an exhausted government and a previously assured prime minister who
had lost his political touch.

The downfall of the Callaghan government in 1979, and the manner
of the events leading up to it, left an indelible imprint on British Labour
history and the future attitude of Labour leaders to government–union
relations. When Labour finally returned to power after 18 years in opposition, it was as 'New Labour', under a bright young leader who had no
particular links with, and little sympathy for, the British trade union
movement. New Labour had been carefully and thoroughly distanced
from the 'Winter of Discontent' and all that went with it (McKibbin,
1991: 12). In 1997 and beyond there would be no looking back to the
chaotic 1970s, remembered as an era of national decline, poor economic
performance and unbridled trade union power that had helped bring
down three governments. In opening his 1997 election campaign, Tony
Blair spoke out: 'naturally the Tories want to refight the election of 1979,
rather than fight that of 1997.' Instead, he unequivocally endorsed the

Thatcherite trade union legislation of the 1980s (*The Times*, 31 March 1997).

Yet, from across the globe different lessons were clearly drawn from the British experience of the last years of Jim Callaghan's Labour government. In 1978, Ralph Willis, Australian Labour Party (ALP) shadow minister for economic affairs, visited Britain on an important fact-finding tour, including meetings on economic and industrial policy with Callaghan, Healey and senior TUC officials. His objective was to put together a realistic anti-inflation strategy for the ALP preparing for government back home. On his return, his highly influential report fed directly into fundamental ALP debates on industrial relations. The social contract in Britain had fallen apart during the British 'Winter of Discontent' due to the imposition of a totally unrealistic 5 per cent pay norm. Nevertheless, the more constructive aspects of government–union co-operation, as evidenced in Britain, could be incorporated into a more widely based and all-embracing policy in Australian Labour politics. Willis's pioneering work in Britain, where a disastrous incomes policy in the end contributed to the fall of James Callaghan's Labour government, led, in sharp contrast, to 'The Accord' successfully negotiated between government and unions in Australia. From 1983 to 1993 this comprehensive and long-lasting policy agreement on wages, prices, social welfare and employment became the successful foundation stone on incomes policy and associated issues of the Bob Hawke and Paul Keating Labour governments (Singleton, 1990: 155–76; Scott, 2000: 231–7).

References

Ashton, J. (2000), *Red Rose Blues: The Story of a Good Labour Man* (Basingstoke: Macmillan).

Bartram, P. (1981), *David Steel: His Life and Politics* (London: W. H. Allen).

Beckett, A. (2010), *When The Lights Went Out: What Really Happened to Britain in the Seventies* (London: Faber and Faber).

Benn, T. (1991), *Conflicts of Interest: Diaries 1977–80* (London: Arrow).

Butler, D. and Kavanagh, D. (1980), *The British General Election of 1979* (London: Macmillan).

Callaghan, J. (2006), *Time and Chance* (London: Politicos).

Campbell, J. (2007), *Margaret Thatcher: Volume One: The Grocer's Daughter* (London: Vintage).

Clark, G. (1979), 'The Nation's Choice: a Conservative woman Prime Minister' in The Times, *Guide to the House of Commons May 1979* (London: Times Books).

Crewe, I. (1979), 'The Voting Surveyed', in *The Times* (eds), *Guide to the House of Commons May 1979* (London: Times Books).

Donoughue, B. (2008), *Downing Street Diary: With James Callaghan in No.10* (London: Jonathan Cape).

Dorey, P. (2001), *Wage Politics in Britain: The Rise and Fall of Incomes Policies since 1945* (Brighton: Sussex Academic Press).

Ferguson, N., Maier, C. S., Manela, E., and Sargent, D. J. (eds) (2010), *The Shock of the Global: The 1970s In Perspective* (Cambridge, MA: The Belknapp Press of Harvard University Press).

Harvie, C. (1981), *No Gods and Precious Few Heroes: Scotland 1914–1980* (London: Edward Arnold).

Hattersley, R. (2009), 'Callaghan, Leonard James [Jim]. Baron Callaghan of Cardiff (1912–2005), *Prime Minister'*, in *Oxford Dictionary of National Biography* (Oxford: Oxford University Press).

Hay, C. (1996), 'Narrating Crisis. The Discursive Construction of the "Winter of Discontent" ', *Sociology*, Vol. 30, No. 2, 253–77.

Hay, C. (2009), 'The Winter of Discontent Thirty Years On', *Political Quarterly*, Vol. 80, No. 4, 545–52.

Hay, C. (2010), 'Chronicles of a Death Foretold: The Winter of Discontent and Construction of the Crisis of British Keynesianism', *Parliamentary Affairs*, Vol. 63, No. 3, 446–70.

Healey, D. (1991), *The Time of My Life* (London: Penguin).

Jones, J. (1986), *Union Man: The Autobiography of Jack Jones* (London: Collins).

Kavanagh, D. (2005), 'The Making of Thatcherism, 1974–1979', in Ball, S. and Seldon, A. (eds), *Recovering Power: The Conservatives in Opposition since 1867* (Basingstoke: Palgrave).

Kellner, P. (1979), 'Not a Defeat, a Disaster', *New Statesman*, 18 May.

King, A. (1979), 'The People's Flag has Turned Deepest Blue', *Observer*, 6 May.

Labour Party (1979), *Report of the Seventy Eighth Annual Conference of the Labour Party* (Labour Party: Brighton), 167–8.

Leonard, D. (1981), 'The Labour Campaign', in Penniman, H. R. (ed.), *Britain at the Polls, 1979: A Study of the General Election* (Washington and London: American Enterprise Institute for Public Policy Research).

Market and Opinion Research International (MORI) (1979), *British Public Opinion: General Election 1979 Final Report*.

Meacher, M. (1979), 'Was it really the winter of discontent that cost Labour the election?' *Tribune*, 18 May.

McKibbin, R. (1991), 'Homage to Wilson and Callaghan', in *Labour Review of Books*, 24 October, 13–15.

Michie, A. and Hoggart, S. (1978), *The Pact: The Inside Story of the Lib-Lab Government, 1977–8* (London: Quartet Books).

Mitchell, A. (1993), 'A Night to Remember, More Like a Night to Forget', *The House Magazine*, Vol. 18, No. 612.

Morgan, K. O. (1997), *Callaghan: A Life* (Oxford: Oxford University Press).

Morgan, K. O. (2007), Michael Foot: A Life (London: HarperCollins).

Norton, P. (1980), *Dissension in the House of Commons 1974–79* (Oxford: Clarendon Press).

Norton, P. (2004), 'Parliament', in Seldon, A. and Hickson, K. (eds), *New Labour, Old Labour: The Wilson and Callaghan Governments, 1974–1979* (London: Routledge).

Owen, D. (1992), *Time to Declare* (London: Penguin).

Owen, D. (2011), 'Stick to Your Principles and Damn Your Party', *New Statesman*, 24 January.

Sandbrook, D. (2012), *Seasons in the Sun: The Battle for Britain* (London: Allen Lane).

Scott, A. (2000), *Running on Empty: 'Modernising' the British and Australian Labour Parties* (Annadale, NSW and West Wickham, Kent: Pluto Press Australia and Cromerford and Miller).

Shepherd, J. and Laybourn, K. (2006), *Britain's First Labour Government* (Basingstoke: Palgrave).

Shore, P. (1993), *Leading the Left* (London: Weidenfeld and Nicolson).

Singleton, G. (1990), *The Accord and the Australian Labour Movement* (Carlton Victoria: Melbourne University Press).

Steel, D. (1980), *A House Divided: The Lib-Lab Pact and the Future of British Politics* (London: Weidenfeld and Nicolson).

Taylor, R. (1993), *The Trade Union Question in British Politics* (Oxford: Blackwell).

Taylor, R (2008), 'When the sun set on Labour the last time', *Tribune*, 19 September, 28.

Thatcher, M. (1989), *Speeches to the Conservative Party Conference 1975–1988* (London: Conservative Party Centre).

Thomas, J. (2007), 'Bound by History: The Winter of Discontent in British Politics, 1979–2004', *Media, Culture and Society*, Vol. 29, No. 2, 263–83.

Trades Union Congress (TUC) (1979), *Cause for Concern* (London: TUC).

Williams, S. (2009), *Climbing the Bookshelves* (London: Virago).

Wood, F. (1989), 'Scottish Labour in Government and Opposition, 1964–1979', in Donnachie, I., Harvie, C. and Wood, I. (eds), *Forward! Labour Politics in Scotland 1888–1998* (Edinburgh: Polygon).

Worcester, R. (1979), 'What Happened? Post-election Aggregate Analysis', in Market and Opinion Research International (eds), *Campaign Polling Presentations* (London: MORI).

Wrigley, C. (1996), 'The Winter of Discontent: The Lorry Drivers' Strike, January 1979', in Charlesworth, A., Gilbert, D., Randall, A., Southall, H. and Wrigley, C. (eds), *An Atlas of Industrial Protest in Britain 1750–1990* (London: Macmillan).

7
The Fall of the Brown Government, 2010

Timothy Heppell

Defeat at the general election of May 2010 brought to an end 13 years of power for Labour and the longest period of continuous government in the history of the party. It also brought to an end the New Labour project, which had delivered two parliamentary landslides in 1997 and 2001 (majorities of 179 and 167 respectively), and one solid parliamentary majority of 66 in 2005. During the Blair years (1997–2007) Labour could claim that they had replaced the Conservatives as the natural party of government (Bentley, 2007: 111). Central to their electoral appeal had been the ability of Labour to colonise political territory traditionally assumed to belong to the Conservatives. The strategy of triangulation in an age of economic prosperity allowed Labour to successfully claim to advance both economic efficiency *and* social justice, thereby creating both a new electoral strategy and governing approach for the party (Gamble, 2006: 300). Their capacity to appeal both to its traditional working-class, trade unionist base and to parts of the traditional Conservative middle-class base was built around improving public services without increasing income tax, while satisfying the aspiration of individuals to climb up the social ladder alongside the creation of a fairer society (Fielding, 2010: 657–8). In assessing this decade-long period of New Labour governance under Blair, Beech described it as the 'politics of dominance' (Beech, 2008: 1–3).

While Labour would enter office in a set of circumstances that had been denied to previous incoming Labour administrations – a benign economic environment and a demoralised and discredited Conservative Party – we need to acknowledge that, while in office under Blair, Labour did acquire three characteristics not normally associated with the party when in office. The Blair administrations could legitimately claim to be *competent* (especially in the sphere of economic management); *united*; and *effectively led*. Until its third term in office, Labour could argue that, under its stewardship, the economy had maintained steady growth and low inflation rates and that it had presided over falling unemployment. The prudence that it displayed during its first term in office helped to establish credibility with the financial markets and sustain its image of economic competence with the electorate, most notably the middle classes. Critically, it had avoided the kind of financial crises that had undermined Labour governments in the past (Gamble, 2010: 648). In addition to establishing a reputation for economic competence, the first term was characterised by a degree of unity that his predecessors could only have envied (Cowley and Stuart, 2003: 317). Acquiring and sustaining a reputation for governing competence and internal unity enhanced the reputation of Blair as an effective political leader. Indeed, in an age of valance, rather than positional politics, in which election campaigning has become so focused around the character and competence of political leaders, it could be argued that Blair came to personify New Labour. Party strategy was strongly influenced by inspiring in the electorate trust in his abilities. Blair was the consummate political communicator. He was adept at parliamentary debate and the set piece party conference speech, but, most importantly, he excelled as a television performer (Finlayson, 2002: 586–99).

However, the factors that contributed to Labour's political dominance were actually eroding before the party secured its third term in 2005. Embryonic signs of governing degeneration were evident, and question marks around these three aforementioned themes of competence, unity and leadership began to emerge (Heppell, 2008: 589–93). First, on competence, the inability of the government to contribute to securing a swift resolution to the conflict in Iraq, and the apparent absence of a post-invasion strategy and exit route, led to serious questioning of the intelligence gathering and decision-making that had justified war. Second, the internal unity of the Blair government was undermined by significant opposition among Labour MPs towards Blair's approach to Iraq. That disunity would spread in the late Blair era. There were increasing divisions over education (tuition fees), health (foundation hospitals) and identity cards. Finally, the perception that Blair was an effective political leader became questioned and satisfaction ratings fell significantly after 2003 (King, 2006: 153–4). Concerns about his health, plus the ongoing demands from Gordon Brown that he step aside, contributed to Blair's 'humiliating' and 'weakening' decision to announce in September 2004 that he would not seek a fourth term should he be elected for a third term (Blair 2010a: 553; Allen, 2011: 3). Norton concludes that, rather than being dominant in the way that Beech implies, it could be argued that Labour was actually vulnerable in 2005. It was saved from being removed from office by two factors: the enduring strength of the economy and the continued weakness of the Conservatives as an alternative party of government (Norton, 2009: 32, 43).

According to the terms of the so-called Blair–Brown deal on the Labour Party succession, Brown had expected to acquire the premiership during the mid-point of the second term. What explained his obsessive desire to remove Blair, which was to be a particularly corrosive aspect of party dynamics in the 2004–07 period, was his fear that 'he would get the premiership too late to make a success of it' (Rawnsley, 2010: 280). Despite an initial short honeymoon period, which lasted a matter of months in the summer of 2007, his administration was to be undermined by two seismic crises – the banking collapse and the subsequent recession, and then the scandal of parliamentary expenses (Kenny, 2009: 671). These events would greatly undermine the capacity for Brown to stimulate political renewal within a governing party whose decline was already evident before he assumed the premiership. Recognising the insinuation by McAnulla that Blair left a toxic legacy to his successor, this chapter thus charts the further decline of Labour and its fall with reference to the Brown era of 2007–10 (McAnulla, 2011).

Governing failure: The transition from Blair to Brown

Prior to 1997, Conservative elites had repeatedly constructed a narration of crisis around Labour in office due to its economic failures – the devaluations of 1949 and 1967; the financial crisis of 1976 and the IMF loan; and the Winter of Discontent in 1979. With ten years of continuous quarters of economic growth being recorded between 1997 and 2007, Labour could legitimately claim to have provided a 'superior economic performance than that achieved by any previous Labour government' (Lee, 2008: 8). By presiding over such prolonged economic stability, it had denied the Conservatives the trigger that could allow them to demonstrate the economic incompetence of Labour. In doing so, it stymied Conservative electoral strategy (Gamble, 2006: 308). Much of its success in establishing itself as the party of economic competence, and thereby governing competence, had to be attributed to Brown as chancellor. Economic stability, and the avoidance of what Brown repeatedly derided as 'Conservative boom and bust' economic management methods, had meant that there was scope for investment in the public services, notably health and education (Heppell, 2008: 590).

However, despite such assertions, by the middle of the decade there was growing unease about the impact of Labour's economic strategy *vis-à-vis* social justice. Such criticisms emanated from some of the traditional Labour working-class voters, who felt disconnected and questioned whether Labour was improving their conditions. Here the insights of Coates are illuminating. Regarding the attempt to marry economic efficiency and social justice, Coates argued that there had been serious shortcomings in policy on poverty and inequality and that Labour policies worked less well than was claimed (Coates, 2008: 3–16). The Coates critique highlighted three limitations in terms of the traditional Labour vote base. First, although poverty did decline during the first two terms, it increased again during the third term. The 2004 figure of 12.1 million defined as beneath the unofficial poverty line started to increase up to 12.7 million. Moreover, within that, child poverty increased from 3.6 million to 3.8 million. Second, the strategy in terms of income differentials was questionable; the minimum wage was set at too low a level, and both Blair and Brown showed an unwillingness to curb high salaries. Third, the Coates verdict is that without Labour in office inequality might well have increased, but with them it stabilised at Thatcherite levels, although post-2005 the gap between rich and poor widened again (Coates, 2008: 13–14).

Scepticism was also emerging from among the middle classes who had transferred their allegiance to Labour in 1997. Fielding notes that, as government spending increased from 40.1 per cent of gross domestic product in 1997 to 44.1 per cent after a decade of Labour governance, so there was a discernable shift in electoral attitudes on the balance between taxation and spending (or investment) (Fielding, 2010: 658). By the time of Labour's third term, the electorate was increasingly moving towards favouring reductions in taxation over further increases in spending. Fielding concludes, therefore, that by its third term Labour was 'already losing the support of swing voters' and 'having made but a modest difference to the lives of most core supporters', the impending financial crisis would threaten to 'completely unravel the New Labour coalition' (Fielding, 2010: 658).

As the economic downturn unfolded, Brown was undermined by his rhetoric from the age of affluence. For example, as chancellor he had informed the 2002 Labour Party Annual Conference that:

> all past Labour governments were forced to retrench, cut back, and were overwhelmed by world conditions in 1924, 1931, 1951, 1967 and 1976 ... [but] it is because we painstakingly built the foundations

in economic management we are the first Labour government with the strength to be able to plan for the long term on the basis of stability not stop-go.

(Toye, 2009)

Brown was to be politically damaged by his previous rhetoric and his repeated exhortations about the dangers of re-electing the Tories due to their record of boom and bust (Fielding, 2010: 657). The bankruptcy of Northern Rock and the subsequent decision to nationalise in early 2008 was portrayed as an Old Labour nationalisation (Kavanagh and Cowley, 2010: 51). The subsequent decision to recapitalise parts of the banking sector did secure a degree of international recognition, although praise was not forthcoming from a sceptical electorate, who felt that Brown was 'bailing out the bankers' while the economy fell into recession (Kavanagh and Cowley, 2010: 23).

Labour was to be politically damaged by three other issues relating to the fall-out of the economic crisis: regulation of the finance sector; its contorted rhetoric in terms of cuts; and the tax issue. First, Labour had missed an opportunity to adequately regulate the finance sector of the economy, and in doing so it had failed to make 'a more socially democratic case for responsible capitalism' (Beech, 2009a: 9–10). In assessing how its management of the economy in 1997–2007 would have to be reassessed, Beech concluded that:

The extended period of economic growth under New Labour was in part built upon the housing bubble, high levels of personal indebtedness and a reliance on corporate tax receipts from the finance sector – especially those in the City of London where an active policy of minimal regulation was followed ... The most successful social democratic government of modern times has succumbed to the ways of British finance capitalism, and both had praised a sustained period of growth, profits and expansion but, as time would tell, the incessant desire for greater and greater profits and larger individual bonuses culminated in high lending practices and a general lack of oversight and fiscal rectitude.

(Beech, 2009b: 528)

As the economic position deteriorated, Brown remained reluctant to accept responsibility. He was keen to emphasise how the downturn was due to global financial failure, and expressly not due to his own handling of public finances (Seldon and Lodge, 2010: 253–4). The fiscal stimulus that he had deemed necessary, and the scale of the recession in terms of its impact on the public finances, had left a ballooning government deficit (Heffernan, 2011: 167). This created the second big political issue which Labour and Brown struggled to address: the issue of public spending cuts. Brown had framed party competition on economic matters during his time at the Treasury as being a choice between investment under Labour and cuts under the Conservatives (Rawnsley, 2010: 654). It was felt that the 'cuts versus spending' strategy was a central explanation for the three election victories in 1997, 2001 and 2005 (Kavanagh and Cowley, 2010: 64). Therefore, for emotional and strategic reasons, Brown was reluctant to enter into the vocabulary of cuts (Seldon and Lodge, 2010: 359–60). On this issue, Brown was in conflict with chancellor, Alistair Darling, and Business Secretary Lord Mandelson. The latter would later admit that the anti-cuts strategy that Brown wanted to retain 'created the impression we would simply keep on spending, borrowing and taking on debt' (Mandelson, 2010: 477).

During the course of the second part of 2009, Darling and Mandelson did manage to force Brown towards their position of framing the debate around *how* cuts should be made. Rather than spending versus cuts, Mandelson encouraged Brown towards a distinction between 'progressive state reformers versus ideological state retrenchers'. An unhappy Brown would attempt to interpret that distinction as 'nice Labour cuts versus nasty Tory cuts' (Seldon and Lodge, 2010: 360–2). On the electoral significance of the shift from spending versus cuts to nice or nasty cuts (i.e., speed and where), Seldon and Lodge concluded that the reticence of Brown on this issue limited the ability of the government to portray Labour as the party of progressive cuts as well as the party of investment (Seldon and Lodge, 2010: 372).

In addition to criticism of their light touch regulation of the financial sector and this difficulty in discussing cuts, Labour and Brown also had to face up to the taxation issue. As the full magnitude of the financial position that the government found itself in became apparent, so the debate on cuts had to run alongside tax increases. In November 2008, Darling announced that he would increase the top rate of income tax from 40p to 45p (from 2011), and later, in April 2009, stated that he would raise the top rate to 50p (Fielding, 2010: 657). After Labour had fought so hard to redefine the image of the party away from tax and spend, many erstwhile supporters openly condemned such reversals. As Fielding noted:

> The Murdoch press presented these measures as marking the end of New Labour. In November 2008, *The Sun* pictured a tombstone on its front page on which was carved 'RIP New Labour'. The accompanying story surveyed 'The life and death of Blair's baby' which had, it claimed, finally succumbed to 'socialism'.
>
> (Fielding, 2010: 657)

Interestingly, Brown initially appeared keen to distance himself from Blair and the era of New Labour. As the popularity of Blair had waned in the post-Iraq era, Brown had ensured that he retained a 'stranglehold' by emphasising that he was more 'authentically' Labour than Blair. This implied a distancing, not only from the departing leader and the rhetoric of New Labour, but also from the governing approaches of the Third Way (Theakston, 2011: 90). Therefore, as Brown sought to emphasise his moral compass and his status as a conviction politician, so many within the party assumed, indeed hoped for, a radical new narrative for the post-Blair era. Watt encapsulated the thinking within Labour about what it expected from Brown: 'he had been so desperate to become Prime Minister, and had plotted so meticulously and ruthlessly to get to No. 10...we all assumed that he knew what he was going to do when he got there'. Tragically, for Labour, Watt concluded that it soon emerged that there was 'no vision, no strategy, no grand plan...Gordon was simply making it up as he went along' (Watt, 2010: 7–8).

Ultimately, the Brown premiership would be characterised by policy confusion and the absence of a coherent agenda shaped by clearly defined and ideologically informed objectives. Initially, the policy direction seemed to be shaped by political calculation. For example, Brown felt that there was an electoral need to retain the support of the moderate centrist middle England voters who possessed socially conservative instincts. To appeal to this constituency of *Mail* and *Times* readers, Brown reversed the position of Blair on super casinos; the reclassification of cannabis; and 24-hour drinking laws. Brown also felt that there was a need to appeal to the more natural Labour territory of *Guardian* readers, so socially liberal moves were made on constitutional reform, with a commitment to establishing a 'new constitutional settlement' and the strengthening of parliament (Seldon and Lodge, 2010: 17). However, by the time of the 2007 Labour Party Annual Conference there was a sense that such measures were designed simply to differentiate Brown from Blair: that this was a 'political strategy, not a programme for government', and such rhetoric was 'symbolic'. Therein was the central problem, according to one advisor: 'having policy deliberately designed to contrast with Blair was enough to get us through the first weeks, but it was no agenda for the future' (Seldon and Lodge, 2010: 30).

To assess the Brown premiership in terms of policy direction requires a broader analysis than just the economic overview identified earlier in the chapter. Moving beyond the economic, it is best to examine the agenda in terms of some of the defining themes of the Blair era: constitutional reform; law and order; and education. Brown had entered Downing Street keen to push forward on constitutional reform, which would involve strengthening the power of the legislature *vis-à-vis* the executive, a desire to address concerns about the democratic deficit, and a longer-term aspiration for arguing the case for a written constitution (Seldon and Lodge, 2010: 17). However, Flinders accurately argues that, although Brown 'may have had the political inclination', he lacked 'the capacity to deliver far-reaching reform' (Flinders, 2010: 58). His proposals for electoral reform also fell by the wayside, although the commitment to the alternative vote model resurfaced by the time of the general election, perhaps in anticipation of appealing to the Liberal Democrats in the case of a hung parliament (Seldon and Lodge, 2010: 418).

Law and order had been a key component of the New Labour project. However, concerns about being associated with the Blair legacy meant that this was another policy area which lacked a clear agenda or any impetus under Brown. Therefore, the Respect agenda of the Blair years and the emphasis on attacking anti-social behaviour were downplayed, with resulting electoral implications, as Brown limited his 'appeal to the manual working-class' who were the 'main sufferers from lawlessness' (Seldon and Lodge, 2010: 423). As Labour sought re-election, crime figures were at their lowest level for nearly 30 years, but fear of crime was increasing 'almost out of control' (Kavanagh and Cowley, 2010: 33). Education was to be another pivotal policy arena of the Blair agenda that Brown struggled to develop effectively. Brown appointed to the rebranded Department of Children, Families and Schools Ed Balls, a known supporter, whose mindset appeared to be based on running the department in a non-Blairite way. As a consequence, the language of choice, diversity, academies and empowering parents, which had defined the thinking of Blair, was downplayed. As Seldon and Lodge note, however, this did not result in an alternative or coherent agenda emerging (Seldon and Lodge, 2010: 420).

Seldon and Lodge partly attribute this failure to construct a viable policy agenda and impart a sense of governmental direction on 'the seismic impact of the economic crisis of 2008 and the expenses scandal of 2009' (Seldon and Lodge, 2010: 426). However, they do suggest that Brown was overly influenced by 'what he was against' – that is, Blair – rather than 'what he was for' (Seldon and Lodge, 2010: 426). So what of his predecessor, the (co-) architect of New Labour? Blair commented that 'the fundamental problem' with Brown was that he 'simply did not understand the appeal of New Labour, in anything other than a polling strategy, election-winning sort of way. He could see that it worked, but not *why* it worked' (Blair, 2010a: 616). Of the three years between 2007 and 2010, Blair laments the 'watering down' of the academies programme; the 'downplaying' of crime and anti-social behaviour; and the fact that ID cards were 'scaled back' (Blair, 2010a: 680). He concludes that had we 'struck out to a new level of New Labour and not wandered down into a cul-de-sac of mixed messages and indecision, we would have been so much better placed for the economic crisis; and so far ahead of the Conservatives in thinking' (Blair, 2010a: 656). For the consequences of failing to do so, Blair attaches much of the blame to the limitations of Brown as a political leader:

> Why did Labour lose the 2010 election? The answer to that, I'm afraid is obvious. Labour won when it was New Labour. It lost because it stopped being New Labour... Had he [Brown] pursued New Labour policy, the personal issue would still have made victory tough, but it wouldn't have been impossible. Departing from New Labour made it so. Just as the 2005 election was one we were never going to lose, 2010 was one we were never going to win – once the fatal strategic decision was taken to abandon the New Labour position.
>
> (Blair, 2010a: 679)

Brown had entered the leadership and the premiership with high expectations. He had ten years of Cabinet service in which to acquire the necessary experience for the office of prime minister. The years of waiting to be prime minister should have ensured that he was well prepared and that he was in possession of a clear political programme to implement (Foley, 2009: 502; Allen, 2011: 67). Although the first three months of his prime ministerial tenure passed with positive media interpretations of his leadership and an increase in the opinion polls for Labour, thereafter he was undermined by a litany of 'self inflicted crises' compounded by 'poorly judged responses to them' (Kettell and Kerr, 2008: 492). The impact on Brown's reputation as he moved from the Treasury to Downing Street was best encapsulated by Vince Cable, when he noted Brown's 'remarkable transformation from Stalin to Mr Bean, creating chaos out of order, rather than order out of chaos' (Allen, 2011: 10). To assess the significance of Brown as prime minister to the removal of Labour from office, it is worth considering his leadership in terms of how he communicated the aforementioned political narrative; his political methods and decision-making processes; and whether he was an asset or a liability to the party when campaigning for re-election.

If Labour was undermined by the sense of the message being incoherent, then it also suffered from the limitations of Brown as the messenger. He was to suffer in three key comparative ways. First, there was the comparison with Blair (Radice, 2010: 209). Mandelson would later reveal that Blair had reservations about Brown in terms of his communication skills. Blair was of the view that Brown lacked political intuition, or 'what to do; when to do it; how to say it; and how to bring people with you' (Mandelson, 2010: 10). Second, the Conservative Party leader David Cameron was widely admired for his political communication skills, and Brown frequently struggled to compete against him, notably at Prime Minister's Questions (Jones, 2010: 107; Theakston, 2012: 195–7). Finally, during the televised leadership debates of the general election campaign of 2010, Brown was also to suffer in comparison to the Liberal Democrat leader, Nick Clegg. Opinion polling suggested that in each of the leadership debates he came last, scoring the following ratings as the best performer: 19 per cent in the first debate; 29 per cent in the second; and 25 per cent in the third and final debate (Fielding, 2010: 661).

The leadership debates highlighted his lack of natural skills as a public communicator, which was a huge limitation in terms of seeking to be a successful modern leader (Rawnsley, 2010: 525). Brown was aware of his perceived communicative limitations as he entered Downing Street, and Labour made various attempts to address this. Initially they proclaimed his lack of spin, as an antidote to the Blair era. Early on in his premiership he proclaimed that: 'I have never believed presentation should be the substitute for policy' (Price, 2010: 394). In rejecting the politics of celebrity and the over-emphasis on image, Labour tried to make a virtue of his limited communicative skills, by the 'not flash, just Gordon' poster campaign (Fielding, 2010: 655).

Brown may not have been flash, but was to become gaffe-prone. His public image was badly damaged by mistakes and persistent criticism about how uneasy he seemed for a public figure. In April 2009, he was openly mocked for 'adopting odd facial expressions and smiling awkwardly' to camera during a statement on MPs' expenses that had been uploaded onto YouTube (Jones, 2010: 206). He was humiliated during Prime Minister's Questions in December 2008 due to a slip of the tongue. When discussing his involvement in saving the world's banking system, he accidentally claimed that 'we not only saved the world' (Seldon and Lodge, 2010: 210). However, the ultimate Brown gaffe occurred within the general election campaign itself. After an exchange with Gillian Duffy, an elderly and traditional Labour supporter from the marginal constituency of Rochdale, Brown got into his ministerial car, unaware that his live microphone remained on. Irritated by the fact that Mrs Duffy had asked him questions about immigration, Brown was heard to describe her as 'a sort of bigoted woman'. To compound the mistake, Brown was filmed during a BBC Radio Two interview with his head in his hands as the tape was played back to him (Fielding, 2010: 662).

Sympathy within the party towards Brown for his presentational limitations was limited due to his political methods. The long years waiting for Blair to step down, and his fear of an alternative to himself emerging as a possible successor, had contributed to his use of 'faction boss methods' and his 'mastery of machine politics'. His tendency towards 'petty infighting' and 'narrow calculation' had contributed to a tactical and short-term political mindset which would culminate in allegations of bullying (Price, 2010: 240; Rawnsley, 2010: 510).

However, while such events did much to hurt his reputation, many would come to believe the cancelled general election of the late summer of 2007 would fatally shape perceptions of him (Foley, 2009: 500). Speculation mounted that Brown would call a snap general election to establish his own mandate to lead and step out of the shadow of Blair. Brown and his advisors allowed speculation to mount, as they hoped that the immediacy of a rumoured general election, when Labour was leading in the opinion polls, would destabilise Cameron (Richards, 2010: 290–2). However, when the Conservatives announced their new policy on inheritance tax, the seven-point Labour lead was wiped out inside a matter of days and a small Conservative lead was established (Cole, 2008: 34). Having dithered about whether to dissolve parliament when the political circumstances were to his advantage, Brown had to withstand the charge that he was indecisive. What was to really damage his political credibility was that, having decided not to hold a snap general election, he denied that his decision was influenced by the changes in the opinion polls over the previous week (Riddell, 2008: 10).

Many in the Parliamentary Labour Party and political journalists began to indentify a correlation between the 'loss of governing competence resulting from policy failure' and the 'capabilities' of Brown as prime minister (Kettell and Kerr, 2008: 492). Within a year of his becoming prime minister, there was a degree of media speculation on whether he could survive through until the general election (Coates, 2009: 423). By the summer of 2008 Labour had entered into a vicious circle: the Brown administration would be undermined by an event which led to a questioning of its competence; the PLP would be rumoured to be mobilising an attempt to unseat him; and then it would hit the brick wall of the procedures which make it so difficult to unseat the incumbent. To succeed him an alternative leader had to challenge him directly, without first using a stalking horse candidate to wound the existing leader. In order to challenge Brown, the support of 20 per cent of the PLP would be needed, which is a remarkably high threshold to participate. Moreover, even if this could be passed, if Brown refused to step down then a challenge would only activate the Electoral College, which takes months to complete. Various plots failed because they did not, or could not, engage with the procedures for leadership challengers as they existed, and were trying to circumnavigate procedures that aided the leader and undermined challengers (Heppell, 2010: 185–92; Quinn, 2012: 86–94).

That the PLP so openly questioned the leadership abilities of Brown demonstrated that Brown was a liability to its re-election chances (Dorey, 2010: 429). Conservative strategists would ruthlessly exploit his leadership limitations and make Brown a central plank of their negative campaigning. Personalising Labour around the unpopularity of Brown informed the Conservative poster campaigning approach during the general election campaign. Their line of attack was to imply that a vote for Labour was a vote for another five years with Brown as prime minister. To frame such a question in negative terms, a series of posters were placed picturing Brown alone with statements on his 'achievements' and an appeal to support him: 'I've doubled youth unemployment. Vote for me' or 'I let 80,000 criminals out early. Vote for me' or 'I doubled the tax rate for the poor. Vote for me' (Dorey, 2010: 411).

Party failure: Disunity, organisational chaos and depleted finance

For New Labour strategists, the predilection for internal debate and dissent that characterised Old Labour was the antithesis of what was required of a successful party of government. For Blair, the desire for unity was virtually all-consuming. Shortly before securing power, he reminded the party of the implications of its past behaviour – 'ill discipline allowed us to be painted as extremist, out of touch and divided' – and promised that under a New Labour government there would be 'no return to the factionalism, navel gazing or feuding of the seventies and eighties' (Cowley and Stuart, 2003: 327). In governing terms, Blair was referring to the 1974–79 Labour administrations, during which the scale and frequency of rebellion hit 21 per cent, which was a significant increase on the single-figure rebellion rates that had characterised governing parties in the 1940s, 1950s and 1960s (Cowley and Stuart, 2010: 1). Blair did manage to secure parliamentary cohesion initially. The 1997 PLP developed a reputation for acquiescence, as the number of parliamentary rebellions was the lowest since the 1950s. While this could be seen as evidence of the effectiveness of Blair at party management, some questioned the excessive loyalty of backbenchers, who were accused of being 'timid, acquiescent, gutless, sycophantic, cowardly and lacking in backbone' (Cowley and Stuart, 2003: 318).

However, that level of internal cohesion was not sustainable for a variety of reasons. Longevity in office was a factor. Upon entering government many aspiring parliamentarians were tempted towards loyalty in the hope of ministerial office. When, two terms in, the call from Downing Street had still not come, many were tempted into rebellion as they realised that there would be no reward for loyalty. Alongside those 'never possessed' came another grouping with an increased propensity towards rebellion in multi-term administrations – the 'dispossessed' former ministers, some of whom wanted to exact revenge upon Blair for ending their ministerial careers (Seldon and Lodge, 2010: 257). As Cowley and Stuart have painstakingly outlined, there was a significant increase in the level of rebellions in the second Blair term, with that low figure of 8 per cent increasing to 21 per cent – ironically, the same figure that the Wilson/Callaghan governments suffered in the 1974–79 period (Cowley and Stuart, 2010). As the rate of rebellions increased in the second term, Brown apparently feared 'inheriting a party in which discipline has entirely collapsed' (Rawnsley, 2010: 342).

Those fears were to be realised. Discipline within the PLP became a constant problem for Brown (Seldon and Lodge, 2010: 257). His ability to effectively deal with such PLP tensions placed a considerable burden on the liaison and disciplinary functions of the Whips' Office. However, between 2007 and 2010 the Whips' Office became widely viewed as 'dysfunctional' and was unable to stem the tide of rebelliousness, meaning that at times Labour's majority was 'paper thin on contentious issues' (Seldon and Lodge, 2010: 107). This was a problem that was compounded by a high number of retiring parliamentarians and a growth in abstentions and absentees. In an environment that placed a considerable emphasis on persuasion to bring potential dissenters around, the Whips' Office was not helped by the 'graceless management' techniques of the prime minister, which were to 'exacerbate an already difficult position' (Seldon and Lodge, 2010: 257). As a consequence, the 2005–10 parliament would experience the highest level of parliamentary dissent of any governing party (at 28 per cent) in the post-war era (Cowley and Stuart, 2010). What is particularly noteworthy is that many of the most high-profile rebellions were self-inflicted by Brown's poor prime ministerial decision-making. Three illustrations spring to mind.

The first humiliating and divisive issue that would undermine the Brown administration was what became defined as the '10p fiasco'. Electoral calculation and political posturing seemed to be evident in the last budget that Brown delivered as chancellor in 2007 (Rawnsley, 2010: 439–40). Here Brown had cut the basic rate of income tax from 22p to 20p, while also abolishing the 10p rate at which earners start to pay tax. Such earners would now start paying at 20p. Cutting from 22p to 20p would ensure that Brown would go down in history as a tax-reforming chancellor (Seldon and Lodge, 2010: 93). The measures would not come into force until April 2008, by which time the social impact of the measure, within the context of the recession, was becoming apparent to Labour parliamentarians. Armed with a Treasury Select Committee report which argued that over 5 million low earners would be made worse off, a major party rebellion against the measure gathered momentum. The authority of Brown and Darling was further damaged when they backed down, issuing a compensation package in a mini-budget presented in May 2008 (Fielding, 2010: 656). The second humiliating, divisive and self-inflicted divide that was created was over the issue of detention without trial for terrorist suspects. Here Brown wanted an increase from 28 to 42 days to show that he was 'tough on terrorism' (Seldon and Lodge, 2010: 106). The parliamentary division was scheduled for June 2008, at a time when the PLP was increasingly rebellious, and many who were unhappy with Brown were arguing that the vote should be used as a referendum on his prime ministerial leadership – that is, defeat might be a method of securing his removal (Seldon and Lodge, 2010: 109). Chris Mullin would reveal how Brown was seeing individual Labour MPs to persuade them of the need to back the government, with 'extraordinary tales of inducements' being offered (Mullin, 2011: 249). Although the intelligence of the Whips' Office led the party to expect defeat, it secured a narrow parliamentary majority due to the support of Democratic Unionist parliamentarians, although the press focused on the 36 Labour parliamentarians who rebelled. Ultimately this was to be a Pyrrhic victory, as the motion was defeated in the House of Lords and the 28-day limit was retained (Seldon and Lodge, 2010: 109). The third humiliation did result in a parliamentary defeat when 27 Labour parliamentarians supported a Liberal Democrat Opposition Day motion on improved settlement rights for Gurkha veterans. Mullin would record that defeat was due to a 'cock-up' in the Whips' Office, which failed to realise the number of rebels (Mullin, 2011: 325).

The focus on parliamentary rebellions demonstrates the existence of backbench discontent, but unless ministers are willing to resign it does not fully capture the nature and scale of divisions within ministerial ranks. For the duration of the Brown premiership political commentators were frequently discussing the lack of confidence within the Cabinet between the prime minister and his ministers. It was widely recognised that key Cabinet elites such as Harriet Harman, Jack Straw, David Miliband, Alan Johnson, Bob Ainsworth, Hazel Blears and John Hutton had doubts about Brown's prime ministerial abilities (Seldon and Lodge, 2010: 489–91). It was equally well known that Brown had lost confidence in Darling as chancellor and that he wanted to shift him to the Foreign or Home Office in the 2009 reshuffle (Mandelson, 2010: 463). However, the refusal of Darling to accept any other Cabinet position other than chancellor, and David Miliband briefing that he did not want to be moved from the Foreign Office, made for an unedifying spectacle. Brown was so politically weak that his Cabinet colleagues seemed to be dictating to him, rather than accepting the traditional prime ministerial authority to allocate portfolios (Seldon and Lodge, 2010: 280). The Cabinet was also split on electoral strategy; on the language of investment versus cuts (as discussed earlier); and on whether to prioritise equality, fairness and the vulnerable (as advocated by Harman) or focus on the middle income earners, as argued by John Denham (Fielding, 2010: 658). Even in the aftermath of the general election, the Cabinet was divided between those seeking to advance coalition talks with the Liberal Democrats and those (notably Andy Burnham and Jack Straw) who argued that Labour should accept that it had lost (Seldon and Lodge, 2010: 455).

Divided at both backbench and frontbench level, Labour was also undermined by a gradual decline in its organisational effectiveness and its finances. The infrastructure to mount an effective re-election campaign was lacking. Being in government, and for so long, had meant that many of its most talented and able staff had been drawn into government positions. Kavanagh and Cowley note that its ability to attract high-quality staff was undermined by resource constraints and the fact that retaining power 'seemed a doomed enterprise' (Kavanagh and Cowley, 2010: 61).

The symbolic evidence of a party in retreat was provided by its membership numbers. When New Labour entered office on a wave of optimism membership was at 400,000, but by the time Brown replaced Blair that figure had fallen to 176,000 (2007), and it would fall to 160,000 by late 2009 (Pugh, 2010: 412). Reduced membership, of course, carried with it financial implications. Prior to Brown assuming the leadership, the National Executive Committee had attempted to address the financial meltdown facing the party. In 2006 it had budgeted for an income of £4 million in donations but had raised only £700,000. Mullin noted, in the aftermath of the cash for honours crisis, that 'with the police knocking on the door, no one is willing to help' (Mullin, 2011: 115). He would then muse upon the organisational and financial legacy of the Blair era, with a deficit of £14.5 million and membership halved. Bankruptcy became a serious concern in the 2005–07 period, as acknowledged by the then general secretary, Peter Watt (Watt, 2010: 89–103). His successor, Ray Collins, would admit to Mullin that the situation remained 'precarious' thereafter (Mullin, 2011: 115, 128, 299).

These membership and financial pressures had been seen to be one of the contributing factors to the cash for honours crisis that had so embarrassed Blair. The origins of that crisis could be traced to the financing of the 2005 general election campaign. Andrew Rawnsley noted that, leading up to the campaign, Blair had been in a 'state of panic' about Labour's limited financial base (Rawnsley, 2010: 357). The party would later be found to have raised £14 million in loans, not donations, from a dozen millionaires, some of whom were subsequently nominated for elevation to the House of Lords. This would lead to a criminal investigation, including the questioning of Blair himself, although ultimately no formal charges were brought (Watt, 2010: 37–68). There was a hope and an expectation that the transition from Blair to Brown would bring to an end the damaging political fall-out surrounding cash for honours. However, just like his predecessor, Brown would be forced to explain alleged financial wrongdoing. It was alleged that £630,000 had been provided to Labour through intermediaries, which contravened the principles of transparency that were deemed to be central to the guidelines on party funding. Just as with cash for honours, a police investigation would follow, and once again would result in no convictions. However, as before, it carried with it huge political fall-out. Brown dismissed Watt as general secretary in an attempt to distance himself from the scandal (Rawnsley, 2010: 519). The scandal would have significant implications for Labour in terms of its financial planning for the 2010 general election campaign. Brown would become 'hypersensitive' on the issue of donations, to such an extent that it 'became difficult to attract money as the Prime Minister was reluctant to make himself available to potential donors or to entertain them at Downing Street' (Rawnsley, 2010: 518).

Therefore, it was a 'cash-strapped' party that entered the 2010 general election campaign (Seldon and Lodge, 2010: 444). In this context, it is worth reflecting upon the importance of party finance to the debate about whether to hold a general election in the autumn of 2007. Although the opinion polling feedback was the primary consideration for Brown, he would also have been aware of the view of Watt, who noted, on the question of 'electoral capability', that the 'longer Labour went without calling an election the greater the gulf in spending with the Tories' (Seldon and Lodge, 2010: 35). This view was shared by Home Secretary Jacqui Smith (2007–09), who was defending a marginal seat and would be targeted by the Conservatives through what Labour disparagingly referred to as the 'Ashcroft' money (Rawnsley, 2010: 499). The substantial amount of money provided by Michael Ashcroft, the Conservative Peer, was later seen to reflect the considerably greater 'financial muscle of the Conservatives, who used this to send personalised copies of their manifesto to 3 million voters in marginal seats', which resulted in the defeat of Smith and many other marginal Labour seats (Seldon and Lodge, 2010: 446). One of the criticisms that can be levelled at Brown is the damage that was inflicted upon limited party resources by the election that never was. Operating on the assumption that Brown would dissolve parliament, 5 million leaflets at a cost of £1 million were printed for marginal constituencies; billboard sites for advertising were booked at a similar cost; and additional staff were employed at Labour Party Headquarters in anticipation of the campaign (Rawnsley, 2010: 506; Richards, 2010: 295). A party with limited organisational and financial capacity could ill afford to waste scarce resources, especially if the external environment was working against them (Watt, 2010: 171–5).

Time for change: A hostile climate and a resurgent Conservative Party

One of the most significant changes that the architects of New Labour had achieved in the 1994–97 period was securing the backing of the majority of the British press. Six out of ten backed Labour, most memorably *The Sun*, whose conversion after its aggressive anti-Labour propaganda in 1992 was electorally advantageous to Labour, even if many party activists felt uncomfortable about it (Scammell and Harrop, 1997: 158–60). By the time of the 2010 general election, Labour had lost the support of all but *The Mirror*. *The Sun* returned to the Conservatives, while *The Guardian* endorsed the Liberal Democrats (Scammell and Beckett, 2010: 280–3). Overall, the Conservatives commanded 74 per cent support from the total daily circulation of papers, and, while this did not convert into a parliamentary majority overall, we should note that the swing from Labour to Conservative among *Sun* readers was 13.5 per cent, as compared with the national 5 per cent swing (Wring and Deacon, 2010: 451). *The Sun* may not have 'won it' as it claimed in 1992, or 'swung it' as in 1997, but Cameron 'had cause to be grateful to Rupert Murdoch's support' (Scammell and Beckett, 2010: 284).

However, rather than arguing that the climate was working against Labour because the press had switched its allegiance back to the Conservatives, it would be easier to say that the climate was moving against the political class. Whilst sleaze and corruption had engulfed British politics on many occasions before – most notably at the tail end of the last Conservative administration – the expenses scandal of early 2009 led Alexandra Kelso to comment that the 'collapse in public trust in politicians [was] so comprehensive that the entire basis of parliamentary democracy might well be in jeopardy' (Kelso, 2009: 453–4). Public dissatisfaction levels with the political system increased from a 2001 level of 30 per cent to 63 per cent in the aftermath of the scandal (Flinders, 2010: 61).

The expenses scandal hurt all of the main political parties, although commentators judged that Cameron managed this process more effectively than Brown (Rawnsley, 2010: 648). While Cameron was focused on apologising to the electorate for the wrongdoing of Conservative parliamentarians, and ensuring that those exposed paid back dubious claims, Brown was slower to respond and thus lost the initiative in the 'all important battle to influence the news agenda' (Jones, 2010: 204). Part of the problem for Brown was the reaction of his own parliamentarians. Earlier Brown had given his support for full disclosure, and, as such, many of his own backbenchers felt he was partly responsible for the furore. Moreover, as Seldon and Lodge note of the PLP:

It wanted Brown to protect its members against the baying press and public, not hang them out to dry. Most of them continued to argue that they had acted within the rules...and that this was a political plot against Labour by the right wing press...Brown was caught between a rock and a hard place, and ended up failing to be tough enough to placate public outrage, but too tough for the parliamentary Labour Party.

(Seldon and Lodge, 2010: 266)

Seeking a fourth term after the impact of the economic crisis and the expenses scandal meant that Labour had to find a response to the rallying call for change (Radice, 2010: 233). In one of his limited contributions to the re-election campaign, Blair informed the electorate that:

The tough thing about being in government, especially as time marches on, is that disappointments accumulate; the public become less inclined to give you the benefit of the doubt; the call for a time for a change becomes *easier* to make, and the prospect of change becomes more attractive.

(Blair, 2010b)

Blair dismissed change as a vacuous slogan. He asked the electorate to think about the obvious question – change to what? (Blair, 2010b). If Blair thought change was a vacuous slogan, it was not just the Conservatives whom he was criticising. He was also implicitly criticising Brown. Despite having been chancellor for a decade, Brown entered Downing Street with a bold attempt to present himself as the agent of change. This was a strategy fraught with risk, given the opinion polling evidence provided by Deborah Mattinson of Opinion Leader Research. Her 2007 focus group work had informed Brown that 'change' was the 'most popular word', which made the Brown pitch seem logical (Rawnsley, 2010: 459). However, while her findings did identify that the electorate regarded Brown as different from Blair, the feedback was not necessarily helpful to the cause of New Labour. It suggested that Brown was less well equipped to sustain that fragile New Labour electoral coalition. In addition to viewing Brown as 'bullying' and 'scheming', they 'felt that he was to the left of Blair and themselves' and that they were 'concerned' that he was 'Old' Labour (Rawnsley, 2010: 461). A year later, further focus group findings by Mattinson informed Brown that the Conservatives retained underlying vulnerabilities and that they had 'not yet closed the deal', and thus it was 'still possible for Labour to win' (Rawnsley, 2010: 568). Any optimism that this message may have carried came with continued electoral 'craving' for 'change' and the sense that Brown 'could not bring this about', as he was 'associated with the past' (Mattinson, 2010: 174).

As the General Election drew closer, further private polling data were presented to the Cabinet by famed New Labour strategist, Philip Gould. They reaffirmed the central message of the Mattinson findings. Gould could not mask the negativity that surrounded them:

> The central driver of the electoral dynamic is hostility to Labour and its leadership. This hostility blocks any appreciation of Labour's record and protects the Tories from proper scrutiny. Appreciation of Labour's achievements is negligible.
>
> (Kavanagh and Cowley, 2010: 64)

However, Gould outlined areas where private polling showed that the Conservatives were weak: the public do not believe that the Tories have changed; they are not sure what the Tories stand for; they do not fully trust the Tories on their values; and the Tories still put the better off first (Kavanagh and Cowley, 2010: 64). As Green concludes, 'by the time of the 2010 campaign many voters wanted change, but could not yet put their faith in a government run by the Conservatives' (Green, 2010: 668).

The era of opposition for the Cameron-led Conservatives was characterised by three stages: first, 2005–07 in a benign economic environment against a paralysed and departing Blair, when they converged with Labour on economic management; second, between late 2007 and late 2008, when they restricted themselves to critiquing Labour on the economy; and from late 2008 onwards, when a clear divergence emerged. That it was a period of convergence, critique and divergence indicates the turbulent political times and the reactive nature of Conservative thinking (Lee, 2009a: 45–6; 2009b: 63–77).

In the first period, the Conservatives had made a clear assumption. As the economy had been growing for more than a decade and Labour was being endorsed for its economic competence, there was no political capital to be gained by challenging Labour on its economic record (Lee, 2009b: 58). That being the case, the focus should not be economic, but social, with the implication being that Labour had presided over social decline (Lee, 2009a: 45). Through the focus on the social, it was clear that Cameron was seeking to 'reach out' beyond his core constituency and 'establish credibility on issues long considered the territory of opponents' (McAnulla, 2010: 295). To 'secure permission to be heard' on such matters (Bale, 2010), Cameron set about decontaminating 'the brand', which he did by utilising a number of themes such as 'compassionate conservatism', 'progressive ends-conservative means' and 'social responsibility' in order to negate the Conservatives' image as the 'nasty' party (Seawright, 2010: 173; 2012: 38). For example, their 2006 revamped statement, entitled *Built to Last*, identified the key principles that would inform Conservative policy development as eliminating poverty through raising quality of life for all; fighting social injustice; tackling environmental threats; improving the quality of public services; bolstering internal security; human rights; and enabling communities (Kerr, 2007: 50–1). Ensuing rhetoric on the environment; feminisation; championing the National Health Service; supporting state schools; attacking 'fat cat' salaries; and defending professional autonomy in the public sector constituted 'reach out' rhetoric that was designed to symbolise how the Conservatives were dissociating themselves from the age of Thatcher and the ideology of Thatcherism (Lee, 2009a, 2009b). Through such modernising strategies the decade and a quarter of flatlining in the opinion polls ended. When all opinion polls since the election of Cameron to the Conservative Party leadership from December 2005 to June 2007 were aggregated, the projected Conservative share of the vote had stabilised above 35 per cent and had regularly approached 40 per cent. By the time Brown was selected to replace Blair, pollsters were indicating the projected Conservative share was 40 per cent, and that they possessed a lead over Labour which stretched into double figures (Bale, 2010: 329). Such leads indicated that the Conservatives could secure victory at the next general election, and that they could secure an overall majority, albeit a relatively small one (Kerr, 2007: 47).

The second period of opposition – late 2007 up to late 2008 – would see that convergence replaced with a strong Conservative critique. Part of the Conservative strategy had been about competing with Labour on public expenditure, to negate the investment versus cuts strategy that had propelled Blair through three successful election campaigns. Cameron had pledged to increase public expenditure, especially on health and education, to break the association with Thatcherism, and to demonstrate that the Conservatives were genuine in their desire to 'tackle social fragmentation and inequality' and thereby mend what they defined as 'broken Britain' (Dorey, 2009: 260). However, such 'comfortable narratives' appear to 'assume, indeed necessitate' continued economic growth (Dorey, 2009: 261). The subsequent response of the Conservatives to the ensuing economic crisis was not entirely convincing. Indeed, McAnulla goes as far as to suggest that it was 'almost as embarrassing for the Conservatives as it was for the Labour government' (McAnulla, 2010: 291). It was embarrassing for them, as the financial services sector had been deregulated in the era of Thatcherism. Lee concludes that, as such, the Conservatives could only escape culpability through an 'extraordinary act of political and historical amnesia' (Lee, 2009b: 74). This left the Conservatives with a critique built around attacking Labour for 'allowing' the crisis to happen. The language was explicit – the Brown government was accused of a 'borrowing binge' and 'maxing out our nation's credit card' (Lee, 2009b: 68–71).

The third period would see the Conservatives clearly abandon their strategy of matching the spending commitments of Labour (Lee, 2009a: 46). By 2009 the rhetoric had shifted to cuts in the age of austerity (Lee, 2009b: 77). Ultimately, the turbulence of the 2007–09 period de-stabilised the pre-determined strategy that Cameron and the modernisers had carefully crafted in the 2005–07 period. The consequence was that policy development became opportunistic as they sought to exploit the failures of the Brown government. That shift from convergence to critique to divergence appeared to be reactive, rather than proactive, and suggested the absence of a coherent political vision (Lee, 2009a: 59). This may well explain why 'there was not a simple translation of concerns' from Labour and the economic downturn 'towards trust in a Conservative government to solve [such] economic problems' (Green, 2010: 680). As Dorey notes:

> although the vast majority of voters accepted the necessity and inevitability of significant cuts in public expenditure after the General Election, there was considerable concern about the severity or speed of the cuts that might be imposed by a Conservative government, which Labour naturally sought to exploit by warning of the danger of a 'double dip' recession being caused by the Conservatives choking Britain's tentative, fragile, economic recovery.
>
> (Dorey, 2010: 414)

Given the severity of the recession, it would have been understandable for the Conservatives as the opposition party to have secured an opinion poll lead. While the Conservatives did possess an opinion poll lead on the question of comparative economic competence, it was a marginal lead, which narrowed as the general election drew closer (Dorey, 2010: 413; Green, 2010: 412). That there were limits to the appeal of the modernised Conservative Party was further evident when considering the comparative appeal of the parties on the most salient electoral issues: National Health Service (Labour lead 33–24); unemployment (Labour lead 30–24); education (Conservative lead 29–28); immigration (Conservative lead 28–17); the economy (Conservative lead 29–26); and taxation (Conservative lead 26–25) (Dorey, 2010: 412).

Narrow leads on four of the six most salient electoral variables reflected the limitations of the Conservative campaign and the failure of their supposedly unifying narrative – 'the Big Society'. It was meant to provide coherence to their agenda of decentralisation and involvement of the voluntary sector in addressing the problems of 'broken Britain' (Green, 2010: 683). However, as an election slogan 'Big Society, not Big Government' did not connect with voters and completely failed to symbolise the 'national mood'. It did not resonate with voters, and even Conservative activists and parliamentarians 'on the stump found it to be "woolly" and "lacking in clarity" (Seawright, 2012: 39). The quiet distancing from the 'Big Society' theme as the campaign developed indicated the limits of the strategic recovery that Cameron and the modernisers had tried to stimulate. As a long-serving government seeking re-election, Labour was not in the same position as the Conservatives had been in 1997, when opposed by New Labour. The extent to which 'change' had occurred within the Cameron Conservatives was not as advanced as had been the case under Blair and New Labour. According to Bale, the renewal of New Labour involved a 'reengineering' of the party, based on a changed policy/ideological outlook and political approach. Identifying the notion of a 'Clause IV' moment, which has been lacking under Cameron, Bale suggests that change within the Conservative Party has been less pronounced in both policy and political/ideological terms. Where New Labour was a 'reengineered' party, Cameron has merely 'restyled' the Conservatives (Bale, 2010).

The comparison between 1997 and 2010 is intriguing. New Labour had been swept to power on the back of a discredited prime minister (John Major); a governing party whose reputation for economic competence had been destroyed (by Black Wednesday in September 1992); and an avalanche of sleaze. Those same factors were at play by the tail end of the Brown administration, but 2010 was not 1997 in reverse, as, while Labour lost, it 'did not see its parliamentary representation decimated to the same extent as the Conservatives thirteen years before' (Johnston and Pattie, 2011: 204). Labour secured a considerably higher level of parliamentary representation (at 258) than the Conservatives had in 1997 (at 165) despite securing a lower percentage vote share (29 per cent for Labour in 2010 as compared with 31 per cent for the Conservatives in 1997) (Table 7.1).

Table 7.1   The general election of 2010

Party	Votes won	MPs elected	Share of vote (%)
Conservative	10,726,555 (2005: 8,772,473) (2001: 8,357,622) (1997: 9,602,857)	307 (2005: 198) (2001: 166) (1997: 165)	36.1 (2005: 32.4) (2001: 31.7) (1997: 30.7)
Labour	8,606,518 (2005: 9,547,944) (2001: 10,724,895) (1997: 13,516,632)	258 (2005: 356) (2001: 412) (1997: 418)	29.0 (2005: 35.2) (2001: 40.7) (1997: 43.2)
Liberal	6,836,518 (2005: 5,981,874) (2001: 4,812,833) (1997: 5,242,894)	57 (2005: 62) (2001: 52) (1997: 46)	23.0 (2005: 22.0) (2001: 18.3) (1997: 16.8)
Others	3,518,148 (2005: 2,801,972) (2001: 2,473,448) (1997: 2,924,214)	28 (2005: 30) (2001: 29) (1997: 30)	11.9 (2005: 10.4) (2001: 9.3) (1997: 9.3)

Note: Figures for 1997, 2001 and 2005 in brackets.
Source: Kavanagh and Cowley, 2010: 350–1.

Although the Labour vote share went down by 6.4 per cent overall across all constituencies, much of this decline was in constituencies where it had already been defeated at the polls in 2005. It recorded double-digit declines in many of these constituencies held by other parties. The level of decline was lower than the overall figure of 6.4 per cent in the constituencies that it was defending (Johnston and Pattie, 2011: 226). While this still resulted in the loss of 91 constituencies – the Conservatives gained 53 seats where Labour was defending a constituency with a gap between 4 and 15 points, but the Conservatives failed to gain a further 26 that fell into this category (Johnston and Pattie, 2011: 235) – in regional terms Labour increased its vote share in Scotland (42 per cent being a 2 per cent increase from 2005) and its decline in London was only 2 per cent, at 37 per cent to the Conservatives at 35 per cent. While the vote share declined in the North East (down by 9 per cent) and North West (down by 6 per cent), these were regions in which Labour retained a lead over the Conservatives – 20 per cent in the North East, and 7 per cent in the North West. Leads were retained in Wales and also in Yorkshire and the Humber, but elsewhere the Labour vote was badly eroded, and it performed especially poorly in the South West and South East of England, with 15 per cent and 16 per cent shares respectively, meaning it picked up only eight of the 136 seats contested (Worcester et al., 2011: 278–80).

Ultimately, however, a positive interpretation can be made with regard to the loss of office in 2010. That positive interpretation flows from the level of fear about the scale of defeat that existed in the 2008–09 period. Given this, many felt that Labour did better than they had expected (Hickson, 2011: 256). Defeat was thus not seen as an 'unmitigated disaster' for Labour; and, as Worcester et al. noted in 2011, there are few people asking 'can Labour ever win again' (Worcester et al., 2011: 275).

Conclusion

The aim of this chapter has been to analyse the decline and fall of the Labour government in its third term as the transition from Blair to Brown coincided with the politics of dominance giving way to the politics of degeneration. Having analysed the Brown era of governance between 2007 and 2010 against the criteria that have informed this historical comparative evaluation of how Labour governments fall, we can now consider the extent to which these variables were factors in their losing office.

The absence of a clear policy direction, alongside the negative image of Brown as party leader and prime minister, were clearly factors in the defeat of 2010, and these were tied to the erosion of Labour's lead on economic competence. Throughout his three-year tenure, with the exception of a brief honeymoon period before the election that never was, the Brown administration could never fully shake off an image of being accident-prone and directionless. Defining Brown as not Blair amounted to a short-term tactical position, rather than longer-term strategic vision. This was significant because, in the absence of a clear narrative, Brown suffered a loss of authority and respect within the Labour movement. The constant speculation on how to replace him undermined the party's electoral prospects. It is difficult to persuade the floating voter to endorse Labour when the leader has been exposed to such high-profile and prolonged criticism within his own party.

The doubts that many within Labour had about Brown, many of which had pre-dated his entry into Downing Street, were clearly justified. With modern elections placing such a premium on the charisma and likeability of the party leader, Labour placed itself at a disadvantage by being led by a politician with limited communication skills. Labour had two obvious choices, having ensured that Brown was elected unopposed in 2007. First, it could show remarkable self-discipline and loyalty and back him throughout, or, second, it could swiftly and brutally remove him once it had realised that he lacked an electorally appealing narrative and the personal charisma to sustain the New Labour electoral coalition. That first option was beyond the abilities of a PLP split by the decade-long feud between Blairites and Brownites. The second option was the desired option of many, but the time, financial and unity costs of challenging directly meant that the party leadership procedures protected Brown from a challenge. Instead, the PLP opted for a suicidal third option of telling the electorate how flawed and unelectable Brown was and then leaving him in post. Trapped by its inability to endorse Brown or to remove him, the PLP critically undermined the chances of the party securing a fourth term of office. It entered the campaign with the Brown problem unresolved: only 13 per cent of the electorate thought he was likeable as opposed to 40 per cent for Cameron. Even more worryingly for Labour, while 40 per cent thought that the Eton-educated Cameron was in touch with their concerns, only 21 per cent thought Brown was (Kavanagh and Cowley, 2010: 250).

Labour had tried to circumnavigate the leadership issue surrounding Brown by defining him as a politician of substance and policy as compared to the stylistics of Cameron (and indeed Blair). Such a strategy made competence the central claim around which the electorate should identify with Brown. The banking collapse and subsequent recession eroded the Labour claim to economic competence, and thus Brown's claim to leadership competence. The double-digit lead over the Conservatives that they had held in previous elections was removed. However, indicating the limits of Conservative recovery, Labour was only marginally behind in opinion polling data on the party best equipped to manage the economy. That benefit for Labour was offset by the existence of an 'overwhelming' desire within the electorate for change. That desire for change appears to be as much a reaction to a long period of one-party governance and a discredited leader as it was against the actual positions that Labour were seeking to promote. For example, as the general election began, over 35 per cent of the electorate agreed that 'Britain needed a fresh team of leaders', which implied a desire to reject Brown (Fielding, 2010: 659). However, demonstrating the contradictory nature of the electorate, only 30 per cent were supportive of the Conservative intention of immediate cuts, as opposed to the Labour position of securing the recovery before embarking on cuts, which was supported by approaching 60 per cent (Dorey, 2010: 415).

It was immensely difficult for Labour to adequately respond to the desire for change when it had been in office for 13 years. The ability to renew while in office was undermined by the fact that party elites who shaped and presented policy had become subsumed within governmental, and departmental, concerns. Longevity in office had made the 'time for a change' argument more relevant. This made it harder and harder for Labour to persuade the electorate that it was the only party with a policy platform which could address those enduring economic, social and political problems. In 2001, and to a lesser extent in 2005, blaming those enduring problems on the legacy of a four-term Conservative administration between 1979 and 1997 gave them some political space, and during that period of economic affluence the electorate was willing to give Labour the benefit of the doubt. After three terms, and in an age of austerity, the ability to deny culpability in 2010 did not really exist.

That lack of a clear policy direction, the negative image of Brown, and the desire for change compounded three limitations within the Labour Party. Here, we can argue that its public disunity was a factor that did contribute to its removal from office. Labour developed a reputation for disunity, just as the Conservatives began to rediscover the importance of public unity after a decade and a half arguing about the legacy of Thatcherism. While Labour in 2005–10 was the most rebellious parliamentary party of government in the post-war era, what probably resonated with the electorate more than backbench rebellion was the ongoing feuding between the supporters of Blair and Brown. Similarly, it can be argued that the organisation and financial difficulties that Labour experienced were factors that undermined its capacity to effectively contest a conventional general election campaign.

Effective leadership and a strong economy may well have been the trump cards for Labour under Blair, but those strengths were consolidated by the lack of a credible alternative. As Norton acknowledges, the Conservatives in 2001 and 2005 were simply not electable (Norton, 2009: 31–42). In 2010 the Conservatives had significantly improved their image and redefined their narrative. However, enduring reservations existed about the impact of their economic strategy and their values and ethics. In this sense, electoral hostility towards the political class in the aftermath of the parliamentary expenses scandal was significant. That is because Cameron could not 'politicise' the issue and use it against Labour in 2009–10, in the way that Blair had been able to in 1994–97 when sleaze and corruption engulfed the Major administration.

Ultimately, however, the most significant issue in the fall of Labour was the leadership of Brown. It is worth recalling that Labour only lost office because the dynamics in the aftermath of the result meant that Liberal Democrats were almost forced into negotiating with the Conservatives first. Had Labour been able to improve its vote share by only 2–3 per cent (up to 31–32) and perhaps increase its representation to around 280–300 seats, then, with the Conservatives pulled slightly lower, the nature of the post-election negotiations would have been different. Can we argue that with an alternative leader this could have been achieved? This is difficult to prove, but what we can confirm is the following. Opinion polling data showed that Cameron was a relatively popular leader and his ratings surpassed those of his party. Conversely, Brown was considerably more unpopular than Labour (Dorey, 2010: 419, 429). The problem for Cameron was the image of his party; the problem for Labour was the image of its leader.

References

Allen, N. (2011), 'Labour's Third Term: A Tale of Two Prime Ministers', in Allen, N. and Bartle, J. (eds), *Britain at the Polls 2010* (London: Sage).

Bale, T. (2010), *The Conservatives from Thatcher to Cameron* (Cambridge: Polity Press).

Beech, M. (2008), 'New Labour and the Politics of Dominance', in Beech, M. and Lee, S. (eds), *Ten Years of New Labour* (Basingstoke: Palgrave).

Beech, M. (2009a) 'A Puzzle of Ideas and Policy: Gordon Brown as Prime Minister', *Policy Studies*, Vol. 30, No. 1, 5–16.

Beech, M. (2009b), 'No New Vision: The Gradual Death of British Social Democracy', *Political Quarterly*, Vol. 80, No. 4, 526–32.

Bentley, T. (2007), 'British Politics after Tony Blair', *British Politics*, Vol. 2, No. 2, 111–17.

Blair, T. (2010a), *A Journey* (London: Hutchinson).

Blair, T. (2010b), 'Campaign Speech at Sedgefield', 30 March.

Coates, D. (2008), 'Darling, It is Entirely My Fault! Gordon Brown's Legacy to Alistair and Himself', *British Politics*, Vol. 3, No. 1, 3–21.

Coates, D. (2009), 'Chickens coming Home to Roost? New Labour at the Eleventh Hour, *British Politics*, Vol. 4, No. 1, 421–33.

Cole, M. (2008), 'The Brown Factor in Elections and Public Opinion: The Return of the Electoral Cycle', in Rush, M. and Giddings, P. (eds), *When Gordon Took the Helm: The Palgrave Review of British Politics 2007–2008* (Basingstoke: Palgrave).

Cowley, P. and Stuart, M. (2003), 'In Place of Strife? The PLP in Government, 1997–2001', *Political Studies*, Vol. 51, No. 2, 315–31.

Cowley, P. and Stuart, M. (2010), 'A Coalition with Wobbly Wings: Backbench Dissent since May 2010', www.revolts.co.uk (accessed 16 November 2010).

Dorey, P. (2009), 'Sharing the Proceeds of Growth: Conservative Economic Policy under David Cameron', *Political Quarterly*, Vol. 80, No. 2, 259–69.

Dorey, P. (2010), 'Faltering Before the Finishing Line: The Conservative Party's Performance in the 2010 General Election', *British Politics*, Vol. 5, No. 4, 402–35.

Fielding, S. (2010), 'Labour's Campaign: Things Can Only Get…Worse?', *Parliamentary Affairs*, Vol. 63, No. 4, 653–66.

Finlayson, A. (2002), 'Elements of the Blairite Image of Leadership', *Parliamentary Affairs*, Vol. 55, No. 3, 586–99.

Flinders, M. (2010), 'Bagehot Smiling: Gordon Brown's New Constitution and the Revolution that Did not Happen', *Political Quarterly*, Vol. 81, No. 1, 57–73.

Foley, M. (2009), 'Gordon Brown and the Role of Compounded Crisis in the Pathology of Leadership', *British Politics*, Vol. 4, No. 4, 498–513.

Gamble, A. (2006), 'British Politics after Blair', in Dunleavy, P., Heffernan, R., Cowley, P. and Hay, C. (eds), *Developments on British Politics 8* (Basingstoke: Palgrave).

Gamble, A. (2010), 'New Labour and Political Change', *Parliamentary Affairs*, Vol. 63, No. 4, 639–52.

Green, J. (2010), 'Strategic Recovery: The Conservatives under David Cameron', *Parliamentary Affairs*, Vol. 63, No. 4, 667–88.

Heffernan, R. (2011), 'Labour's New Labour Legacy: Politics after Blair and Brown', *Political Studies Review*, Vol. 9, No. 2, 163–77.

Heppell, T. (2008), 'The Degenerative Tendencies of Long Serving Governments', *Parliamentary Affairs*, Vol. 61, No. 4, 578–96.

Heppell, T. (2010) *Choosing the Labour Leader: Labour Party Leadership Elections from Wilson to Brown* (London: I. B. Tauris).

Hickson, K. (2011), 'The End of New Labour? The Future of the Labour Party', in Lee, S. and Beech, S. (eds), *The Cameron-Clegg Government: Coalition Politics in an Age of Austerity* (Basingstoke: Palgrave).

Johnston, R. and Pattie, C. (2011), 'The Local Campaigns and the Outcome', in Allen, N. and Bartle, J. (eds), *Britain at the Polls 2010* (London: Sage).

Jones, N. (2010), *Campaign 2010: The Making of the Prime Minister* (London: Biteback).

Kavanagh, D. and Cowley, P. (2010), *The British General Election of 2010* (Basingstoke: Palgrave).

Kelso, A. (2009), 'Parliament on its Knees: MPs Expenses and the Crisis of Transparency at Westminster', *Political Quarterly*, Vol. 80, No. 3, 329–38.

Kenny, M. (2009), 'Taking the Temperature of the Political Elite 4: Labour, Chronicle of a Defeat Foretold?', *Parliamentary Affairs*, Vol. 62, No. 4, 663–72.

Kerr, P. (2007), 'Cameron Chameleon and the Current State of Britain's Consensus', *Parliamentary Affairs*, Vol. 60, No. 1, 46–65.

Kettell, S. and Kerr, P. (2008), 'One Year On: The Decline and Fall of Gordon Brown', *British Politics*, Vol. 3, No. 4, 490–510.

King, A. (2006), 'Why Labour Won – Yet Again?', in Bartle, J. and King, A. (eds), *Britain at the Polls* (London: CQ Press).

Lee, S. (2008), 'The British Model of Political Economy', in Beech, M. and Lee, S. (eds), *Ten Years of New Labour* (Basingstoke: Palgrave).

Lee, S. (2009a), 'David Cameron and the Renewal of Policy', in Beech, M. and Lee, S. (eds), *Built to Last? The Conservatives under David Cameron* (Basingstoke: Palgrave).

Lee, S. (2009b), 'Convergence, Critique and Divergence: The Development of Economic Policy under David Cameron', in Beech, M. and Lee, S. (eds), *Built to Last? The Conservatives under David Cameron* (Basingstoke: Palgrave).

Mandelson, P. (2010), *The Third Man: Life at the Heart of New Labour* (London: HarperPress).

Mattinson, D. (2010), *Talking to a Brick Wall: How Labour Stopped Listening to the Voters and Why We Need a New Politics* (London: Biteback).

McAnulla, S. (2010), 'Heirs to Blair's Third Way: David Cameron's Triangulating Conservatism', *British Politics*, Vol. 5. No. 3, 286–314.

McAnulla, S. (2011), 'Post-Political Poisons? Evaluating the Toxic Dimensions of Tony Blair's Leadership', *Representation*, Vol. 47, No. 3, 251–64.

Mullin, C. (2011), *Decline and Fall: Diaries 2005–2010* (London: Profile Books).

Norton, P. (2009), 'David Cameron and Tory Success: Bystander or Architect?', in Beech, M. and Lee, S. (eds), *Built to Last? The Conservatives under David Cameron* (Basingstoke: Palgrave).

Price, L. (2010), *Where Power Lies: Prime Ministers and the Media* (London: Simon and Schuster).

Pugh, M. (2010), *Speak for Britain! A New History of the Labour Party* (London: The Bodley Head).

Quinn, T. (2012), *Electing and Ejecting Party Leaders in Britain* (Basingstoke: Palgrave).

Radice, G. (2010), *Trio: Inside the Blair, Brown, Mandelson Project* (London: I. B. Tauris).

Rawnsley, A. (2010), *The End of the Party: The Rise and Fall of New Labour* (London: Penguin).

Richards, S. (2010), *Whatever It Takes* (London: Fourth Estate).

Riddell, P. (2008), 'Brown's First Year', in Rush, M. and Giddings, P. (eds), *When Gordon took the Helm: The Palgrave Review of British Politics 2007–2008* (Basingstoke: Palgrave).

Scammell, M. and Beckett, C. (2010), 'Labour No More: The Press', in Kavanagh, D. and Cowley, P. (eds), *The British General Election of 2010* (Basingstoke: Palgrave).

Scammell, M. and Harrop, M. (1997), 'A Tabloid War', in Butler, D. and Kavanagh, D. (eds), *The British General Election of 1997* (Basingstoke: Macmillan).

Seawright, D. (2010), *The British Conservative Party and One Nation Politics* (New York: Continuum).

Seawright, D. (2012), 'The Conservative Election Campaign', in Heppell, T. and Seawright, D. (eds), *Cameron and the Conservatives: The Transition to Coalition Government* (Basingstoke: Palgrave).

Seldon, A. and Lodge, G. (2010), *Brown at 10* (London: Biteback).

Theakston, K. (2011), 'Gordon Brown as Prime Minister: Political Skills and Leadership Style', *British Politics*, Vol. 6, No. 1, 78–100.

Theakston, K. (2012), 'David Cameron as Prime Minister', in Heppell, T. and Seawright, D. (eds), *Cameron and the Conservatives: The Transition to Coalition Government* (Basingstoke: Palgrave).

Toye, R. (2009), 'Gordon Brown and the Credit Crunch in Historical Perspective', *History and Policy* (www.historyandpolicy.org/papers/policy-paper-83.html, accessed 27 November 2011).

Watt, P. (2010), *Inside Out: My Story of Betrayal and Cowardice at the Heart of New Labour* (London: Biteback).

Worcester, R., Mortimore, R., Baines, P. and Gill, M. (2011), *Explaining Cameron's Coalition: How it Came About* (London: Biteback).

Wring, D. and Deacon, D. (2010), 'Patterns of Press Partisanship in the 2010 General Election', *British Politics*, Vol. 5, No. 4, 436–54.

8
Conclusion

Timothy Heppell and Kevin Theakston

What common explanations can be identified across the falls of the Labour governments in 1924, 1931, 1951, 1970, 1979 and 2010? With the exception of the 1924 government, economic problems and crises provide a common thread through the history of Labour governments and a major negative factor in explaining their fall. The 1929–31 MacDonald government was unable to cope with the onset of the Great Depression, had no real answer to rapidly rising unemployment, and fell apart when the 1931 international financial crisis struck – the 'National' government that replaced it promptly abandoning the gold standard Labour had ineffectually tried to defend. The economic record of the 1945–51 government was in many ways creditable, as it increased industrial production, maintained full employment and boosted exports in the drive for economic recovery after the war. But a big political price was paid because of the way consumer spending was held down – provoking a backlash against 'austerity' that cost middle-class and female votes in suburban and south-eastern seats even while the party's working-class vote held solid – and with successive blows to the government's economic credibility (the 1947 fuel crisis, the devaluation of the pound in 1949, the budgetary effects of massive rearmament because of the Korean war in 1950–51). Wilson's 1964–70 government came in with ambitious plans for economic modernisation, but in practice had to battle with balance of payments crises, another devaluation of the pound, problems with inflation and unemployment, patchy economic growth, public spending cuts and poor industrial relations. The fact that many of the economic problems it faced were inherited, the result of external pressures and not (or not entirely) of its own making, and that there were some positive economic signs by 1970, was not enough to save it, however. The same story of economic crisis management and

171

failure applies to the 1974–79 government, again one whose economic inheritance when it came into office was dire. 'Stagflation', low growth, strikes and union problems, and the need to call in the IMF to arrange a large loan shredded Labour's chances of being able to pose as competent managers of the economy. Key to New Labour's successful re-election in 2001 and 2005 was its delivery of the economic goods and keeping its reputation for economic competence, and the lead over the Conservatives it had won on this indicator after 1992. In contrast to the story under previous Labour governments, 'New Labour did not make any dramatic mistakes. There was no currency crisis; no flight of capital; no balance of payments crisis; no recession; no failure to control either public spending or inflation' (Sanders et al., 2001: 801).

After 2007, of course, with the financial crisis and recession, concerns over Labour's management of the economy and its economic competence returned and ate away at its support (Allen, 2011: 5). The fact that New Labour's economic (and electoral) strategy was overwhelmed by the 2008 global economic crisis demonstrates the impact of what can best be described as external shocks. These external shocks intensify the gap that exists between the expectations of the electorate and what the governing party can realistically deliver. After all, New Labour had only been able to sustain their increases in public expenditure through the proceeds of economic growth. As the tax yield fell as the economy slipped into recession, the Brown government bailed out the banking sector and racked up unprecedented levels of debt, while trying to retain their commitment to investment in public services (Heffernan, 2011: 167). Such external shocks can manifest themselves in different forms. For example, the Attlee government saw its domestic social policy objectives undermined by the defence costs associated with the Korean War (Laybourn, 2000: 94–5). The Brown government was particularly unfortunate as, in addition to the external shock of the global financial crisis, it was also undermined by the parliamentary expenses scandal of 2009, which was to hit Labour, as the governing party, more profoundly than the Conservatives (Rawnsley, 2010: 648).

Labour governments have also been undermined by two types of external factors. First, when entering opposition in 1924, 1929, 1945, 1964 and 1974, the Conservative Party has demonstrated remarkable powers of recovery and has traditionally been able to initiate highly effective processes of change, whether of policy, organisation or personnel (Ball and Seldon, 2005). The parliamentary arithmetic and its vulnerability as a minority government was the dominant explanation for Labour's removal from office in 1924, and their impotence and divisions in the face of the economic crisis explain their fall in 1931. However, it is noteworthy that the Conservatives adopted an effective strategy when in opposition, ensuring that they were 'united, possessed an effective organisation [and] had attractive policies – moderate social measures in 1924, and tariffs after the economic crisis in 1931' (Ball, 2005: 162). The whole-scale processes of change that were initiated after the defeat of 1945 and the subsequent shift to centre ground and the emergence of New Conservatism served to blunt the Labour attacks that had worked so effectively in the 1945 general election (Evans and Taylor, 1996: 76). Similar processes of policy adaptation and strategic positioning occurred when Edward Heath and Margaret Thatcher acquired the Conservative Party leadership in 1965 and 1975, respectively (Denham and O'Hara, 2007). Heath managed to initiate a process of policy appraisal that was sufficient to provide a new narrative of Conservatism, and which was able to exploit the economic failings and internal divisions of Labour under Wilson. A more enduring impact was evident in the way that Thatcher helped to politically manufacture a perception of crisis around Labour's governing capabilities in the late 1970s. Here the Conservative right effectively constructed a narrative in which Keynesian social democratic solutions could not address the problem of an overextended, overloaded and ungovernable state held to ransom by excessive trade union power (Hay, 2010: 451).

An additional consideration in terms of party competition would be how Labour governments have historically had a competitive disadvantage flowing from their inferior party organisational structures and financial base (Ball, 1994: 308–9). Incumbent Labour governments have been disadvantaged by the fact that the Conservatives had invested considerable time and resources when in opposition towards maintaining activism at the grassroots level of the party structure (Evans and Taylor, 1996: 278). Seeking to retain office for Labour was also difficult, given that the Conservatives have traditionally used opposition to develop innovative approaches to news management and advertising. This was particularly in evidence when Labour lost office in 1979, after the use of negative campaigning and more sophisticated public relations campaigning culminated in the infamous 'Labour isn't working' billboards (Ramsden, 1998: 436).

The second external disadvantage that Labour has suffered when seeking re-election has been the enduring press bias against it and in favour of the Conservatives. Indeed, political historians have often mentioned that a chief obstacle to sustaining a positive image of Labour in power in the twentieth century (pre-New Labour) was the way in which a capitalist popular press negatively reported upon the record of Labour in office (Thomas, 2005). The increasingly partisan behaviour of the Conservative-supporting press, which by the 1980s had circulation figures three times those of Labour-supporting papers, created a bias worth a 1 per cent switch in voting intention from Labour to Conservative (Harrop, 1986, 1987). The cumulative effect of superior Conservative Party organisation, financial muscle and press bias can be seen to have tilted the odds against Labour holding on to office, especially when its removal has been by a small margin, such as in 1951 and 1970.

However, the fall of Labour governments is not all down to external factors. Brian Brivati (1997: 194–5) has suggested that, historically, Labour's statecraft has been less successful than the Conservatives', and that – until the Blair era – in the pursuit of power the party had just not been particularly good at communicating effectively, campaigning hard, timing elections correctly, keeping the party united and the government energised. Leadership failures and mistakes certainly seem to be a recurrent feature in the fall of Labour governments. As Martin Pugh (2010: ix–x) puts it, 'an historical perspective suggests that Labour's perennial problems with leadership have been a significant impediment to its success.' To take just one indicator, as Brivati (1997: 192–3) says, Labour prime ministers have not had a good record in terms of timing general elections to maximise party advantage, Attlee making poor choices in 1950 and 1951, and Wilson miscalculating in 1970, with Callaghan in 1978 and Brown in 2007 fatally deciding to hang on only to see their electoral prospects get worse, not better. In the post-war period probably only Heath, on the Conservative side, has mistimed an election, in February 1974. In a larger sense, Attlee in 1950–51, Wilson in 1970, Callaghan in 1979 and Brown in 2010 failed to provide the clear sense of direction, and the energy and new ideas, needed to win further terms of office. Internal party splits, disunity, ideological faction-fighting, and disputes over policy (and leadership) have marked most periods of Labour government and contributed to their downfall. The Labour Cabinet split right down the middle over the handling of the financial crisis in 1931. In 1951 the Bevan/Gaitskell feud (and damaging Cabinet resignations) overlay ideological arguments over future policy direction. Labour in the 1960s was weakened by leadership plots against Wilson and by clashes with the trade unions (over incomes policy and union reform). Left–right, party–government, and union–government tensions and disputes all sapped Labour's credibility throughout the 1974–79 government. The Blair–Brown feud diverted Labour energies after 1997, and the plots and attempted coups against Brown after 2007 weakened his authority and standing (Quinn, 2012, 72–6).

Given that the Introduction identified the influence of the Seldon book entitled *How Tory Governments Fall: The Tory Party in Power since 1783*, it is worth asking how the fall of Labour governments compares with that of Conservative governments. Table 8.1 gives basic data on the six 'exits' from government since 1922 for both Labour and the Conservatives.

In terms of vote loss at the general election at which governments were defeated and left office, Labour's biggest loss was in 2010 (−6.2 per cent on its 2005 vote and fully −14.2 per cent on its 1997 vote when it had triumphantly first entered office), its vote-share falling to the lowest (29 per cent) of any losing government in this period – lower than the Conservatives' total in the 1997 wipe-out and lower even than Labour itself got in the disastrous 1931 election when its 'National' opponents united against it. In 1924, and again in 1951, Labour lost office at a general election in which its vote share actually increased but its number of MPs fell – in both cases the overall result was affected by a slump in the Liberal vote which worked out to the advantage of the Conservatives. It is striking that, historically, the Liberals have usually done badly after periods of Labour government, while a Liberal recovery seems to have been a factor in the Conservative defeats of 1929, 1964 and 1974 (Seldon, 1996: 458). Set against the big Labour vote haemorrhage of 2010 are the Conservative double-figure percentage vote losses of 1929, 1945 and 1997, though the 1964 result suggests that multi-term governments may not always end in an electoral meltdown. Labour's biggest seat-loss on eviction from office in this period was in the special circumstances of 1931, the next biggest being seen in the 2010 election, underlining again just what a poor result that was for the party.

The Conservatives saw their biggest culls of MPs when they lost in 1945 and 1997 – both of them taking bigger hits in that respect in those defeats than Labour did in 2010. It is also worth noting that during Labour's one successful multi-term period of government (1997–2010) it did not succeed in pulling off an equivalent to the Conservatives' record in 1951–64 and in the 1980s. Labour's experience under Blair and Brown was one of attrition – steadily losing votes and losing seats (albeit at first only marginally on the second measure) as it defended its record at subsequent elections (comparing 1997–2001–2005–2010). In the 1950s the Conservatives increased their majorities in parliament at successive elections (1951–1955–1959) and saw a slight increase in percentage

Table 8.1 Losing office: Comparing loss of votes and seats

	Duration	Per cent vote on taking office	MPs on taking office	Per cent vote on finally leaving office (+/−)	MPs after losing office
Labour governments					
1924	9 months	30.5	191	33.0 (+2.5)	151 (−40)
1929–31	2 years, 3 months	37.1	288	30.6 (−5.5)	52 (−236)
1945–51	6 years, 3 months	47.8 (1945)	393 (1945)	48.8 (+1.0 on 1945; +2.7 on 1950)	295 (−98 on 1945; −20 on 1950)
		46.1 (1950)	315 (1950)		
1964–70	5 years, 8 months	44.1 (1964)	317 (1964)	43.0 (−4.9 on 1966)	287 (−76 on 1966)
		47.9 (1966)	363 (1966)		
1974–79	5 years, 2 months	37.1 (February)	301 (February)	36.9 (−2.3 on October 1974)	269 (−50 on October 1974)
		39.2 (October)	319 (October)		
1997–2010	13 years	43.2 (1997)	418 (1997)	29.0 (−14.2 on 1997; −6.2 on 2005)	258 (−160 on 1997; −98 on 2005)
		40.7 (2001)	412 (2001)		
		35.2 (2005)	356 (2005)		
Conservative governments					
1922–23	1 year, 1 month	38.2	345	38.1 (−0.1)	258 (−87)
1924–29	4 years, 7 months	48.3	419	38.2 (−10.1)	260 (−159)
1931–45	13 years, 11 months	55.2 (Cons: 1931)	473 (Cons: 1931)	39.8 (−15.4 on 1931; −13.9 on 1935)	213 (−260 on 1931; −219 on 1935)
('National' government)	53.7 (Cons: 1935)	432 (Cons: 1935)			
1951–64	13 years	48.0 (1951)	321 (1951)	43.4 (−6.0 on 1959)	304 (−61 on 1959)
		49.7 (1955)	344 (1955)		
		49.4 (1959)	365 (1959)		
1970–74	3 years, 8 months	46.4	330	37.9 (−8.5)	297 (−33)
1979–97	18 years	43.9 (1979)	339 (1979)	30.7 (−11.2 on 1992; −13.2 on 1979)	165 (−171 on 1992; −232 on 1983)
		42.4 (1983)	397 (1983)		
		42.3 (1987)	376 (1987)		
		41.9 (1992)	336 (1992)		

vote-share. Thatcher in the 1980s suffered a relatively modest loss of votes but greatly increased her parliamentary majority in a 1983 result that more or less guaranteed two more terms in office. Labour has only twice managed to increase its number of MPs while in government – in 1966 (increasing its majority from five to 97) and in October 1974 (when minority government status was swapped for a majority of just three) – and in both cases lost office at the next election.

The 'cost of ruling' literature (Paldam, 1986; Sanders et al., 2001: 797) suggests that normally the popularity of all governments is inexorably eaten away by policy failures, adverse events and disappointed expectations. Unless it can be countered by conspicuous successes, the normal expectation would be of a downward trend of vote loss over the course of time. In the post-war period, only the Attlee Labour government has not experienced a fall in electoral support over its full term of office, actually managing to increase its vote by 1.98 million between 1945 and 1951 (the equivalent of gaining 26,408 votes per month). Other governments have seen various rates of voter attrition between the elections at which they gained office and the defeats triggering their exits. On this basis, the embattled Labour government of 1974–79 actually lost only 1,829 votes per month, whereas Wilson's Labour government of 1966–70 had lost votes at the rate of 17,409 per month. The New Labour government lost votes at the rate of 31,484 per month over its whole period of office from 1997 to 2010 (a breakdown shows that the fastest rate of vote-loss was over the first term: $-45,790$ per month in 1997–2001; $-19,873$ per month in 2001–05; $-15,765$ per month in 2005–10). In comparison, the Conservatives lost votes at the rate of 10,999 per month over the course of the 1951–64 government, Heath lost 28,930 votes per month in 1970–74, and over 1979–97 the vote-loss figure ran at $-18,967$ per month (votes being lost under Major in 1992–97 at the catastrophic rate of $-74,867$ per month).

It is not clear, however, that Labour and Conservative governments fall in fundamentally different ways or for different reasons. The key factors that Seldon (1996: 453–62), for instance, picks out as contributing to the fall of Conservative governments also help explain how and why Labour governments end. The Conservative examples of *failures of leadership and/or leadership unpopularity*, including Home in 1964, Heath in 1974 and Major in 1997, are matched by Brown in 2010, with Attlee in 1950–51 and Callaghan in 1978–79 arguably making serious leadership mistakes even though they were assets to the party in terms of their personal popularity and ratings. Just as *confusion or uncertainty over policy direction* was a factor in Conservative defeats in 1929, 1945, 1974 and

1997, the same could be said for Labour in 1931, 1951, 1979 and 2010. While *internal disunity and party divisions* damaged the Conservatives in 1964 and 1997, there are perhaps more examples of Labour problems on this measure, including 1931, 1951, 1979 and 2010. Just as Home and Major faced the challenge of a *revived opposition*, so did Attlee and Brown. In 1945, 1974 and 1997 a *hostile intellectual and/or media climate* seems to have contributed to Conservative defeats, and the same could be said for Labour in 1924, 1931, 1951, 1979 and 2010. *Economic problems* and concerns over the government's economic management record have been a negative force for both the Conservatives (1964, 1974, 1997) and Labour (1931, 1970, 1979, 2010). Seldon (1996: 461) argues that *poor party organisation* and *depleted party finances* do not seem to be common factors in Conservative election defeats, that party generally always having an advantage. On the other hand, problems with Labour's party machinery, finances, and effectiveness as a campaigning organisation did not help Labour's re-election chances in the Wilson–Callaghan period or again in 2010. Labour governments (1951, 1979, 2010) seem just as vulnerable as Conservative governments (1964, 1997) to the charge of being stale and the feeling of '*time for a change*'. Finally, it is worth noting that the idea that disputes and clashes with the trade unions are a factor in the fall and defeat of governments seems to apply only to a specific period from the mid-1960s to the late 1970s – with Labour (1970 and 1979) and the Conservatives (1974) suffering alike.

However, contrasting Labour and Conservative governments may be interesting, but the opening paragraphs of the Introduction to this book focused on the idea that New Labour was the great exception. It is clear that in the period between 1997 and 2007 the Blair governments had two substantive differences from Old Labour governments, which gave credence to the suggestion that they were an exception within Labour Party history. First, they had survived to become multi-term administrations, and, second, they presided over a prolonged period of economic prosperity. These factors enabled them to successfully claim to be the party of economic competence, and thereby argue that they were the natural party of government. Advocates would argue that such longevity in office justified the policy, organisational and positional changes that New Labour had initiated in opposition and which had sustained them in government. It legitimised their Third Way accommodation with the legacy of Thatcherism; their emphasis on news management and nullifying the aforementioned negative impact of the press; and their pursuit of the centre ground in British politics (Hay, 1999; Heffernan, 1999; Hindmoor, 2004).

The crucial question, therefore, is: did New Labour fall in a way that was different from other Labour administrations? The cataclysmic economic failings that happened to coincide with the Brown prime ministerial tenure ensured that, just as previous Labour administrations had a symbolic economic failure attached to them, so did New Labour. Just as Conservative electoral strategy had for generations revolved around citing 1931, 1947, 1967 or 1976–79 as a means of showcasing the economic ineptitude of Labour in office, so Cameron and the Conservatives now had a modern-day equivalent trigger. However, any claim about New Labour and economic competence post-1997 should acknowledge the following. The previous five times Labour had entered power, it had done so in either politically or economically constraining circumstances, which undermined its ability to demonstrate competence once in power. The parliamentary arithmetic in 1924, 1929, 1964 and 1974 for the incoming Labour administrations meant that they were politically constrained, in the 1920s being minority administrations and the Wilson governments having only a small majority in 1964 and being in a minority in 1974. Nor did they enter power in economically prosperous times. While the incoming Attlee administration benefitted from having a strong parliamentary majority, it was economically constrained due to the aftermath of the war. New Labour benefitted from entering power in strong parliamentary circumstances, but, critically, it inherited a strong economic environment, which was to be sustained for the next decade. New Labour was also fortunate in comparison to its predecessors in terms of its opposition. The Conservatives were intellectually bankrupt and ideologically divided in 1997 to an extent that had not been evident in previous periods when they had entered opposition (Seldon and Snowden, 2005). Also, the Major administration had offered Labour a symbol of its governing failure – Black Wednesday and its forced removal from the Exchange Rate Mechanism in September 1992. For all the skill with which New Labour spin doctors emphasised the brilliance of their leader and the strategy, they benefitted greatly from the record of the Major administration: its divisions, its sleaze and corruption, and the perception of weak leadership by Major (Dorey, 1999).

New Labour is distinct from previous periods of Labour governance due to its duration; its policy/ideological approach; and the period of press bias in its favour. It also had the good fortune to enter power in a benign economic environment when facing a demoralised, discredited and divided Conservative opposition unable to accept the need to modernise. Ultimately, however, despite the argument that New Labour is distinct from other periods in Labour history, some common themes can be seen between its fall in 2010 and previous evictions from office, with economic difficulties, leadership failings and internal disputes being key contributing factors.

References

Allen, N. (2011), 'Labour's Third Term: A Tale of Two Prime Ministers', in Allen, N. and Bartle, J. (eds), *Britain at the Polls 2010* (London: Sage).
Ball, S. (1994), 'The National and Regional Party Structure', in Seldon, A. and Ball, S. (eds), *Conservative Century: The Conservative Party since 1900* (Oxford: Oxford University Press).
Ball, S. (2005), 'Democracy and the Rise of Labour: 1924 and 1929–31', in Ball, S. and Seldon, A. (eds), *Recovering Power: The Conservatives in Opposition since 1867* (Basingstoke: Palgrave).
Ball, S. and Seldon, A. (eds) (2005), *Recovering Power: The Conservatives in Opposition since 1867* (Basingstoke: Palgrave).
Brivati, B. (1997), 'Earthquake or Watershed? Conclusions on New Labour in Power', in Brivati, B. and Bale, T. (eds), *New Labour in Power: Precedents and Prospects* (London: Routledge).
Denham, A. and O'Hara, K. (2007), 'The Three Mantras: Modernisation and the Conservative Party', *British Politics*, Vol. 2, No. 1, 167–90.
Dorey, P. (ed.) (1999), *The Major Premiership: Politics and Policies under John Major, 1990–1997* (Basingstoke: Macmillan).
Evans, B. and Taylor, A. (1996), *From Salisbury to Major: Continuity and Change in Conservative Politics* (Manchester: Manchester University Press).
Harrop, M. (1986), 'The Press and Post-War Elections', in Crewe, I. and Harrop, M. (eds), *Political Communications: The General Election Campaign of 1983* (Cambridge: Cambridge University Press).
Harrop, M. (1987), 'Voters', in Seaton, J. and Pimlott, B. (eds), *The Media and British Politics* (Aldershot: Gower).
Hay, C. (1999), *The Political Economy of New Labour: Labouring under False Pretences* (Manchester: Manchester University Press).
Hay, C. (2010), 'Chronicles of a Death Foretold: The Winter of Discontent and Construction of the Crisis of British Keynesianism', *Parliamentary Affairs*, Vol. 63, No. 3, 446–70.
Heffernan, R. (1999), *New Labour and Thatcherism* (Basingstoke: Macmillan).
Heffernan, R. (2011), 'Labour's New Labour Legacy', *Political Studies Review*, Vol. 9, No. 2, 163–77.
Hindmoor, A. (2004), *New Labour at the Centre: Constructing Political Space* (Oxford: Oxford University Press).
Laybourn, K. (2000), *A Century of Labour: A History of the Labour Party* (Stroud: Sutton).
Paldam, M. (1986), 'The Distribution of Election Results and the Two Explanations of the Cost of Ruling', *European Journal of Political Economy*, Vol. 2, No. 1, 5–24.
Pugh, M. (2010), *Speak for Britain! A New History of the Labour Party* (London: The Bodley Head).

Quinn, T. (2012), *Electing and Ejecting Party Leaders in Britain* (Basingstoke: Palgrave).

Ramsden, J. (1998), *An Appetite for Power: A History of the Conservative Party since 1830* (London: Macmillan).

Rawnsley, A. (2010), *The End of the Party: The Rise and Fall of New Labour* (London: Penguin).

Sanders, D., Clarke, H., Stewart, M., and Whiteley, P. (2001), 'The Economy and Voting', *Parliamentary Affairs*, Vol. 54, No. 4, 789–802.

Seldon, A. (1996), *How Tory Governments Fall: The Tory Party since 1783* (London: Fontana).

Seldon, A. and Snowden, P. (2005), 'The Barren Years 1997–2005', in Ball, S. and Seldon, A. (eds), *Recovering Power: The Conservatives in Opposition since 1867* (Basingstoke: Palgrave).

Thomas, J. (2005), *Popular Newspapers, The Labour Party and British Politics* (Abingdon: Routledge).

Index

Printed and bound by CPI Group (UK) Ltd, Croydon, CR0 4YY